Make Great Music with Ease!

The Secret to Smarter Practice, Confident Performance, and Living a Happier Life

Jennifer Roig-Francolí

Praise for *Make Great Music with Ease!*

"In this highly illuminating book, the author shares with daring vulnerability her journey of self-discovery that inspires her innovative, all-embracing approach to personal growth, freedom, and artistic mastery. I've witnessed firsthand the power of The Art of Freedom® Method to help my students learn and play with more ease, and I've also had great success in experimenting with the ideas for myself. With this book in hand, any musician can unlock the confidence and flow that deliver a whole new level of facility and joy in life and music!"

~ Cynthia Roberts, Concert Baroque Violinist and Faculty at The Juilliard School of music

"Most performing musicians I know suffer from performance anxiety and chronic pain, including myself. We try to deal with these potentially debilitating problems the best we can. Jennifer Roig-Francolí's book offers us a holistic, natural way to free ourselves from bondage of our own creation! Her work with musicians online has long created a stir among performers fortunate enough to participate in her workshops, and now her expertise is available to all of us in book form. I am looking forward to implementing her suggestions in my own practice, and to offering it to my developing students so that they can avoid the pitfalls of pain and anxiety that often await us."

~ Kathie Stewart, Principal Flute for Apollo's Fire, Teacher of Baroque Flute at the Cleveland Institute of Music and Indiana University Jacobs School of Music

"Jennifer Roig-Francolí is both an accomplished violinist and an experienced Alexander Technique teacher. With this dual background, she identifies clearly many of the things that hold musicians back, whether physical discomfort, mental distress or lack of confidence. She offers insightful solutions for musicians to rekindle joy in their music-making and in their life."

~ Noah Bendix-Balgley, Concert Violinist and 1st Concertmaster of the Berliner Philharmoniker

"You do not need to be a musician to benefit from this beautiful book. With Jennifer's help, I was able to move gracefully and confidently before a large audience to win a ballroom dance competition when I had never done anything like that before. I felt totally present and able to just be.

I am a psychiatrist of over thirty years. I believe that if more people understood Alexander Technique, especially through Jennifer's insightful lens, there would be less anxiety, depression, and struggle with body image. I highly recommend this gem of a book."

~ Tracey G Skale, MD, psychiatrist / Chief Medical Officer, National Speaker for Mental Health

"Jennifer Roig-Francolí offers compelling 'Awareness Etudes' that serve as powerful lessons in self-mastery through musical practice. Brava!"

~ Michael J. Gelb, Author of *BodyLearning: An Introduction to the Alexander Technique* and *How to Think Like Leonardo da Vinci*

"The impact of this captivating book is profound, granting readers the opportunity to create better music and embrace life to the fullest by tapping into their inner wisdom and finding a natural state of ease within. Having collaborated with exceptional musicians worldwide, I can vouch for the universality of the challenges musicians face, as presented in this book. This book deserves a cherished spot in every musician's library."

~ Karen Kamensek, Grammy Award-winning Conductor

"Centered in joy, *Make Great Music with Ease!* is a valuable addition to any musician's bookshelf. With this volume, Roig-Francolí shares a systematic approach to fearless and freedom-filled self-expression. My personal experience with The Art of Freedom® Method and Primal Alexander™ has changed my approach to singing, teaching, and life in general. I am forever grateful for the tools I now have, and I use them every day."

~ Dr. Quinn Patrick Ankrum, Mezzo soprano, Assistant Professor at the University of Cincinnati College-Conservatory of Music

"Successful music-making is not technical mastery but embodiment, presence, and sensitivity to the musical moment; it calls on the heart, mind, and body to be activated and aligned, which is just what Jennifer Roig-Francolí teaches in this astonishing book. Musicians (and others!) will benefit profoundly from her wisdom in the areas of mindfulness, creativity, and mind-body awareness."

~ Ingrid Matthews, Visiting Associate Professor of Historical Performance and Baroque Violin, Jacobs School of Music, Indiana University, co-founder and Music Director Emeritus of Seattle Baroque Orchestra

"I am a professional composer and conductor with over 40 years of work behind me. I did not realize how much freedom there is within before I started to learn from Jennifer Roig-Francolí's teaching how to direct my efforts and find inner peace. She is a remarkable coach who understands a musician's inner thoughts and what makes one spend hours in the quest of perfection (and why perfect playing is perhaps not the right or only quest). Jennifer's book, like Jennifer, is a miracle. Her written words sound just like her speaking—concise, warm, directed, and encouraging. To have her book by my side is a forever gift—and I hope others will find in her warm and dynamic teaching the calm we all seek while never forgetting how to enrich our innate gifts."

~ Michael Shapiro, Composer and Conductor

"Jennifer Roig-Francolí is a first-class musician, equally at ease with the modern and baroque violins, equally at ease playing Bach or 'Gypsy Jazz.' Her expertise in ease and freedom is invaluable for her listeners and for her students—and now, also for her readers!"

~ Pedro de Alcantara, Musician, Writer, and Teacher

"What I have gained from learning The Art of Freedom® Method and Primal Alexander™ as described in this book is above and beyond what I ever could have imagined. I highly recommend this book not only for its vibrant, inspirational language and storytelling, but also for its positive, encouraging, and holistic perspective. I guarantee you will be moved. . . If you are a musician looking to find more joy, peace, health, assuredness, and serenity . . . read this book and begin your gratifying journey!"

~ Martie Perry, Baroque violinist; Co-concertmaster, North Carolina Baroque Orchestra; Principal Second Violinist, Indianapolis Baroque Orchestra

"This magnificent book is a valuable resource for any musician looking to improve their well-being and artistry while making a joyful difference in the world. The reader will experience the essence of one musician's deeply insightful and spiritual journey into the panoptic realm of a musician's life. A truly valuable book, not to be missed!"

~ Tommy Thompson, Certified Alexander Technique Teacher (ATI), former Faculty Member, Harvard University

"Jennifer Roig-Francolí has masterfully created a space for musicians of all levels to discover their true potential. A musician herself, Jennifer has a deep understanding of the musician's mind as well as the experiences of intense training. She gives us important insight into the non-habitual possibilities we can all achieve. Curiosity and a positive attitude permeate all that she writes. Her music-making comes from love and joy—and this book is definitely a joy to read!"

~ Debi Adams, NCTM, ATI Certified, ISMETA MSME, pianist, Alexander Technique Program Director, Boston Conservatory at Berklee

"Jennifer Roig-Francolí's Art of Freedom® Method is truly groundbreaking. It has the inherent power to bring about profound changes in one's approach to music and life. It stands apart as a unique pathway that enables musicians to perceive their craft through a spiritual lens, unlocking thought-provoking insights and growth. Personally experiencing her teachings, I can confidently attest to their incredible effectiveness. The techniques have seamlessly integrated into my daily musical practice. I highly recommend this book to all musicians!

~ Nandini Shankar, internationally acclaimed Indian Classical Violinist

"After nearly fifty years of teaching the Alexander Technique, I have immersed myself in countless books on the subject. However, there are a select few that stand out as truly exceptional and worth adding to one's collection. *Make Great Music with Ease!* breathes a much-needed gust of fresh air into the realm of Alexander Technique literature and serves as an extraordinary resource for our Alexander community. What sets it apart is its comprehensive approach, addressing not only the physical and mental aspects but also delving into the emotional and, importantly, spiritual dimensions of both musicianship and human existence."

~ Michael D. Frederick, Senior Alexander Technique teacher and Founder of the Alexander Technique International Congress

"This book will be a gift to so many who suffer from misguided instruction and thoughts leading to poor body use and injury. I highly recommend taking the ideas to heart; having had earlier access to the methods she describes would have changed my own career path."

~ John Wion, former Principal Flute for New York City Opera, Emeritus Professor at The Hartt School, University of Hartford

Make Great Music with Ease! is an exceptional book! Jennifer Roig-Francolí is both a top level Violinist and an excellent Alexander Technique teacher who now shares her knowledge with us, acquired from many years of professional experience and personal introspection. This book is a wonderful resource for all musicians who want to dive into their own physical, mental, and emotional selves and thus enrich their playing.

~ Maaike Aarts, Former Violinist in the Royal Concertgebouw Orchestra, The Netherlands, and Alexander Technique teacher

"If you are a musician and you feel you are not playing at your full potential, or are experiencing pain while practicing or playing, or are experiencing performance anxiety, this is a must-read book. It could make your life a lot easier and could literally save your career."

~ Robert Rickover, Alexander Technique teacher, Author of *Fitness without Stress: A Guide to the Alexander Technique*

"I'm so excited that finally there's something tangible I can highly recommend to my students to read about Primal Alexander and so much more! This book is a wonderful road map to guide musicians into more Ease, Flow and Freedom in practice and performance."

~ Fiona Tree, Harpist and Alexander Technique Faculty at the Royal Conservatoire of The Hague, Netherlands, where Primal Alexander is now part of the core curriculum for musicians

"Thank you, Jennifer Roig-Francolí, for offering a safe and nurturing space through this book for musicians to experience the joy (and infinite possibility!) of a heart-centered approach to artistry!"

~ Katie Fittipaldi, faculty at the Eastman School of Music, Alexander Technique teacher (AmSAT), cellist

DOWNLOAD THE AUDIOBOOK FREE!

READ THIS FIRST

To thank you for getting this book, I would like to give you the Audiobook version 100% FREE!

I know you're more likely to finish this book if you have the audiobook. I even narrated the book myself so it will feel like we are having a conversation!

Instead of paying $10-$20 for the audiobook, I'd like to give it to you for free...

www.ArtOfFreedom.me/Audiobook

VIDEO TRAINING

Want a video training that will teach you the fundamental mind-body awareness skills taught in this book?

Check out this mini-course to make your life and your music easier right away!

In this training we'll cover 3 things:

What you're doing unconsciously that's holding you back

How to let go, think and move differently to get different results

How to get inspired, feel better, and enjoy your music more

www.ArtofFreedom.me/VideoTraining

Make Great Music with Ease!

The Secret to Smarter Practice, Confident Performance, and Living a Happier Life

PAPERBACK - ISBN: 979-8-9890273-0-9

EBOOK - ISBN: 979-8-9890273-1-6

AUDIOBOOK - ISBN: 979-8-9890273-2-3

HARDCOVER - ISBN: 979-8-9890273-3-0

For more information, email Jennifer@ArtofFreedom.me.

Cover designer: Jomel Pepito

Cover photography: Tina Gutierrez

Editor: Margaret A. Harrell: https://margaretharrell.com

Published by Creative Muse Publishing

To Love

Contents

Foreword
By Mio Morales

Music is a gift that reflects the intrinsic, ineffable beauty of life itself. It connects us in unique ways, bridging cultural and personal divides, and can even connect us back through time.

Music is an energy that can influence our mood, mindset, and behavior. It can reduce stress levels and improve mental health and has the power to energize, stimulate, and help maintain focus during all kinds of activities.

It enhances memory, improves focus, fosters creativity, triggers all manner of new experiences. And as a universal language, music can evoke emotions, thoughts, and experiences that transcend words.

Which begins to explain why every culture in every epoch of human history has given birth to its own unique musical dialect. It's a testament to how much we have always valued music as indispensable and inseparable from the human experience itself . . .

MUSIC IS A MIRACLE!

It would thus stand to reason that if music is indeed a miracle, then we, as musicians, are the miracle workers. For those of you who might be feeling a little less miraculous right now due to:

Intense competition, financial instability, irregular schedule, unhealthy work-life balance, physical or mental health challenges, self-promotion issues, lack of job security, unfortunate career trajectory, lack of recognition, creative blocks, artistic struggles, dealing with rejection, maintaining motivation or . . . POLITICS!

FEAR NOT!

The book you're about to read speaks so clearly and eloquently about the miracle and the mess of being a musician that you will be stunned by its simplicity and utterly amazed by the depth and richness of its counsel.

Jennifer Roig-Francolí's book *Make Great Music with Ease!* reflects the amazing journey she's been on since childhood. It provides a clear roadmap that you can use to guide yourself and a nifty compass that comes in handy for the inevitable times you find that you've somehow wandered off road.

Make Great Music with Ease! draws from a rich variety of sources, focusing primarily on:

- The discoveries of F.M. Alexander, commonly known as The Alexander Technique (AT)
- Primal Alexander™, my approach to AT that does not require hands-on guidance, and
- Jennifer's own Art of Freedom® Method

Combined, these three learning techniques, enriched by Jennifer's fresh perspective on various subjects from posture to perfectionism, construct a readable and incredibly enlightening narrative that is as inspiring as it is practical.

Regardless of where you are on the musical spectrum, from a complete beginner to an experienced professional, this book promises to uplift your musical abilities by teaching you how to use your love of music to improve the way you do everything else in your life.

Music is a dangerously evocative medium. Gorgeously expressive and brutally revealing. As musicians, we are blessed with the incredible opportunity to connect with the sheer beauty and immense power of music. We may encounter physical, emotional, and creative challenges along the way, but it is within our grasp to utilize them to grow.

In navigating the intricate dynamics of this expressive and demanding medium, we often discover that the biggest obstacle we face is not external, but within ourselves. This realization is not meant to discourage us, but rather to inspire a shift in our mindset. Just as Einstein wisely said, "We cannot solve our problems with the same thinking we used when we created them," we understand that it's new perspectives that lead to breakthroughs.

Make Great Music with Ease! is a compendium of the kind of mindset shifts that are the key to better habits, better choices, better feelings, better actions, and better music.

We must recognize that the transformative potential of music lies not only in the external elements such as instruments, composers, collaborators, and audiences, but mainly within our very own selves.

Every note we play or sing, every emotion we convey, and every choice we make as artists speaks volumes about our personal growth and evolution. It is through this vulnerability that our music becomes a true reflection of our journey.

Although it may feel daunting at times, we are entrusted with the extraordinary power to shape and mold the very essence of music. We are the conduits through which this art form is brought to life, capturing the essence of our thoughts, feelings, and experiences in every performance. It is this paradoxical nature of being both powerful and vulnerable that gives music its profound cultural significance.

Plato famously said, "Music gives a soul to the universe, wings to the mind, flight to the imagination and life to everything." Those of us privileged to have the talent for playing music know it all started with a passion for enjoying music, ignited by musicians before us who shared their love of music with us.

Musicians and non-musicians alike get to partake in the beauty, power, and grace innate to music. In a similar way, the lessons to be learned in this book are techniques and strategies that can be put to use by anyone looking to bring more ease, clarity, and joy to all the things they do in their life.

Introduction

I'll never forget the moment during one of my first lessons as an Alexander Technique student when I thought to myself: *Wow . . . what a beautiful profession! I could never do that!* It felt a lot like the moment, a few years later, when I was stopped in my tracks by the stunning vision of colorful, geometrically embroidered Japanese "temari" balls in a display case at the public library, and again I thought: *Wow . . . those are so beautiful! I could never do that!*

. . . And when (just one month after graduating from my Alexander teacher training) I was asked if I wanted to design a research study on the Alexander Technique for surgeons—except that time, despite my internal terror as I thought to myself: *What?! Me?! But I barely know what I'm doing yet!* I found my mouth instantly replying with a "yes," being well aware how important such a study could be and what a golden opportunity had just fallen into my lap.

I'd learned mind-body skills for conscious self-control in my Alexander training.

A few days later, I somehow managed to apply them to get past my fear of fainting (a habitual reaction to medical situations that began when I was ten years old), just long enough to watch the graphic video of laparoscopic surgery that was mandatory in preparation for doing the research.

In each scenario above, I wound up doing the very thing I believed I couldn't, not long after being presented with the challenge. Clearly—like a carrot dangled before a rabbit—my motivation led the way to fulfilling my desires.

Precisely this is what happened to F. M. Alexander, who all his life had wanted more than anything to become an actor. But he hit a stumbling block: his voice became hoarse every time he went to perform. Because of his intense passion for his goal, spending years in pursuit of a solution, he eventually did the unthinkable, solving his problem through the power of his mind and creative ingenuity, along with the systematic practice of self-observation and experimentation, and—finally—accessing natural ease and flow within himself by learning to let go.

I've written this book to encourage you to get in touch with your own desires and learn how to get past any unhelpful habits and instinctive reactions (like my default "I can't"), so that you can overcome the challenges you face as a musician and thrive—whether you're a professional or an amateur. Or maybe you're an Alexander teacher interested in exploring new ways to help your musician students better. I want you to discover that you, too, can do amazing things you may have thought were out of reach!

What's in the book?

When my students come to me, they have a strong desire to make better music—a desire that's being thwarted. Their joy is interrupted by pain, performance anxiety, or something else that gets in their way. And they haven't yet figured out how to solve the problem on their own.

Part 1 of this book presents the most common obstacles musicians encounter on their way to artistic mastery, along with what works to overcome them and what doesn't.

Part 2 takes you on my personal journey from young violinist to "Rising Star" featured in *TIME* magazine; from stuck and struggling in my early adulthood to some years later feeling far freer and happier than I ever could have imagined, thanks in large part to discovering the Alexander Technique and touch-free Primal Alexander™.

Lastly, Part 3 shares very practical and effective tools I use with myself and my online students to improve practice and performance, avoiding common pitfalls and enjoying the process of effortless musical mastery by thinking constructively and prioritizing mindful awareness in the moment over everything else.

Throughout the book, I will be illustrating the concepts with colorful examples gleaned from my lifetime as an award-winning violinist, ongoing interest in personal development, and twenty years of experience with the Alexander Technique.

I've included plenty of stories, shared with permission from many of my former and current Art of Freedom students (with some details altered to protect privacy), in the recognition that we're all in this together: you are anything but alone in your struggles—whether primarily physical, mental, emotional, spiritual, or artistic. Each of us is battling our own private Doubt Monsters while yearning to express our souls through music in the most beautiful, meaningful, and joyous way possible.

How to approach this book

As you read, my first job is to inspire you, like I do with my students, to think outside the box and open up to All-Possibility. Personally, I *do* believe anything is possible, so it's not hard for me to encourage others to entertain the idea.

Even so, to get the most out of this book, you don't actually have to *believe* anything is possible; just be *open to the possibility* that anything is possible! Having an open mind is an indispensable prerequisite for learning, along with curiosity and a willingness to experiment, toying with new ideas that may at first glance go against the grain!

If anything in this book just seems plain wrong to you, that's OK . . . but try not to throw the baby out with the bathwater. Take a moment to check in with your heart and return to the book a little later. The most important thing is to let yourself open up again when you're ready, and let yourself ponder the ideas without hurry, and without any preconceptions. (Of course, if you're not open to learning something new, please put this book down right now!)

Download the free resources through the links located in multiple places throughout the book, try out the suggestions, and see what happens when you give yourself a little bit of time to explore. After all, finding buried treasure requires a bit of digging!

That said, I'm far from claiming to have all the answers. I'm well aware that despite all my efforts to be as accurate as possible, some errors may have crept in! Please be generous in forgiving any errors you may find among these pages, and please do get in touch with me personally so I can consider correcting them in any future editions.

You'll see there's a lot of repetition of the core concepts because repetition is SO important for ideas to stick and new habits to be formed . . . and because many of the ideas in this book, while sometimes blatantly obvious and ridiculously simple once you think about them, may be radically different from how you were brought up or how you were trained to teach or make music, and therefore they can be easily misunderstood or forgotten.

So, let yourself drink the repetitions in and trust that they're cleaning out some of the muck stuck in your unconscious that's blocking you from growing into your full potential.

As this is a rather long book, don't feel pressured to read every word from start to finish—we're all very busy these days and time is precious! There's a common thread that runs through the whole book, which I think you'll appreciate no matter at what point you pick it up—as long as you're approaching it in the positive spirit of open-minded curiosity, healthy detachment, and willingness to learn.

While letting your interest guide you to read the sections that capture your attention in any order—you're certainly free to skip around—I do recommend that you work your way through from the beginning. That way, you'll find it easier to grasp unfamiliar concepts—especially as I'll be using some jargon here and there that requires definition; if you miss the explanations, you might feel a bit lost when you come across words like "inhibition" (in the sense meant here) or "ConstructiveThinking™" or "Primary Concern" and you have no idea what I mean.

A universal perspective

Speaking of which, there's one very important word I'd like to address now to clear up any possible confusion. That word, which I use abundantly throughout to refer to what I consider the source of creative Inspiration, is *Spirit*. This will be the best word for many readers, but depending on your associations, it might not be the best for YOU.

I invite you to use the word "Spirit" like I do or to substitute a word that's more meaningful for you. Here are some other words you might wish to substitute for "Spirit" whenever you come across it in the book: God, Source, Nature, Great Mystery, All-Possibility, Infinitude, Creator, Essence, Grace, Universe, Higher Power, Higher Self, Divine Energy, Life, or simply . . . LOVE. To me, these words are all synonyms for the special, ineffable spark of Life that inspires our every breath, thought, and action on this earth and brings meaning to our existence if we want it to.

The Art of Freedom® Method, like the Alexander Technique, is available to all people interested in making the best use of their life, creating the most wondrous music with their whole self. And it isn't limited to any particular belief or value system. I'd like to share a favorite quote of mine, found on the first page of Alexander's first book, *Man's Supreme Inheritance*:

> The theory and practice of my system are influenced by no particular religion nor school of philosophy, but in one sense may be said to embrace them all. For whatever name we give to the Great Origin of the Universe, in the words of a friend of mine, "we can all of us agree . . . that we mean the same thing, namely, that high power within the soul of man which enables him to will or to act or to speak, not loosely or wildly, but in subjection to an all-wise and invisible Authority." The name that we give to that Authority will in no way affect the principles which I am about to state. In subscribing to them the mechanist may still retain his belief in a theory of chemical reactions no less than the Christian his faith in a Great Redeemer.[1]

To me, that says it all.

1 F. M. Alexander, Man's Supreme Inheritance (Penguin Books), 1918: 1.

What I am *not* promoting

This book is overflowing with advice culled from my own personal life and professional experience, along with spiritual concepts I've absorbed from many sources over the years. I'd like to make it abundantly clear that even though some of my formulations may be unique, "there is nothing new under the sun" and I don't consider myself a "guru" of any kind, beyond the basic definition of the word, which simply means "teacher" in Sanskrit.

In no way do I intend for what I'm sharing to be a substitute for a formal religious or other spiritual practice, including meditation, should you have one or wish to embark on such a path—something I encourage you to do. What I share in this book will be essentially compatible with—and can enhance—any of those as you understand and practice how to free yourself and be yourself . . . through a combination of appropriate effort, positive direction, and the presence of a Grace beyond our understanding and control.

I very much hope you'll enjoy this book and that the ideas will lift you up to a higher vantage point, from where you can get a bigger, broader perspective on your experience and your struggles as a musician and receive sturdy reassurance that solving them can be much easier, and much quicker, than you think! My greatest wish in writing this book is that it will help you be yourself—so you can make great music with effortless ease and joy!

Now, let's dive in! Let's begin by considering some of the common obstacles you might be facing as a musician and get a first glimpse of the underlying source of those problems and their ultimate and universal solution!

Part 1

The Challenges of Being a Musician

In Part 1 of this book, we'll take a look at some of the common challenges musicians face today, as we strive for artistic success and personal fulfillment in bringing greater beauty, meaning, and positive change to a modern world all too often dominated by selfish materialism and hardness of heart. v

Being a Musician

Common desires and obstacles to success

Who am I and what am I doing here?

~ *Everybody's Question*

What if you could wave a magic wand and improve any aspect of your life while vastly improving the quality of your art? As a musician, what one wish would you make today?

. . . Maybe it would be to overcome pain or improve your posture so you can relax while you play and enjoy a long, healthy career.

. . . Maybe you wish you could toss off those fiendishly difficult technical passages with effortless ease or luxuriate in your unique, personal sound whenever you pick up your instrument.

. . . Maybe you yearn to express your musical emotions freely and fearlessly from your heart—whether onstage in front of a thousand people or at home in your living room.

Or maybe you long to stay calm, poised, and centered, undaunted when in the throes of financial stress. Or maybe it's to tackle interpersonal conflict in a healthy way, instead of tensing up, bottling up your emotions or overreacting.

Well, I can't offer you a magic wand . . . exactly. But I can help you master a tool you already have within you! *One that's even better.*

This tool is your natural, human capacity for awareness, combined with your innate potential to choose how you think, move, and express yourself. In this book, I will show you how your capacity for awareness and *clear self-direction* is what allows your creative dreams to come true.

Most of us haven't yet realized our full potential. We don't yet know how to consciously, easily *direct* our mind, body, and spirit for maximum freedom of expression, joy, and success.

By "direct," I mean harnessing the power of our imagination and actively allowing our creative energy to flow as nature intended, along the lines of least resistance required to realize our goals with integrity.

As a coach for musicians, I daily help scores of people around the world realize their birthright, in applying this creative freedom in their everyday life and music. The same creative birthright is yours. I've written this book to help you become aware of the miraculous results that come when you prioritize a healthy curiosity and a conscious awareness of your moment-to-moment experience, replacing your habitual reactions, personal preferences, and especially unexamined beliefs.

Whether you're a world-class performer or music educator, an aspiring musician just setting out on a new career, or an amateur at any skill level, the approach I describe in this book will *help bring healthy balance to your life and increase your joy and success in everything you do*.

Music shouldn't hurt, but many musicians suffer in silence

As a professional violinist and a certified Alexander Technique teacher, I've had countless conversations and worked with musicians globally: soloists, ensemble players, students, and music educators at every level—from private studio owners to university-level faculty. From this, I've gained a unique perspective into the myriad challenges that musicians face today. It's because of the solutions I came up with that my coaching practice is devoted exclusively to helping musicians.

Even though I enjoyed a lot of success as a musician before the age of twenty and was called "a rising star" by *TIME* magazine, with solo appearances at Carnegie Hall and with world-renowned orchestras, my career hasn't always been smooth sailing. Discovering the Alexander Technique in my early thirties was a real before/after experience for me. It changed *everything* for the better.

Until I discovered this technique, I used to think of music-making as primarily a mental activity. For some reason, I had an irrational prejudice that so-called mental activities were "better" than physical activities, which was tantamount to judging *the mere idea* of running away from a tiger as more valuable than actually running away—as if you could have one without the other!

I knew I needed to use my arms and fingers to play the violin. Naturally. But what did my legs or hips have to do with playing octaves in tune?!? I was oblivious as to how the rest of my body was involved. After all, my feet seemed so far away . . .

Unfortunately, being ignorant of what was happening throughout my whole body while playing the violin meant that I didn't notice when my toes were curled and gripping the floor, my knees were locked, or my hips were thrust forward, creating a swayback posture (which I thought at the time was "good posture" but now I know introduces tremendous strain on the body), thereby breaking the flow of energy throughout my system, compromising the free flow of my musical technique.

I was unaware of a chain of tension beginning in my neck, jaw, and shoulders, which continued down to my arm muscles, causing them to contract and my fingers to be stiffer than necessary, all of which made it harder to play fast, technically demanding passages. I also didn't realize how often I held my breath when I played. My shallow breathing, too, was preventing me from shaping musical phrases with the natural ease, subtlety, and flowing beauty I expected of myself . . . but I had absolutely no idea all of this was going on!

To be honest, this is not unusual. I've witnessed a lot of physical and emotional suffering from inside the trenches of the music profession. Sadly, it's common for musicians to experience unnecessary pain, but it's not so common for them to find a lasting solution that relieves their suffering, allows them to feel more fulfilled in life, AND helps them become better artists!

Working with my students, I teach them specific mind-body techniques based on the F. M. Alexander Technique. A brilliant, time-tested and research-proven holistic awareness and movement discipline offered privately and at top educational institutions around the world (such as The Juilliard School and Royal College of Music), the Alexander Technique helps people from all walks of life improve their well-being and find more ease, joy, and success in whatever it is they wish to do. Practicing these tools on their own, they are able to accurately identify the source of their pain and struggles and know exactly how to overcome them with ease.

Being a musical artist puts very high demands on the mind, body, and creative spirit. It requires intense levels of emotional expressiveness and very precise physical movements that are as highly specialized as any elite athlete's. In fact, I think musicians are unrecognized athletes. Sadly, it's almost taboo for musicians to admit their suffering.

The comparison with athletes may seem inconsequential, but there are a lot of related problems that make YOUR life as a musician much more difficult when you suddenly need support that isn't readily available, or you're afraid to speak up and seek help. This became evident for many musicians during the pandemic, when musicians notoriously had nowhere to play. No gigs in bars, no grand stages, no Lincoln Center live performances, no city ballet. And they weren't getting much—or any—support from their employers, those that had an employer. Many felt compelled to resort to pain killers, recreational drugs, or therapeutic treatments.

One client of mine, Anne, told me in her initial coaching session that she'd suffered from quite a bit of anxiety throughout the pandemic. *As a section leader for a top-notch professional orchestra, she had never experienced performance anxiety before.*

But when the pandemic began, no one was able to rehearse or perform in person anymore, obviously. Yet how long would that last? No one knew. When would she be called back to work? It was nerve-wracking almost to the point of unendurable. This deviation from her normal practice and performance routines and the heightened uncertainty compelled her to keep practicing, even though she had nothing concrete to work towards. The need to always be on-call and ready to perform caused her enormous anxiety.

To make matters worse, it became clear that the pandemic might continue for many more months—maybe even years. At that point, Anne watched other musicians around her begin live-streaming performances. But it just so happened, she was by nature timid about exposing herself to an invisible, potentially critical worldwide audience she could neither see nor feel. Her anxiety intensified, spiraled.

When she experienced her first crazy troll ripping apart her performance in an online post-performance forum, it was too much to bear; she turned to anti-anxiety medication for the first time in her life.

Initially, the medication eased her anxiousness, but after a few months she stopped taking it because of unpleasant and addictive side effects. Because she continued to experience anxiety and excessive tension in her body that negatively impacted her performance even after returning to her regular schedule, Anne reached out to me. Within just a few days, her nerves settled down substantially. Using the techniques I taught her—and will teach you—she almost immediately began to experience ease and calm within her mind and body.

I shared with Anne that I'd spoken with many musicians during the pandemic who were battling unfamiliar performance anxiety after so many months off stage, and that what she was experiencing wasn't unusual at all.

Knowing that she wasn't alone in this experience that had felt so isolating reassured her, and she mentioned how incredibly important she thinks it is for musicians to open up, dare to be vulnerable, and share details of their sufferings with others so they can offer mutual support.

She shared with me what I've mentioned to you: that it's almost taboo for musicians to admit their suffering, whether that suffering is mental, emotional, or physical, which leaves them to bear any upset in silence and alone. Besides, it's common knowledge that making a living as a musician in a society that chronically undervalues artists isn't always easy, to say the least!

Here's what Anne, a brass player, wants you to know:

"As a musician, tension is devastating to performing and also leads to performance anxiety, it's a terrible cycle. Slowly but surely, I had developed many habits that caused me to experience extreme physical and mental tension. I was no longer enjoying performing or making music, I was simply surviving!

"Out of desperation, Google searches lead me to find Jennifer Roig-Francolí and The Art of Freedom Method. I looked at her impressive website and watched a few YouTube videos and I knew I had found something that could actually help me! I enrolled in a six-month coaching program and started my journey back to ease!

"Rather than treating the symptoms of my anxiety and tension, Jennifer gave me tools that allow my mind to find ease and improve my use of my Primary Instrument—my whole self. I fully accept that life has no arrival or point of being complete: with my ConstructiveThinking tools I'm a work in progress! But I'm no longer in survival mode and I'm experiencing joy in performing once again!"

Finding balance in life is hard when you're uncomfortable

Like with everyone else, the musician's experience ripples into multiple aspects of their lives: physical, mental, emotional, and/or spiritual.

Many professional musicians experience chronic physical discomfort from misuse or overuse of their muscles during long hours of making repetitive movements while playing. Others suffer from emotional problems such as anxiety or depression, hypersensitivity and reactivity, frustration, or even burnout in respect to their professional environment. And in my coaching experience, physical problems including injury are usually intertwined with mental disorganization and emotional discomfort. After all, it's hard to think clearly and feel joyous and free when you're hurting!

It's also common for artists to have difficulty balancing the work they're passionate about with other areas of life. For instance, it can be hard to maintain healthy, loving relationships while on tour or having a packed rehearsal and performance schedule for weeks at a time without any time off. In addition, many musicians work multiple jobs to make ends meet.

On top of their regular duties, music educators can easily become consumed by caring for their students, trying to accommodate parents or an unsympathetic administration, arranging extra recitals and other events, and doing a thousand tasks that add up to being great at their job, at the price of being a stressed-out person who doesn't have time to relax or "have a life."

It can end up taking a real toll on their body as well as their mental outlook.

If you can relate to this, you might ask yourself how your current lifestyle measures up to what you were expecting when you first embarked on your career.

Are you living the dream you set out to create when you were younger? Or are you feeling disappointed or frustrated by your lack of success or slow progress?

Maybe you'd always expected to be in a more creative or electrifying work environment . . . or you'd hoped to get greater recognition.

Do you feel well compensated for all the time and energy you expend in your work, including practice, preparation, and travel time, and the many investments in instruments, equipment, and education over the years? Or would you say you're underpaid, undervalued, and perhaps even resentful towards society and your employers?

Even if you've been fortunate enough to achieve a high level of professional success—with no complaints about your work environment—the stress of being a professional performer or educator can still be truly intense, and your demanding schedule may feel at times relentless. This pressure can wreak havoc on your sense of well-being. We'll be talking more about your purpose, expectations, and life-balance in the next chapter.

Let's talk about pain

Of course, it's not just professional musicians who struggle. Musicians of all skill levels can find themselves faced with a variety of problems that make it harder to feel good about themselves and enjoy their music. In fact, the problems musicians have to deal with usually take root much earlier in life.

When I was on the faculty of a well-respected university music conservatory, I was surprised to come into contact with so many young students who were already contemplating quitting music and changing careers.

Most of these kids were passionate about music. But when they got to the conservatory, they found that they were woefully unprepared to deal with the competitive pressure in that environment. In their private Alexander Technique lessons, they confided to me that the tension was palpable every time they walked through the halls, but they didn't have the knowledge or skills to take care of themselves and stay balanced and healthy in mind, body, and spirit.

These typical college music students came to me regularly with physical problems such as tendonitis, back pain, shoulder and neck pain; mental problems such as difficulty concentrating and organizing their time; emotional problems such as performance anxiety and depression; and—because they were unable to relax while playing—technical problems with their instruments they couldn't get past.

Many of my students suffered from a general sense of overwhelm. None were lazy; in fact, they were typically good students who chose to take my class because they cared dearly about succeeding in life and music.

Of course, applied-instrument teachers have job descriptions that don't go beyond teaching the musical skills required for students to excel at their instruments. Most music teachers aren't professionally trained to help kids with the physical and emotional issues they face daily.

Unfortunately, it's not uncommon for music teachers themselves to unwittingly (or, in rare cases, maliciously) contribute to their own students' problems, by demanding that they practice unreasonably long hours, berating them when they make mistakes or their progress seems too slow, looming over their shoulders during rehearsals, yelling, or threatening them with poor grades and predicting career failure if they don't work harder.

After I left the university and began working with amateurs, aspiring professionals, and career musicians from around the world, I discovered just how common what my university students were experiencing is, and how many people have given up on their musical dreams—or settled for less than what's truly possible—because of it. The problems I've described are actually very common, no matter the artist's skill level, and are not at all unique to the institution where I was teaching.

When musicians come to me for coaching, I very quickly put them at ease. Through a carefully designed, step-by-step process, I help them draw the connection between their mental outlook, emotions, physical sensations and movements, on the one hand, and their artistry.

Fortunately, these musicians quickly come to recognize that they need a more holistic, expansive, and balanced approach to their daily life and music-making. When they come to me, they are curious, ready to learn, and willing to take full responsibility for their experience. This allows them to practice what I teach so they can experience a shift in perspective and a transformation in how they feel and play, often within days or weeks.

After we had just a few sessions together, my university students were able to start changing unhelpful habits. They began to truly enjoy their college experience and look forward to thriving in one of the best professions in the world: music-making!

Musicians all want to enjoy making the best music possible

We musicians all have two major things in common: we want to FEEL good and PLAY better—whether that means giving a stellar performance for thousands at Carnegie Hall or joyfully playing our heart out, alone in a practice room!

I grew up in a musical family: my mother was a Suzuki-method cello teacher, and my dad is an amateur violist, violinist, and trombonist. Both of my parents are now retired, and they've taken to playing multiple instruments in community ensembles, which they thoroughly enjoy!

My parents have always been passionate about music, but they've had their share of struggles like everyone else. For my mother, debilitating shoulder pain forced her to switch from the cello to the clarinet in her retirement . . . while back pain and multiple surgeries have at times made long rehearsals and certain techniques difficult for my father to navigate.

Despite my own occasional physical pain when playing the violin, which I will go into later, my main struggle as a young performer was frustration at my technical limitations. Every night I would listen to recordings of the great violinists like Nathan Milstein or Michael Rabin play my favorite pieces as I fell asleep, but my own playing always fell short, to the point that I could hardly bear listening to a recording of myself!

Have you ever been an audience member at a concert when all you could do was stare in awe at the performer with your jaw dropped, asking yourself: *But how do they make it look so EASY?!?!!* . . . because you KNOW from much practice and personal experience how incredibly hard it is to do what they're doing.

It can be maddening when you see Itzhak Perlman—or a random eight-year-old on YouTube—play with seemingly no limitations, and yet you ask yourself, perplexed: *Why can I not play the music I love with relaxed abandon, confidence, effortless ease? Will I ever?*

I routinely practiced every day for hours, but even though I played at a very high level when young, my progress was never as swift, and my technique was far from being as satisfying, as I wished. Certain pieces and flashy techniques, I seemed unable to play. And I had a feeling that somehow, no matter how long I practiced—over any number of years—never would I be able to conquer them. I could have consented to that, but I didn't really, which is one reason why around the age of nineteen I ended up drifting away from my solo violin career for decades.

Thankfully, today is different. Though many pieces I still can't play, I have a deep, full-bodied understanding of what is interfering with my performing the most challenging passages. Now, I know exactly what steps to take to master those pieces if I really wanted to—a process vastly different from what I thought it was when I was a teenager, which, to me then, basically meant a lot of detailed woodshedding (that is, practicing and practicing till a piece was perfect).

I rarely experience pain or performance anxiety these days, and if I do, I know how to turn it around quickly, so that both I and my music improve as a result.

I now understand how my old mindset—for instance, worrying about what others thought of me and how they might judge my performance—caused excess muscular tension, and that mind-body combination multiplied the difficulties in my playing—and my whole life (!), making *everything* harder, more difficult. And I've learned how to undo that tension, consistently and reliably, whenever I want to get amazing results that make me HAPPY. *I want to teach that to you in this book.*

Are you ready for such a transformation? It can be simply achieved! It all comes down to how you're using your MIND and moving your BODY . . . *right NOW*.

Throughout this book, I'll be describing in detail what I've discovered through my own experience, including playing with and teaching hundreds of musicians. It's no exaggeration to say that what I've found paves the way to resolving *any* of the mental, physical, emotional, or spiritual blockages I've described up until this point—and infinitely more.

I call this comprehensive solution The Art of Freedom® Method for conscious living and masterful artistry. It's largely based on my own experience with the F. M. Alexander Technique as applied to life and music.

In the next chapter, I'll be sharing the five Life-Pillars of The Art of Freedom Method, which shine a light on five fundamental aspects of who you are as a musician.

By looking at your life and artistry through the holistic lens of these five Life-Pillars, you'll begin to see how *all the problems you will ever face as a musician* are intimately connected to every aspect of your whole self and reflected in the everyday world you experience.

The rest of this book will show you how the simple solution to every problem you might face as a musician depends on letting go of what obscures this unifying connection so you can see and appreciate the essential unity of yourself and the world around you. When you shift your perspective away from what's troubling you and *towards* what's already working, easy, and harmonious, suddenly a fresh experience emerges, revealing the ever-expanding, joyful reality perpetually unfolding within you . . . right now.

RESOURCE:

Throughout this book, I will share supplemental bonus materials that you can download online. To begin, you can access an outline of the book with key points from each chapter here: https://www.artoffreedom.me/book/bonusmaterials

Getting to Know Yourself

The Art of Freedom® Method for conscious living and masterful artistry

The privilege of a lifetime is to become who you truly are.
~ *Carl Jung*

The more I live and work as a holistic teacher and coach for musicians, the more it amazes me how similar we human beings are, insofar as basic needs, struggles, and desires; and yet, how absolutely unique our individual life experiences are!

Witnessing the ever-changing variety and constant unfolding of these experiences lends the artist endless material for creative expression. It gives us a very powerful way to help and lift one another up, especially when our curiosity is sparked to see and explore things from a slightly different angle.

This shift in perspective—to one deeper, more universal—can happen gradually or in a flash, suddenly waking up a more fundamental awareness of our essential unity with the world and people around us. If we simply have the desire to watch, learn, and let this goodness happen, this awakening has the potential to lift up our individual spirits and benefit all of humanity in beautiful and unexpected ways.

We musicians are so fortunate to be able to share meaningful, wordless experiences, which is a big reason why many of us are drawn to music in the first place: music allows us to tap into, feel, and communicate experiences in a way that can be profoundly healing.

I've found this to be personally true for myself and most of the musicians I've known and worked with. However, I've also come to recognize our common shortcomings; how we blindly block the free flow of creative energy and unconsciously sabotage our best performances; how we doubt ourselves, hold back and hesitate to share out of fear of judgment; and how ultimately, forgetting the source of our healing, we obscure the shining truth of who we really are.

My vision of the heights of what's possible for us as human beings, along with the awareness of how we all get in our own way to varying degrees, has led me to create what I call The Art of Freedom Method for conscious living and masterful artistry.

This method gives you a new way of practicing with your whole self that allows you to get at the root cause of whatever's holding you back from fearlessly expressing your unique perspective on life and fully realizing your potential.

The five Life-Pillars of The Art of Freedom Method are the following:

1) Purpose

2) Mind

3) Body

4) Spirit

5) Artistry

This unique five-pillared approach focuses on how you can apply yourself to your personal goals, overcome challenges, and improve your musical skills. By integrating the five Life-Pillars of The Art of Freedom, you can experience accelerated success in all areas of your life, including mastering your instrument and finding balance and joy in your relationships and routine activities.

Becoming more aware of the interconnected aspects of who you are as an artist brings with it insights into deep desires that may have previously eluded you. You'll also learn how to take integrated and appropriate action towards achieving both personal and professional goals, resulting in a life of ever-increasing ease, mindful presence, and joy.

In this chapter we'll take a brief look at each of these five pillars and some common challenges that can come up in our musical lives.

The first step to healing and solving each of these problems is to see them with as much objectivity as possible. Just as crystal flaws in a diamond can be removed by heat treatment, the problems we perceive within ourselves begin to dissolve if we shed the light of awareness on them, one day at a time.

Even though it's not really possible to separate these five aspects of who we are, we tend to experience particular problems more strongly within one or another of the Life-Pillars, depending on whether the problems are primarily motivational, mental, physical, spiritual, or artistic.

It all comes down to getting to know yourself better, your habits of being, and—whether the activity is playing double-stops on the violin, doing the dishes, or walking through a forest—how you approach it.

Learning to observe and listen to yourself with warm compassion, finding out what your Inner Wisdom is telling you from moment to moment, will work best for YOUR whole self and your unique situation, regardless of what might be helpful for someone else, and regardless of what others may think you should do. This is the goal and expertise of The Art of Freedom.

"For many, many years, I viewed tension as my main enemy. I felt it was somehow at the root of my problems—from technical limitations with the cello to performance anxiety, from physical pain to depression—and I committed myself wholeheartedly to finding a way out. But despite a huge investment of energy and money and a host of different strategies for overcoming these issues, I found myself getting worse, not better. I just couldn't see that the never-ending struggle to 'fix myself' was actually making me sicker.

"Jennifer offered me a way to step out of this vicious cycle and walk off the battlefield. While it has not always been easy (nothing worthwhile is!), I can say without reservation that learning the Art of Freedom has been (and continues to be) the most rewarding journey of my lifetime. My life has improved in immeasurable and unexpected ways, and my focus has shifted away from unhappily trying to fix myself, to finding immense joy and gratification in the moment-to-moment process of transformation. What a precious and invaluable gift!"

~ Wendy, Cellist and Educator

Pillar #1: Purpose

The first essential aspect of The Art of Freedom is to develop clarity of purpose—know what you want.

To do this, begin by asking yourself "WHY" you're doing what you're doing, because with a lack of clarity about what you want in life—or with foggy musical goals—you simply can't achieve results that are truly excellent and repeatable. Instead, you'll find yourself distracted, scattering your energy, wasting your time focused on things that have very little to do with what you really want.

When you don't have a purpose that resonates from your heart, other desires will compete for your attention; the result is inner conflict that swerves you off-course when things get difficult. No longer will you be able to stay centered, calm, and disciplined if you feel frustrated by a subpar performance, the loss of a promised gig which fell through, a family conflict, or financial troubles.

When your purpose is clear, you'll always have a reliable anchor or inner GPS that gets you back on track, so you can make steady progress instead of sliding backwards, lost, each time you try to get ahead.

You can practice your instrument every day, but if you're disconnected from your purpose, you won't feel fully integrated and aligned in your body or your soul; some niggling dissatisfaction or discomfort will always be at your side, and consequently, the depth of your musical message won't get through.

In addition, when left unconscious or unattended to, lack of purpose and clear intentions will always show up—sooner or later—as physical or emotional discomfort. Or both.

When I ask my students what they want, some of them are very specific (*I want to play this technical passage better, win that audition, or get rid of this pain from an old shoulder injury*), while the intentions of others are more general (*I just want to enjoy my life; I want to make other people happy when I play my music*).

Whether you start from a general purpose or specific, that clarity of intention will support all the decisions you make, keeping you motivated as you aim towards what you know in your heart you really want.

Pillar #2: Mind

One of the most important skills you need is to get better control over the mind through increased awareness of your mental habits. I say this for anyone.

Every single action we take begins as an idea in the mind, whether conscious or unconscious. Whether we're able to turn our dreams into reality or not depends almost entirely on how much conscious control we have over the mind and, by extension, our body and emotions.

If you want to move with more ease and less tension—to relax while playing your instrument, overcome performance anxiety, improve your musical skills, and feel more comfortable being

YOU in any situation . . . one of the first things you need is to develop a powerful mindset for success; for that, you need to learn that most important skill of getting conscious, positive control over your mind.

Have you ever heard the adage, "what you think is what you get"? Well, it's worth exploring; there's a lot of truth to it. In fact, every single thought you have, even if it's a subtle reaction to a fleeting thought that flickers quick as lighting and disappears before you're even aware of it, is instantly reflected by the body.

Since many of our unconscious thoughts are self-critical and subtly corrode our confidence and stunt our personal growth, if you tend to go through your day or play your instrument on autopilot, this lack of awareness can present a real problem and even sabotage your performance.

For example, performance anxiety—while it shows up with physical symptoms: shaking, increased heart rate, or difficulty breathing, for example—always begins with a certain fear-based thought pattern you've been cultivating unconsciously, often over time.

When you have a negative thought (such as, "What if I mess up?" "I'll never learn this," "I'll never be good enough," or "What if my pain never goes away?"), your nervous system is instantly activated towards some degree of fight-flight-freeze response, or *startle pattern*.

As a result of negative thoughts like these, you'll experience increased muscular tension (just what you don't want before a concert) and other uncomfortable symptoms in various parts of your body. Living with a fearful frame of mind makes everything you do more difficult because your body is full of tension, blocking ease and freedom of movement. Unfortunately, much of that systemic tension lives below the level of your conscious awareness, which is one reason why simply relaxing the body directly whenever you feel tension doesn't work for very long.

Also, when your mind is fretting about a potential negative future or remembering an unpleasant experience in the past, it's harder to stay aware in the present moment, which is the only one you actually have control over. This makes it all too easy to lose sight of how much is in fact going well, so that it's nearly impossible to relax and enjoy yourself, resulting in tenseness the audience picks up on.

The Art of Freedom helps you to harness the power of your conscious mind. It does that by showing you that you're free to *choose where to place your awareness*. That is, you can learn to pay more attention to how you're thinking, what you're experiencing in your body, and what direction you're going in, free of expectation and self-judgment.

Through this integrative approach, you come to understand that you really are free to choose your own thoughts and thereby experience more of what you want. It's up to YOU to find out which of your thoughts are hurting you and which ones are taking you in the positive direction of a life that's healthier, happier, and free to enjoy music-making the way you've always longed to!

Pillar #3: Body

The third essential aspect of The Art of Freedom Method is the body. Since your body reflects the state of your mind, it follows that your body and your emotions will be in harmonious balance only when your mind is calmly under your conscious control and in alignment with your fundamental purpose.

Becoming more balanced and aligned in your whole self means learning how to expand your awareness to include the whole body, listen to its wisdom, and nonjudgmentally accept what you're feeling. Wishing the body were different in some way—denying it—will always lead to suffering sooner or later, whether that takes the form of mental chaos, emotional discomfort, physical pain, or all of the above.

The source of our biggest problems originates from forgetting that everything within ourselves and around us is intimately connected as one infinite cosmic substance. Our sense of separation is superficial, not essential.

Not only do we pretend that different parts of the body are unrelated and tension in one area doesn't affect the rest, but we split ourselves into different parts, too . . . taking the mind, body, emotions, and spirit to be unrelated, isolated entities. In reality, everything influences and needs everything else for full expression to occur.

For example, if I want to lift my violin, it's because the desire first enters my mind, which lights up areas of my brain, which activates the nervous system, which stimulates muscles to change their shape in order for my arm to finally lift up my violin. When I want to move my fingers to play a musical phrase, again it's the idea that initiates a sequence of events culminating in expressive movement.

As mentioned in Chapter 1, I used to think of music-making as primarily a mental activity. I had absolutely no idea I had to include the whole body in my awareness for best results—without fail!

In including the body in our awareness, we need to remember that the body is essentially innocent. All too often we blame our aching body for our pain or technical problems, but the body is simply doing what it's designed to do, which is to carry out the mind's intentions and manifest the consequences of past thoughts or actions into our current experience.

When we experience uncomfortable feelings of tension or pain, it's simply the body giving us valuable information signaling us to course-correct.

It's so important that we not ignore the signals our body is sending! We need to learn to appreciate and pay attention to what our body's telling us and respond with wise choices based on that information.

Mindlessly ignoring pain or pushing through it is a way of shutting ourselves down and ignoring the inner wisdom inside of us, and it will just make the healing and learning process that much slower.

We need to cultivate a quiet internal stillness in mind and body so that we can open up and listen to the wisdom being revealed by the body in every single moment. And then, to learn how to stop doing what isn't working, and instead make new, responsible choices that are tailored to our unique situation, taking into account what we discover by listening to our whole self—mind, body, emotions, and all.

Pillar #4: Spirit

When I was a kid, my violin teachers sometimes said, "Play with spirit!"

Also, sometimes I would see "con spirito" written into the sheet music I was playing from.

Play with spirit. What did it mean? I didn't have a clearly defined idea, but I somehow understood in my heart what it meant, since getting in touch with the deep meaning of music and its central role in life had always come naturally. It was easy for me.

As if there really were such a thing as a mystical Muse or Genius spirit who wanted to give my music an extra-special spark and connect me to something mysterious and much grander than myself, I knew intuitively from a young age that I needed to let go and let the music speak through me.

My teachers instilled in me the need to be sensitive and stay true to a composer's intentions, as if my role were simply to be a conduit for expressing the "spirit of Bach," for example, through a pure and sincere interpretation and faithfulness to his musical ideas.

My parents had always emphasized that the most important reason for performing was to communicate with the audience, and that communication needed to come directly from the heart.

I understood that only if I were first moved by the music *myself* could my audiences be touched, inspired, and moved by the music in turn. Even though I did this naturally, I really had absolutely no idea HOW I was doing it, or how this process of inspired communication worked. All I knew was that somehow I had to get out of the way and let the composer's ideas flow through me the best I could.

Now, after a lifetime of exploration in the realm of ideas, creativity, the arts, meditation and spirituality, I've learned the conscious aspect of this—that it is possible to consciously activate Inspiration and convey deep meaning with awareness and consistent intention; one of the most effective ways being by adopting the holistic strategies I practice and teach my students, which actualize the whole self as a vehicle for expression and dynamic flow.

So that Inspiration can flow easily through us, it's essential to know how to get out of the way. This skill enables us to create the musical life we want, stimulate the healing we need, and communicate universal Love to the world.

I believe truly great artistry simply isn't possible without connecting to and sharing our creative spirit openly with ease and humility. This conviction is at the core of everything I teach.

Pillar #5: Artistry

The way we live, share ideas, and gracefully express ourselves through the medium of music is the fifth pillar of The Art of Freedom Method: Artistry.

When I think of artistry, I think of how we live and express ourselves with grace and meaning. I like to remember how ancient cultures taught people to integrate art and music into their whole lives and combine different art forms as one. They didn't restrict their definition of music the way we tend to do in modern times.

Let's take a look at what the musical arts are according to the thirteenth-century text *Sangita-Ratnakara*, considered a reliable source on ancient Indian music. It identifies three formats of music: *Gitam* (vocal), *Vadyam* (instrumental) and *Nrtyam* (dance)—the three collectively being *Sangita* (music).[2] To this day, Indian classical musicians are inspired by this three-fold definition of music, the performance of which is also considered an act of spiritual devotion.

Through singing and dancing, the musician experiences that the whole body is involved in making music. One of the most important things I learned during my very brief foray into Indian classical violin lessons was that Indian musicians must learn how to sing before they are allowed

2 Rare Book Society of India, https://www.rarebooksocietyofindia.org/postDetail.php?id=196174216674_10157080022386675. Also see Sangita-Ratnakara, https://en.wikipedia.org/wiki/Sangita_Ratnakara.

to begin learning an instrument. In this way, the instrument becomes like a second voice—the external expressing the internal.

When we look to Western history, we see that the ancient Greeks understood music to be a gift from the heavens, promoting harmony. They spoke of a music of the spheres, planets, and other celestial bodies. To them, music was both completely natural and utterly heavenly. I agree!

These ancestors included dance, lyrics, and the performance of poetry in their concept of music. In Greek tragedy, for example, the chorus is an intricate aspect, alternating with the dialogue, and not just any form of dialogue; it's in iambic trimeter or other form of verse or rhythmic speechverse.

> It is often forgotten that the writings at the root of Western literature—the epics of Homer, the love-poems of Sappho, the tragedies of Sophocles and Euripides—were all, originally, music.
>
> Dating from around 750 to 400 BC, they were composed to be sung in whole or part to the accompaniment of the lyre, reed-pipes, and percussion instruments.[3]
>
> Pythagoras firmly believed that music is not only mathematics and harmony but can be applied as medicine.
>
> He first observed that certain tunes and rhythms can calm the mind and the soul. Others can invigorate a person. Once he had discovered the basics of this phenomenon, he started to create compositions for certain purposes, sort of recipes. Like a *playlist* in our modern days.
>
> In his school in Crotona, it was customary to start and end each day with singing. Pythagoreans gathered in a circle with a lead singer in the middle, often accompanied by a musician with a lyre. In the morning they sang songs that helped to wake up and inspire for activities, in the evening those that were relaxing and supported resting.[4]

---

3 Wikipedia, The Sound of Music Greek Style - Archaeology Wiki.
4 "Pythagoras on Music," Pythagoras on music – Popular Beethoven.

He was the first person to prescribe music as medicine.[5]

Auditory music is made up of rhythm, melody, and harmony—plus the ground of silence underneath and in between sounds. The Art of Freedom Method recognizes the transcendent, healing properties of audible and inaudible music, and in the idea of musical living we include creativity in all conceivable art forms.

Singing, dancing, playing an instrument . . . painting, writing . . . or even walking down the street with graceful ease and awareness . . . THIS is what turns life into art and makes life musical to me: having an awareness of any of these creative, musical elements while moving.

To me, music is a natural expression of the mind, body, and spirit. To be human is to be musical, and we all have the capacity to grow through developing our artistry. Making music helps us naturally uplift and transcend our humanity, giving all of us a way to connect to something bigger than our limited, individual personalities.

Everyone has harmony, melody, and rhythm inside, and an urge to express those vibrations in daily life. Learning how to get out of the way of those natural vibrations is a beautiful and centering healing process. Through this process, you become more and more aware of who you are as a whole. ***This is the very definition of healing—becoming whole.***

Just as much for the musician as for the listener, music is healing. It is a vibrant, shared experience, and when you get out of the way of this mutual exchange of energies, you realize that this unifying, loving experience allows us to forgive and transcend our superficial differences.

Everything that is life-enhancing and communicates love brings meaning, joy, and healing to the world—and God knows, the world needs healing these days! I find it truly delightful when I'm able to communicate these ideas and share this experience of love and light with others.

I hope these ideas are making you curious to learn more about how you too can do this! I've created a handy tool to help you reflect on the five Life-Pillars and identify some of the areas that could benefit from a little more of your attention. You can download a Personal Life-Balance Assessment Tool from the Bonus Materials resource page here: https://www.artoffreedom.me/book/bonusmaterials

In the following chapters of Part I, we'll be taking a deeper look into the five Life-Pillars I've presented here, beginning with Pillar #1, Purpose.

---

5 Gabriela de la Mora and Marian Kraus, Pythagoras - anything and more you may have ever wanted to know (delamora.life).

Living on Purpose

Is your reality living up to your dreams?

You are never too old to set another goal or to dream a new dream.

~ *C. S. Lewis*

We musicians are Idealists. Dreamers.

Lovers. Romantics.

Traditionalists. Iconoclasts . . .

. . . and everything else under the sun!

We are human beings whose souls have become enraptured by the ever-changing and infinite variety of shapes, colors, and waves of meaning carried to us on the wings of sound. Our music reflects the entire capacity and richness of the human experience in all its divine glory, as well as its darkest, lowliest misery.

When we chose to become musicians—or music found us—it was because we knew in our hearts there is no better or more beautiful way to connect and share the very depths of who we are.

We live music, breathe music, and risk other parts of our lives and our well-being to pour it all out to the world. Every day, we bare our souls and express ourselves as profoundly as we can.

If you're like most professional musicians, like myself, you've probably spent thousands of hours—maybe an entire lifetime—devoted to your art.

You may have invested tens of thousands of dollars on teachers, university degrees, instruments, equipment, and travel . . . foregoing thousands of hours of leisure time, saying no to endless social activities, holing up alone in a practice room instead.

You've set yourself apart from your neighbors, peers, and loved ones, so you can somehow achieve your goal of transforming your musical ideas into magical sounds and your lifelong dreams into reality.

So, after all these years of passionate dedication and sacrifice, if things still aren't working out, it's no wonder if sometimes you feel desperate for things to finally change for the better, if not a little disillusioned.

It's easy to feel disappointed when the big dreams you had when you were younger turn out to seem unachievable. This inner restlessness is a big reason why the majority of musicians experience physical, mental, emotional, and spiritual suffering over their art.

Here are some of the frustrating situations you might be encountering:

- Your playing still doesn't accurately reflect the music you hear in your mind.
- You're unable to play the music that challenges you most because your technique is stuck at a certain level, and no matter how much or how hard you practice, you just can't break through.
- Even though you feel musical passion in your heart, you can't communicate it freely and fearlessly.
- Your career isn't as satisfying as you thought it would be, and you see few options for advancement.
- You don't receive the recognition you deserve because someone "ahead of" or "better than" you ends up in the limelight instead.
- Audiences, families, and communities don't seem to truly appreciate the value of what you are offering.

On the other hand, you might be so used to life falling short of your expectations that you've accepted this as your reality. And perhaps you decided long ago to settle for the status quo as more comfortable than endless striving on a futile path. Of course, if you're happy, there's nothing wrong with that!

But if you have a niggling suspicion that you aren't truly fulfilling your potential, and deep down you just KNOW you could be enjoying your life more and making better music with more ease and under better conditions . . .

. . . then you might be harboring little whispers under the surface with questions like . . .

Is this it? Is this all there is? Am I really stuck with this lifestyle forever?

What did I do wrong? Am I just not as naturally talented as others, or am I just unlucky?

Why do I still feel like I'm not good enough? Do I just need to practice more and work harder? What am I missing?

If you're having doubts and worries like these about your self-worth and your abilities as a musician, or you're feeling down about the musical profession as a whole, please know that you're not alone. These thoughts are common!

I've played with dozens of orchestras and ensembles, and I've talked and worked with hundreds of musicians, both as colleagues and as my students. Again and again I've seen these kinds of doubts alive in almost all musicians, to some degree or another. But most hide them—even from themselves—because it can be really hard to face the truth that you're not perfectly satisfied with your life and you wish so much things were better.

These thoughts come up to poke you from time to time to keep you from languishing in complacency or digging your heels in deeper, to remind you that there actually IS more for you to achieve and enjoy. Uncomfortable emotions are there to spur you on to make positive changes. As unsettling as these thoughts and feelings are, it's really healthy to look difficulties in the eye, and you're reading this book for a reason.

The truth is, most musicians are NOT living up to their full artistic potential, and everyone can always improve, no matter where they are in life and no matter their musical skill level. As the great Spanish cellist Pablo Casals said when he was asked at sixty-seven, again at eighty, and perhaps later, why he kept practicing, "Because I think I'm making progress!"[6]

What you need to remember is that despite the whispers of your "Doubt Monsters," if you're not making the progress you'd like, and your life isn't shaping up as planned, it's not

6 Garson O'Toole, Quote Investigator, I Feel that I Am Making Daily Progress – Quote Investigator.®

because there's something wrong with you. And it's not because you're lazy, untalented, unlucky, or stupid!

Your sense of lack or deficiency comes from a deep disconnection from your true purpose and a lack of awareness of who you really are; you haven't yet learned how to fully enjoy yourself and your music. The good news is . . . you can always start over and learn how . . . right now! :)

There's a lot of talk about how happiness is a choice, and I agree, even though it can seem totally impossible to be happy under certain circumstances. If I ever begin to doubt this, I'm always reminded of Viktor Frankl, the Jewish-Austrian psychologist known for founding the "third school" of Viennese psychotherapy, following after the first school, of Freud and the second, of Alfred Adler. But Frankl's theory came out of his experience in a concentration camp. He came to the conviction that we are each mainly motivated by a search for meaning in life, a search that, he believed, psychotherapy should be focused on helping us find.

Frankl's trials from the Nazis were many and extreme. Some of what he had to endure included: his wife being forced to abort her child; his father dying in a concentration camp; his being transported, along with his wife and mother, to Auschwitz; being forced to throw away his unpublished manuscript; catching typhoid fever; and keeping himself awake to prevent delirium and a fatal vascular collapse by piecing his manuscript back together on bits of paper he found and a companion stole for him from the Dachau office.

Through self-discipline and extreme vigilance over his thoughts, he was able to uplift his own spirits and the spirits of everyone around him, so they could rise above the horror of their external conditions, despite all odds. (Read the autobiographical *Man's Search for Meaning*.)

The big lesson here is that if you want to be happy, prioritize happiness. Do what it takes to realize it. To me, this means happiness is not only a choice, but also a *skill* that needs conscious practice to experience it more and more. To me, choosing to live life consciously, on purpose, is a prerequisite to happiness and the key to creating more successful experiences for yourself.

In my coaching programs, I explore the idea of purpose with my students. I challenge them to probe into what they truly want. By learning to ask questions and wonder in a way that doesn't demand instant answers, and by practicing specific awareness skills, they learn how to focus their energies efficiently and effectively. They then make noticeable, quicker progress towards the purpose they've uncovered.

When they begin to appreciate how their new direction is influencing the choices they're making in music, frustration wanes. It comes up less and less often as happiness starts to shine again in the practice room and onstage!

It is my sincere wish that reading this book will reignite the flames of your initial passion for music, wake up long-forgotten dreams, and show you step-by-step exactly how to fearlessly and delightfully pursue your creativity. Thus, to enjoy personal and professional success *at a deeper level than you ever imagined.*

That's right. Deeper than you imagined. I've seen it happen over and over.

Before going into what's possible when you apply the ideas in this book, let's take a closer look at a typical musical trajectory, including the common dreams and disillusionments most professional musicians experience at some point.

The musical life you signed up for

The first thing you probably fell in love with when you first set out on the path of becoming a musician was making the music itself.

As you developed a practice routine over time, you got more and more specific about the level of artistry you wanted to achieve. Also, how you wanted your musical career to play out.

Did you excitedly imagine performing for audiences as a soloist? An orchestral musician? a chamber musician? Or maybe you always wanted to run your own studio or teach as a professor at a university.

Maybe you dreamed of playing at Carnegie Hall, winning a big competition, touring the world, or cutting award-winning recordings. Or maybe you imagined playing chamber music with friends in your living room by the fireplace on a snowy wintry evening.

No matter, you probably didn't know how it was going to work out. But one thing was crystal clear: if you were going to achieve your goals, you would need to work hard—probably for a long time—to get there.

If your motivation was strong, you did the work. You found teachers to support you. You put in the practice hours. Maybe you went to a music conservatory or traveled overseas, like I did, to study with top artists in the summertime.

In addition to your music life, you most likely also looked forward to having extra time to enjoy good relationships with friends, family, colleagues, and community.

If you've achieved some—or all—of these things, I heartily congratulate you and hope you really appreciate what you've done because this is no small task! Everything you've achieved you've done by setting your sights on a goal and doing what it took to get there, despite every setback along the way. And setbacks there must have been.

But what if having achieved a lot, you still don't feel happy or successful inside? And what if your original goals now seem completely unachievable, and you don't feel successful at all?

Whether things look great on the outside or not, far too many musicians suffer on the inside. Let's talk about what it looks like for many musicians who don't feel like they're fulfilling their purpose and, therefore, feel neither happy nor successful.

Unconscious beliefs drive your experience of success and self-esteem

Musicians on the whole are very familiar with the concepts of sacrifice, hard work, and suffering. How many of the following expressions did *you* grow up with?

"No pain, no gain"—"You need to suffer for your art"

"Starving artist"—"Musicians are poor"

"Music isn't a *real* job"

"You shouldn't make music for the money"

I remember when I was hired as an extra violinist for the renowned Cincinnati POPS Orchestra one summer, a neighbor of mine naively asked with a casual, quizzical look, "Do you get paid for that?"

Sigghhhh . . .

The problem with growing up in a culture that takes music for granted (just walk into a restaurant where a quite-good unpaid guitarist is gigging for tips) and doesn't value its musicians (at the time I'm writing this book recording artists like myself earn a whopping $0.003–$0.005 on average each time their music is streamed on Spotify) is that our subconscious has been insidiously programmed to blindly accept that popular stereotypes about musicians are actually true.

Not only does this hurt our individual self-concept and work against us in achieving our professional and financial goals, but it subtly affects our overall well-being and the quality of our music, too.

If you've been programmed since childhood to believe that your identity as a musician means you have to suffer, work hard, practice long hours (sometimes until fingers bleed!) . . .

sacrifice friendships, fun, and family activities . . . earn less money than others who have more commonly valued jobs . . . go without luxuries or even starve (!), if necessary, just to prove your worth as an artist . . . well, then you've been hoodwinked!

Unless you decide to question these beliefs and radically shift your perspective to claim your self-worth *independently of what others think*, you're setting yourself up for a less-than-fulfilling, imbalanced life and a painful future.

Unfortunately, a fixed attitude that prizes intensity, hyperfocus, and self-sacrifice, maximizing those to the detriment of natural ease, joy, and well-being, will unwittingly sabotage the quality of your music because you will find it hard to fully enjoy practicing and performing.

It might be hard to detect this chain of events within you because your brain is designed to give you an experience of life that is consistent with your unconscious beliefs. So you will keep finding "proof" that an attitude of hard work and suffering is necessary to become an exceptional artist. Take the stories of the famous French impressionist painter Vincent Van Gogh, who struggled with mental illness and extreme poverty, often trading his paintings for food or art supplies but never selling a single one of his paintings. Or Beethoven, who began to go deaf in his late twenties and couldn't hear his own music at all in his mid-forties. Or one of the most famous American authors of all time, Herman Melville, author of *Moby Dick*, whose success was short-lived and who died poor, with all of his works out of print.

But this is not the point.

If you win an audition after several months of practicing six hours a day, thinking about and doing nothing else, neglecting everything and everyone else around you, what you don't know is that your performance might have been even better with a more relaxed and carefree attitude while also living a more balanced life. To attribute the good fortune to your hard work and intense focus, your intense self-sacrifice alone, then and in the future, is probably a fallacy.

What if you had a more efficient, effective way to prepare for the audition that was integrated with your deeper life purpose? This works, and it is what I am proposing. You might, therefore, have enjoyed the process much more, as well.

Not only that, but your loved ones would have been happier from having more of your undivided attention, your body would feel stronger and healthier (instead of giving you warning hints of impending tendinitis), and after the audition you wouldn't collapse with exhaustion and need days or weeks to recover physically and emotionally.

Unconscious beliefs about our identity and what's possible for us will override what we tell ourselves every time, unless we make our conscious awareness our top priority, and regularly practice applying this awareness to what we're doing in every area of our lives, including the details of how we play our instruments.

So, if you're feeling less than fully satisfied with your life as a musician, it's worth taking some time to question the beliefs you have about musicians and your profession, examining how your culture perceives artists and the arts in general.

You might find it enlightening to ask yourself, "Do I feel valued by those around me? Do I value myself as an artist, and as a human being distinct from my music? Does my life feel balanced in general?" *If you've answered no to any of these questions, you'll be getting a lot of support and powerful solutions in this book!*

Is your life balanced? Do you have enough time for what's important?

One of the biggest indicators that your life is out of balance is that you frequently feel like you don't have enough time. This causes you to rush through your day, under constant pressure, believing that you should be doing more to get things done. Do you give yourself time for the following activities:

- to practice your instrument?
- to play the music you love—just for fun?
- to engage in self-care, including time to meditate, exercise, sleep, and eat well?
- to be with friends and family and nurture other relationships?
- to care for your environment (your instruments, home, garden, car, etc.)?
- to indulge in recreation, travel, hobbies, play, and other creative pursuits?
- to undertake personal development and study?

By the way, if you often feel like you don't have enough time for yourself, then BRAVO to you for making the time to read this book! This book will encourage you to prioritize the things that are most important to you and to become more efficient, saving you lots of time in the long run.

If you take the ideas in this book to heart and start applying them, you'll soon begin to realize that there's really only ONE thing you need to do that really matters, which will make it easier to achieve all of your goals: bring greater conscious awareness to what you're doing with your whole self from moment to moment.

When you start reclaiming your self-worth by putting the focus back on who you are over what you're achieving, meaningless time-and-energy suckers start to fall away; then your life naturally becomes more balanced over time. You'll also learn how to get much more done in less time, giving you back tons of energy for important things that had been falling by the wayside.

Just imagine! What if you could develop a whole new loving relationship with time itself? What if time were your friend instead of a slave driver constantly breathing down your neck?

The paradox about time is that the more you feel strapped for it, the more you need to slow down to "expand" it. In my classes, I like to say, "slow down to speed up!" This advice can be hard to follow if you're addicted to doing things quickly, but in daily life as well as in learning music it's really efficient. It works.

Enjoying the process

People talk about the need to follow your heart, live your passion, and go after your dreams. You may have received these suggestions yourself, and maybe they were a factor that encouraged you to go into music in the first place.

Now, as a more experienced adult, are you still following your heart, living your passion? Even more importantly, are you enjoying the "pursuit of happiness" along the way, or are you stuck, postponing your joy as you work hard now?

Do you have a sense of having "arrived," basking in the self-satisfaction of having "fulfilled" your dreams? Or does the goal post keep moving, rarely allowing you to rest and enjoy a sense of achievement with how far you've already come?

The musicians I know are usually pretty good at congratulating colleagues, celebrating together with drinks or a meal afterward. But sidestepping self-criticism and allowing yourself to feel deep gratitude and appreciation for your *own* accomplishments is much less common. We are typically the first to criticize our own performance, the last to congratulate ourselves on a job well done.

This is because, as a natural survival mechanism to keep us on the lookout for potential predators, the human brain is actually designed to pay more attention to the negative than the positive. Given our habit of minimizing or neglecting the good things in favor of identifying problems and potential dangers, our tendency to move on quickly to tackle our next challenges or dive into the next new project should come as no surprise.

The problem with not letting ourselves feel good along the way—but pushing ahead—is that we don't take the time to fully live and ENJOY the present moment. Plus, when we actually do take the time, our joy is likely to be superficial and short-lived since our brain is already scanning underneath to *plot our next moves in regard to the next problem, in the future*.

This way of living feels "right" to us because of our unconscious beliefs. After all, if on some level you believe you're *supposed* to be a suffering musician, then giving yourself time to rest and feel good will be at odds with that self-concept and you'll be at cross-purposes with yourself.

In psychology, having inconsistent thoughts, beliefs, or attitudes is called "cognitive dissonance"—a very uncomfortable state to stay in. So, we tend to resolve the dissonance by choosing actions more in harmony with our unconscious beliefs—even when they lead us to act in ways that are ultimately self-defeating, out of alignment with our conscious purpose.

Since unconscious beliefs and strong habits will win any fight against a new habit that hasn't taken hold in the brain, you won't be able to permit yourself to feel too good, even when things are going well.

For example, how many times have you played 99 percent of the notes of a piece of music correctly and beautifully in concert, and yet, all you could think about afterwards were the few isolated notes that didn't come out right? Why? Because somewhere inside, your unconscious expected you to mess up. And so, that's what you did. That's your unconscious, working hard to keep your inner world aligned with your self-concept; it's safer that way. Imagine if instead you let down your guard and felt fully excited and gratified about what just happened.

The funny thing is, audiences pick up on your expectations, mirroring them back to you, thanks to how our brains are designed. If you stride onstage feeling joyful, relaxed and fearless, looking forward to a great performance, that puts your audience at ease and they can enjoy your playing, too. In that more relaxed, open state, mistakes are more generously overlooked because everyone is giving the meaning and the essential energy that comes through the music more importance than the small technical details.

On the other hand, if you feel anxious and hurried, worried about what might go wrong, your audience will pick up on your tension and be more likely to care about your mistakes.

In both cases, what you focus on gets magnified. If you are judging yourself, you're more likely to feel judged by your audience, and vice versa. If you don't want to feel judged by your audience, don't *expect* judgment from them, and *don't judge them* if they judge you!

Check in with yourself

Take a moment to skim through the following list. How many of these things cause your energy to dip slightly? How many of them trigger a sense of unease, dissatisfaction, or lack:

- your income and financial situation?
- your career and future job prospects?
- your home and work environments?
- your personal and professional relationships?
- your relationship with yourself (mind, body, spirit)?
- your musical skills, the quality of your music?

Now, go over the list again more slowly. Take a moment to appreciate what actually IS working in each of these areas, and thank yourself for the good work you've done over time to get yourself where you are today. No matter what your situation looks like right now, can you still be grateful for the skills you have, the ideas you have, and the people you connect with?

If you want to make improvements, know that it's actually easier to change things when you're feeling relatively content and grateful, rather than over-focusing on what you don't have or what's not working. Making a habit of counting your blessings and celebrating even the tiniest personal wins on a daily basis is a key to cruising along the road to greater life satisfaction.

When you're practicing . . . why not put down your instrument for a moment and bask in the beautiful sound you just got out of your instrument? Why not feel good about your improving intonation and that newly memorized passage in the moment you get it right, instead of immediately searching for what else might be going wrong that needs fixing in a hurry, before your practice time runs out?

Taking time to pause, acknowledge your achievements, and feel good about yourself is such an important skill to develop. It creates balance and joy, and it's essential to speeding up your progress.

How you react to your external and internal environments influences the quality of your music

If you feel the quality of your music could be better in general—that you're not fulfilling your artistic potential—you might be feeling stuck at a certain level because you can't get past stubborn technical or musical limitations.

You may feel frustrated or embarrassed that your musical product isn't up to the standards others set for you (which you've adopted for yourself), and you may have a niggling suspicion that things will never change and you'll never be good enough, no matter how hard you try to get better.

Most musicians have some level of awareness that they've hit a "technique ceiling," that they're bumping up against some personal limitations in their skills. But even though they can sense they're missing something, they rarely know what it is.

You have a tugging feeling deep down that there MUST be a solution . . . *Why am I blocked? If I could just figure out what it is, I'd be able to finally break free of those limitations. I could finally play the pieces I've always longed to play, move audiences the way I know audiences can be moved.*

If you're like most people, you probably believe the solution is simply to practice more and practice harder.

One of the problems with thinking this way is that you can forget that the quality of your music is greatly affected and shaped by both your external and internal environments. In fact, your success depends much more on how you regulate your reactions to those influences than on how long or how intensely you practice. (More on that in the last chapter, on common myths.)

Bringing The Art of Freedom Method and more awareness of your purpose into your life will help you realize how much your attitude to what's happening within and around you affects the quality of your playing.

You'll become more skilled at noticing how you react to things in your whole mind-body-self. You'll start seeing over time and with practice whether those reactions are taking you in the direction of greater ease and joy, or more dis-ease, tension, and unhappiness.

Here are some external circumstances (past and present) that may cause you to feel insufficiently supported. The way you react to these circumstances may be preventing you from taking appropriate actions to create the life of your dreams. You may find that you lack . . .

- sufficient physical, emotional, spiritual, and/or financial support
- inspiring role models and healthy work situations
- adequate training and education
- financial resources and necessary instruments, equipment, etc.
- professional situations, organizations, and employers who give you what you need to thrive
- the freedom and energy to pursue your dreams, due to an excess of obligations

A lack of outside support can show up internally as a lack of self-knowledge and self-confidence. Do any of the following resonate with you?

- Is it hard to feel enthusiastic and motivated to work towards your goals?
- Are you unclear about the steps needed to get what you want or how to solve the problems getting in your way?
- Do you have a hard time establishing and maintaining healthy boundaries in your personal or professional life?
- Are you confused about how to find a balance between structure and freedom in your life or music?
- Do you feel spiritually off-course, ungrounded, lonely, or disconnected from nature?
- Do you feel the need for more time and space for self-care, self-reflection, and self-direction?

It's clear that both your external and internal environments influence the quality of your life and your ability to evolve. Later in this book, I'll be sharing some specific ways these deprivations can influence your musical practice and performance.

The good news is that, even if past circumstances weren't supportive and your external situation isn't exactly how you want it to be right now, when you work on how you react to both internal and external events, your external circumstances will automatically begin to improve, reflecting the more positive direction you're taking yourself on the inside.

Stephanie's story

When Stephanie joined my private coaching program, she was frustrated with her status quo as an aspiring professional violinist. Despite enjoying long hours of disciplined daily practice, she felt stuck playing in low-caliber community orchestras for free, or playing the odd, unfulfilling wedding gig with other musicians who weren't pulling their weight.

As hard as she tried, Stephanie seemed unable to improve her external circumstances, especially considering that she was the mother of two young children and wasn't willing to move away from the lovely small town where she lived, even though there weren't as many options for her there as in a large city.

Stephanie's dream was to be able to play the repertoire she loves and feel great about her playing, and have other excellent musicians to play with in a professional context. In short, she wanted to enjoy a qualitative performance career, what she'd dreamed of as a student years ago. But she was continually disappointed that the quality of her own playing wasn't improving much, in spite of doing everything "right" and practicing the way she had been taught in music school.

When we started working together, it was very clear to me where she was getting in her own way and I shared with her the exact steps she needed to take in order to increase her awareness, shift her thinking, and experiment with applying The Art of Freedom Method to her daily life and music-making.

I knew the process would work, but I was flabbergasted when Stephanie came to her coaching session after just a few months of working together (mostly without the violin!) and proceeded to play for me. It was like listening to a completely different player as, wide-eyed, I noticed a dramatic improvement in her technique and musicianship. Her bow arm, which had previously been rigid and inflexible, suddenly flowed with smooth bow changes and produced a rich, warm sound from the instrument. Her left hand was more mobile, and her phrasing was nuanced in a way it hadn't been before. Everything was working, and she was loving it!

It was easy for her to make a quantum leap in her playing very quickly because (1) she had such a passionate love of music and (2) she was ready to do whatever it would take to improve—including cultivating the best attitude for learning (as described throughout this book), methodically following all of my suggestions, and humbly trusting the process.

A few months later, Stephanie had a fantastic experience auditioning for a nearby orchestra, and even though she didn't win the orchestra job, she knew she was on the right track because she had superior control over her internal environment—her thoughts, mood, and reactions—even when things on the outside normally would have thrown her off and derailed her performance (including having to bring her kid with her to the audition in the last minute, without a babysitter; and refusing beta blockers from a well-meaning friend driving her to the audition!).

Not long after completing her coaching program with me, Stephanie decided to re-enroll in school to get her master's degree in music performance, and new opportunities began springing up near her. At the time I'm writing this, she has found exciting professional colleagues to perform with in her area, she is in a paying orchestra she's delighted to play in, she has renewed enthusiasm for teaching, AND . . . she sounds better than ever, continuing to use everything I taught her every single day!

As Stephanie's experience illustrates, the best way to change the outward is to shift your focus and prioritize the inward. In doing this, you can capitalize on the incredible power your mind has to design your future. Start paying more attention to the present moment, regardless of your past or current circumstances—what's happening to you right now?—and wait for surprising new good things to appear when you least expect them to!

In the next chapter, we'll take a look at how you think and concentrate, which can either lift you up and take you closer to your goals or, even with the best intentions, can derail your progress.

> "In the last five months, working with Jennifer, I've learned and accomplished so much. I'm playing in ways I never thought would be possible for me. I'm LIVING with a sense of freedom I had no idea would be a benefit of this program! I've taken blindfolded leaps and poured all of my faith into this working for me. And it is. I've played with other people and other orchestras and I feel the new me showing up to those activities.
>
> "It has become so clear how this way of living/thinking can heal your past, present, and future all at the same time. I'm now creating a future without tension. I'm allowing space for my body to react differently than it did before. I'm showing up for the moment I'm in. I'm looking forward to next week! I can't wait to see what happens!"
>
> ~ Stephanie, Violinist and Educator

Meeting Your Mind

Are your thoughts helping or hurting you?

Our mental attitude transforms a situation into either a problem or an opportunity.

~ *Geshe Kelsang Gyatso*

If you've ever had trouble concentrating, trying to focus your thoughts on what you're doing—instead of struggling with mind wandering, getting stuck in "analysis paralysis," or chaotic "overthinking"—then you know how challenging it can be to take charge of your thoughts and gain peace of mind.

Paradoxically, the mind can be both our best friend and our worst enemy. Depending on how we direct our attention, our thoughts can help us manifest our loftiest dreams or throw us into dark prisons of misery, gasping for freedom, light, and air.

When I was growing up, it was instilled in me how much our culture values mental intelligence and how those who passionately pursue their goals achieve distinction in their area of expertise. I was taught to recognize the importance of using the mind well to compete, get ahead, and stand out from the crowd.

Being smart didn't just mean coming up with the right answers and getting good grades in school, though. It also meant having the self-discipline to work and study hard, concentrate for long periods of time, and practice delayed gratification by sacrificing pleasure now for success later.

Of course, there's value in much of this "success-formula"; it served me well. My private motto as a child was, "Worst comes first"; that helped me do my homework or practice my violin before playing outside—which allowed me to get ahead in school and distinguish myself as a musician among my peers.

As an adult, I can now look back at how my growing intensity and ambition slowly became more problematic than beneficial. Even though I was garnering a lot of success, it was subtly feeding a growing perfectionism, competitiveness, and gnawing sense of dissatisfaction within myself.

It's clear to me now that pursuing a kind of "worldly" success defined by professional achievements and material accumulation is only as good as the deeper purpose that supports it from inside. The skyscrapers we build to reach the sky are only as magnificent and strong as the clarity of their internal frameworks and the foundations that support them from underneath.

It wasn't until I came into contact with spiritual ways of looking at life that I realized how torn I was between the desire to experience peace and happiness within me and the cultural drive to get happiness externally, especially through hard work and intense ambition.

None of this is surprising, since when I was a child, I rarely heard anyone talk about the need to prioritize internal success *as a prerequisite* for achieving external success if you want to have both.

Your mind plays a grand role in designing what you want to experience on the outside—your external achievements, professional successes, and material accumulations. But you ultimately have very little control over those things, as in the end they depend on forces beyond your control (employers, colleagues, audiences, institutions, competitors, the economy, the weather, you name it).

The one thing you DO have control over is your mind. No matter what happens, you can always access the ever-present joy and deep heart-intelligence within you that allows your creative spirit to continually create new positive situations on the outside. That is, provided that you have good control over your mind. With the right kind of mental discipline (knowing how to think in flow, with clear direction and ease), you develop flexibility, resilience, adaptability. And a creative spiritual connection.

You see, most people have their priorities backwards: they put the external world first, their internal experience second. That's because we've, most of us, been duped to believe it's necessary to think hard, delay joy, and push ahead now. In that way, we get happiness from the outside and have an easier life later on. *So, the expectation goes*.

True wisdom tells us just the opposite: learn to direct your thoughts with greater simplicity, clarity, and relaxed ease in order to access your internal joy and reach peace now. In so doing, you find the world gradually reflecting that centered goodness back to you, giving you more and more opportunities to grow and share your positive experience in a continual play of energy exchange from within and without.

Like most people, I had my priorities backwards. I had no idea there was a better, much easier way to use my mind, although I did get little glimpses of a kind of mental relaxation from time to time, especially when I accidentally slipped into musical flow while playing my violin.

But I didn't know then how to make that easy flow happen on purpose. Yet I realized there was something deeply special and meaningful hidden in the experience of being swept up into the gushing river of music. I think having tastes of that mystical experience kept me playing the violin and was the main reason I wanted to become a professional. Even so, I didn't yet know there was a conscious way to be carried along by the creative spirit within and around me—one that could support my whole life, not just my violin playing, with ever-present ease.

If, growing up, I'd belonged to a spiritual community, perhaps I would have had a better idea of the importance of developing mental calm, inner peace, and heart-centered happiness. But most of my family members weren't religious or spiritually inclined, as far as I was aware; my friends didn't talk about meditation over lunch at school, and my teachers never mentioned any other way to discipline the mind than through willpower, hard work, and intense concentration.

Lucky for me, there were two things I found at home that piqued my curiosity and motivated me to explore further: a book on yoga on my mother's bookshelf and an assortment of old LPs my dad gave me.

In one of those recordings, the Indian sitar player Ravi Shankar performed at the Monterrey International Pop Music Festival in California in 1967. As described in *The New Yorker*, "Shankar sat cross-legged behind his sitar, calm and focussed, engaging in musical dialogues of thrilling virtuosity with his tabla player, Alla Rakha," along with Kamala Chakravarty playing the tanpura. For four hours, these musicians mesmerized a Western audience unfamiliar with traditional Indian classical music.[7]

I, too, was captivated. I loved that recording! I would lie on my bedroom floor, listening to it with closed eyes for hours upon hours, and I never tired of it. Listening to the intricate interweaving of exotic melodies and soothing rhythms above the constancy of the underlying drone, my wandering mind reconnected with the quiet stillness underneath . . . it was like watching endlessly shifting waves dancing on the ocean's surface and diving down into the deep, calm waters below.

7 Taylor Ho Bynum, "Ravi Shankar, Open Mind," The New Yorker, Dec. 12, 2012.

My body relaxed along with my mind, as I was transported—always—into a state of calm, comfort, and ease, escaping from the crazy intensity of modern education and my personal desires for success. I didn't realize it then, but the time I spent listening to Indian classical music was effectively training me to calm the mind through guided meditation. I'm sure it helped music-making, even then.

There were also two other ways that I remember meditating as a child and teenager, without realizing I was meditating.

After dinner, I would often go up to my bedroom, close the door, turn off my lights, get out my violin—and just play, sometimes deliberately pouring out negative emotions that had accumulated over the day. At other times, I would simply play without working on anything, letting myself melt into a flow state, merging with the music, and time would pass, free of extraneous thoughts.

The second way I used to "meditate" was while riding in the car, sitting quietly in the back seat as we drove home from school. I remember staring out the window one rainy day, when I suddenly noticed that I wasn't thinking. That really captured my attention because it was the first time I realized that *I* was something more than, and beyond, my thinking mind. I could simply BE and witness myself and the world without thinking.

This became a new car game of mine: *could I stop myself from thinking? For how long?* Only for a few seconds. But something in me knew this would be an extremely valuable skill to cultivate.

Not till years later did I learn more about meditation and decide to adopt a formal meditation practice. But I had already learned a valuable lesson: meditation is natural, and yet it is also a skill that needs to be practiced.

When I was growing up in the United States, it was mostly for hippies or religious contemplatives—certainly not a mainstream activity. Although we had computers, we didn't have the internet yet when I was a kid (!), and little research had been done on meditation.

These days, most everyone has heard there are physical and emotional health benefits to it. Doctors and psychologists even prescribe meditation, mindfulness, and yoga, and you can find endless information and research on these topics at the tips of your fingers when you go online or look at the magazine covers at your local grocery store.

Essentially, meditation is a way to bring more objectivity and clarity to your subjective experience by witnessing and gradually quieting the mind.

Through mindfulness practices, you can cultivate more conscious, constructive control (Alexander's words) over yourself, in stillness and activity. With practice, you steadily learn how to harness the power of your mind, directing your energy with focus and precision towards what you truly value and desire most in life, instead of letting your thoughts run rampant, tricking you—leading you in all sorts of directions that waste time and energy, taking you further from your goals.

The Art of Freedom Method doesn't require you to sit quietly on a cushion and meditate for hours. But it does offer meditative practices that help you integrate awareness of your whole mind-body-self AND the world around you simultaneously, so that regardless of whether you're sitting quietly OR engaged in challenging activities like making music, you can enter a stream of ease and flow.

After all, to call upon your ability to be fully awake, creative, and responsive to your fellow musicians and audience, while also centered and calm in mind, body, and spirit—even when you're playing the most technically demanding repertoire—is a skill any musician would love to have!

Developing greater control of the mind

In order to develop more control of the mind (and the body, by extension), you need a number of things, including:

1) Desire: a meaningful goal that motivates you to take action. You may not know exactly what you want right now, but you can be motivated to find out. You need a worthy motivator that will give you the strength to persist with your daily practice and the resilience to get back up when life knocks you down.

2) Healthy curiosity: you may not know what's actually possible for you to achieve or how to get what you want, but you can nurture your innate, childlike curiosity to find out!

3) Humble willingness to learn: you will learn more easily and progress more quickly when you're willing to admit what you don't know, with innocent humility and healthy detachment.

4) Imagination: moving towards your goals with ease requires nurturing your imagination by waking up your creative spirit and letting your inner child explore and play!

By attending to each of these things, you can more readily practice meditation in stillness or activity, learn from what happens, and consciously redirect your whole self with healthy, balanced desire instead of unhealthy ambition. All of the above applies to your music-making as well as your everyday life, of course.

When you know how to bring a holistic, meditative quality to your musical practice and performance, not only can you improve your technique and musicality more effortlessly, but you will be able to slip into a flow state more easily, allowing you to enjoy yourself so much more. This is the special skill that brings grace to your movements and transforms them into art.

When it's hard to concentrate . . .

One of the first things we're likely to notice about ourselves when we meditate (whether in a formal practice or something more spontaneous, such as listening to music or playing our instruments as described above) is that our ability to focus and concentrate isn't always as constant as we'd like: our minds wander, our moods shift, and our bodies fidget.

We get distracted by external stimuli—pleasant or unpleasant—arriving through our senses, or by internal stimuli (thoughts and feelings) created within the mind-body-self.

Examples of external stimuli: noises, smells, lights, temperature, clothing, uncomfortable seats, interruptions.

Examples of internal stimuli: fatigue, aches and pains, and all kinds of thoughts that capture our attention and pull our minds every which way.

As a performer, you know the importance of disregarding unwanted, intrusive stimuli. You want to stay calm and in control instead of getting thrown off by a bellyache, the audience member noisily unwrapping a throat lozenge, or your colleague who forgets to turn the page.

Though meditation in stillness, sitting quietly with the eyes closed, is a great way to develop focus, musicians need to know how to manage the mind while also engaging the body in the very complex activity of playing an instrument.

The ability to immediately notice when your mind has wandered off and then to be able to bring it quickly back to your activity is a crucial skill that involves not only improving your mind-body coordination but also calming your nervous system.

Whether at home alone or onstage performing in front of a thousand people, how are you responding to stimuli? Are you able to choose to change how you're thinking and practice mindful, true concentration in activity?

Unfortunately, despite the usual reprimands—"Stop gazing out the window! Stop daydreaming! LOOK at what you're doing! Sit up and pay attention!"—very rarely (if ever) as children were we told precisely HOW to concentrate. Equally unfortunate, when we heard those admonitions, often delivered in a firm, authoritarian manner intended to get us to change our behavior, we would often startle and bring increased tension to our whole system as we either tried to comply or we rebelled.

Most of us had the following problematic beliefs about concentration drilled into us by our surrounding culture, especially by authority figures (parents, family members, teachers, etc.):

1) Belief: You must pay attention and concentrate on what your caregivers think is important, even if you aren't interested yourself. Do this in order to get positive feedback or attention, or even experience love. This personal attention was directly related to your survival when you were young, not yet able to care for yourself.

2) Belief: If you have difficulty concentrating, something is wrong with you. You should fix this by trying harder or forcing yourself to concentrate, even if you're tired and would rather be doing something else.

3) Belief: The degree to which you are successful in the world is directly related to your ability to concentrate. Those with high levels of intense concentration are smarter, get the best grades and win competitions, so this kind of concentration is considered highly desirable.

The overlooked truth about concentration is that it is not an activity of the mind alone. Because the body mirrors the mind, whatever we do with the mind, the body reflects. The mind and body are inseparable; with intense thinking, increased tension in the body always comes.

In a mind stuffed with a jumble of competing and endless thoughts, the body will reflect that lack of clarity through increased overall muscular tension, and the corresponding secretion of stress hormones into the bloodstream will make it even harder to think straight. Your system has gone into some degree of a fight-flight-freeze-fawn response (see Chapter 2).

Musicians need to develop focus

Ideally, meditation is a tool to bring your attention back to the present moment, emptying the mind of incessant chatter, which can show up as an infinite variety of unnecessary, cluttered, contradictory, irrelevant, or destructive thoughts.

For example, if you're about to go onstage and feeling nervous, you may be thinking things like: *I don't want to be here; I have to go onstage now—the audience is waiting for me; I'm scared—what if I mess up that passage of fast sixteenth notes again? Or: I don't have a choice; I'm not ready! Or: I LOVE the piece I'm about to play—let's get out there right now. I hate waiting backstage!*

Some thoughts are positive, some negative; some are happy and excited, some full of dread; some are pushing you towards the stage, while others imagine a mad dash for the exit.

When you have contradictory desires ("I want to perform" + "I don't want to perform"), your brain is sending contradictory messages, and your muscles will gear up in an attempt to take you in (at least) two different directions at once.

In that inner conflict, you get increased muscle tension, or even start shaking—unless, making a firm decision to choose only ONE way of thinking, you then direct your mind and whole self to follow through, banishing any contradictory thoughts.

If you aren't accustomed to taking charge of your mind to think with more one-pointed clarity on a regular basis, then when you're backstage, fighting with yourself in a last-ditch attempt to override your panic, you certainly won't be able to do it!

Besides contributing to performance anxiety, a lack of mental control will slow down your progress in learning anything because your body won't receive clear messages from the brain.

When you're practicing or performing, you need to be able to think clearly. You need to be able to think one thought at a time (with lightning speed), so as to be fully present and attentive to the notes you're playing as you're playing them, while ALSO being aware of what's coming up, where you've just come from, and what's happening around you.

But . . . HOW do you actually do that?

Concentration is defined as the ability to focus attention on a single object. We all know it's absolutely necessary for a musician to develop this skill in order to learn, play well, and keep improving. In fact, the degree to which our skill evolves is in direct proportion to our ability to concentrate.

But what most people *don't* know is that there are two different ways to concentrate, and our choice is critical to our overall well-being and ultimate success.

Two Modes of Concentration

Mode A: "Habitual Concentration"

"Habitual concentration" is how most of us were taught to concentrate. With habitual concentration, we consider the mind and body as essentially separate and independent; concentration is confined mainly to a mental activity.

Consequently, we narrow our scope of attention to exclude what we consider irrelevant to the task at hand. We become mostly oblivious to how our thoughts and the intensity of our focus are affecting our body, and we tend to block out our feelings or minimize the importance of whatever we do notice.

Habitual concentration has a hard, separative, exclusive, intense quality, and our whole system reacts to this narrowing of the mind with an overall compression or tensing of the body.

As an example, how often have you sat down at the computer to do some concentrated work, only to find yourself still sitting there two hours later, head and neck craned forward like a vulture, jaw tight, back aching, your body stiff. That compression didn't happen all of a sudden. Little by little, your posture drooped; gradually you felt more and more uncomfortable, but you didn't do anything about it because you were deep in "concentration," "hard at work."

Concentrating in this way, you effectively make the activity you're engaged in (your "doing") more important than your well-being (your "being"). You are quite literally thrown off-center when you place the center of your attention outside of yourself—over there with your computer—because your body follows your attention by leaning forward.

You can see this mode of concentration exemplified visually by Rodin's sculpture, *The Thinker* (see below).

The Thinker by Auguste Rodin, Image by Gordon Johnson

Mode B: "True Concentration"

What I like to call "true concentration" is holistic, a way of paying attention with your whole self (not just your mind), which puts your "being" at the center of your experience, more important than your "doing."

This mode of concentration cultivates what Frank Pierce Jones called a "unified field of attention," recognizing that the mind and body are inseparable, all things are interdependent, and relational context is everything.

Consider that the word "concentration" has the same root as the word "concentric"—which literally means to have a center. This mode of concentration makes YOU (your whole mind-body-self) the central, primary focal point of your attention; everything else is secondary, relates back to you, and is included in the whole of your perception.

Things that may seem irrelevant to what you're working on are allowed to enter your expanded awareness, instead of being excluded as in Mode A. This compares to including what happens in your peripheral vision while you're looking at something straight in front of you.

To help you actualize this inclusive mode of concentration right now, try the following experiment:

1. The centering idea. First, think of yourself as located at the very center of your environment, with equal amounts of infinite space extending in all directions from your body. A book, a computer (or even sheet music or a conductor!) is an object out there, located within a circular area organized around YOU: the central focal point. YOU are more important than the book, computer, page, or whatever else is out there, not the other way around.

Now, imagine yourself at the center of multiple concentric circles arranged around you. YOU (your whole mind-body-self) are the central focus of your attention; everything around you is secondary, while also related and connected to you. What's happening to your whole self needs to be central to your experience; everything else is relative to that. This is what it means to be "centered."

2. Now, notice what's happening to you in this moment. Notice that you're reading this book. How is your body arranged in relation to the book? What are you thinking? How's your mood? What are you feeling in various parts of your body? Are you noticing tension or ease? What else do you see around you, beyond the edges of this book?

What you're seeing on the page and what you're taking in from your whole environment through your senses is simply information. That information is transmitted to your brain, where it gives your experience meaning and literally changes the organization of your neural network, which is connected to your whole body.

What you are experiencing in every moment is actually a process of learning, influenced by how you interpret your environment as taken in through your senses. The fresh experience you have in each moment informs your next actions—what you think, what you choose, and how you move.

The internal experience you're having within you right now in response to your environment is infinitely more important than what you think of as "out there." In reality, we never experience the external world directly; our only direct experience is of ourselves—how the mind-body organism is reacting to stimuli.

True concentration makes it easier to know ourselves and recognize how we are relating to the world. It has an expansive, open, receptive, soft, easy, "non-doing" quality. This mode of concentration, the entry point to accessing a natural, energetic flow state, is the key to being "centered." It can be cultivated and reliably achieved through regular practice, which is why I start teaching all my students true concentration from the very first day we work together.

Knowing how to concentrate in a way that expands and unifies our field of attention increases constructive, conscious control over our whole selves. This ability is essential to the quality of our musical experience. It makes all the difference between helping or hurting ourselves.

Importantly, both modes of concentration I've described may carry us towards our specific goals, but only through Mode B—true concentration—can we achieve our goals in a way that is beneficial for the whole self, taking us closer to our long-term goals of ease, well-being, artistic mastery, and a joyful, fulfilling life.

You can see a visual representation of true concentration in the statue of the Buddha below.

White Buddha, Image by Bernd

Symptoms that suggest you need to improve your true concentration skills

When people lack the skill of true concentration, it may appear that they either lack focus or overthink, and perhaps they swing back and forth between the two. In fact, both symptoms indicate they are likely relying on habitual concentration—in which case they need a better understanding of how to discipline the mind with awareness of ease.

Someone who has trouble focusing may tend to procrastinate and appear to be lazy or unproductive; in fact, this lack of clear, forward direction may simply be an intuitive attempt at protecting themselves from overconcentrating in a way that they can sense is unhealthy.

Once a person like this learns the skill of true concentration—which is actually much easier on the entire mind-body system than habitual concentration—the result is likely to be sudden renewed energy and motivation, as well as enthusiasm to engage with work they may have been avoiding.

Since it's not always obvious when you're stuck in a habitual mode of concentration, here are some warning signs so you can catch yourself and shift into an easier, healthier mode of true concentration faster. Consider it a red flag if you . . .

- tend to be very "intense" when you engage in activities you care about
- feel mentally drained or physically fatigued after a period of focused activity
- ignore discomfort or pain while you're working, or don't notice it at all until after you've stopped
- believe concentration is "hard" and force yourself to concentrate
- procrastinate, avoid "mental" work, or consider yourself lazy
- are bored, burned out, lack motivation or enthusiasm about things that used to excite you
- lack curiosity, imagination, or a desire to learn
- experience fuzzy thinking; scattered, disorganized thoughts; mind-wandering; a lack of mental clarity
- have a hard time being inactive, meditating, relaxing, doing nothing
- are often unaware of what you're doing while doing it
- tend to be hard on yourself and others
- suffer from out-of-control negative thoughts and emotions

- are overly reactive in relationships
- suddenly realize that you've been holding your breath while working—for example, it's not uncommon for musicians to hold their breath while playing their instruments
- have erratic rhythm: poor timing, a tendency to rush or get behind in your music
- believe that you have "poor posture" that needs to be fixed; OR . . .
- believe you have "good posture," yet you suffer from back, neck, jaw, or shoulder pain

You may have tried some of these to improve your focus:

- Yoga, exercise, breathwork, meditation, relaxation techniques
- Positive thinking, psychological counseling
- Drugs or medications to help reduce tension and calm your mind or emotions (as mentioned above, pharmaceutical drugs may be a godsend in certain cases, when a person receives an accurate diagnosis and is prescribed necessary medication)

You may have gotten some relief and important insights from the above methods, but none of them will teach you how to practice and apply the skill of true concentration to the specifics of your musical artistry, or how to bring it into your performance with reliable consistency, flow, and effortless ease.

Next Steps

At this point, you have a pretty good sense of the two ways to concentrate, and which one is more effective and healthier. The truth is, it's not hard to learn the skill of true concentration, but as in the development of any skill, you will need to devote yourself to a consistent daily practice to change your habitual mode of concentration and gradually be able to apply the new mode to your daily activities and music.

True concentration is the centerpiece of The Art of Freedom Method, and I teach this skill to all my students from the very beginning. I'll be sharing more specifics about how we do this in Part 3 of this book.

In the next chapter, we'll take a look at pain and other physical symptoms that can show up in the body in musicians, which are very much related to habitual concentration and other unhealthy ways of using the mind.

Getting Physical

Do you blame your body for your discomfort?

You translate everything, whether physical, mental or spiritual, into muscular tension
~ *F. M. Alexander*

I remember well the first time shooting pain ripped through my forearm like a bolt of lightning from the tip of my left pinky. It was while I was playing the violin, and the pain was so excruciating I couldn't put any pressure on my pinky at all, which meant I had to stop playing immediately. No choice.

This novel experience stunned me. But instead of going to the doctor, I chose to rest without playing for a few days. Nearing the end of my bachelor's at Indiana University, thankfully I was able to manage a couple days without playing without repercussions. I told no one about my situation.

After a couple days, I gingerly placed my pinky on the string and eased back into practicing, a little bit at a time. I was lucky. The pain had disappeared. For quite a while, it didn't recur. I kept it mostly at bay after that with gentle yoga stretches, and when it made its surprise appearance again a couple times a year, I was always lucky enough to have time to take a break from playing.

But such an experience isn't that unusual. Unfortunately, many musicians aren't as lucky: their pain doesn't just vanish by itself. After pain first surfaces, far too many musicians can't get back to pain-free playing on their own.

When Serena found me on the Internet, she was at her wit's end. She had tried everything under the sun to heal the pain that plagued her when playing, but nothing worked. She was just about to quit altogether. Not only that, but she was in the middle of working towards a back-up master's degree in musicology, just so she would have a fallback if her performing career became impossible.

Thankfully, her desire to keep performing was strong enough that she was ready to try one last time to overcome her pain. At our initial consultation, she told me she had decided this was it. She would go all in to learn what I had to teach her, but if it didn't work, she'd give up and follow a different career path.

Within the first week of our work together, Serena felt a noticeable difference in her state of being. She felt calmer; her body, she noticed, was starting to relax.

After about a month, she was able to play the viola for about five minutes a day without pain. This was definitely progress! Over the next few weeks, she felt more and more hopeful, as she was able to steadily increase the amount of time she could play pain-free.

By the end of her six-month coaching program, she was ecstatic. Not only was her pain gone, but so was her lifelong performance anxiety.

Now, Serena is devoting her career to running a music school that will help children prevent the kind of pain that for so many years she had to endure.

In Serena's words: "I had my first-ever pain and anxiety-free performance yesterday! I played three Easter worship services in a row at a local Lutheran church. I had several solos and was mostly improvising the entire time. I literally forgot to be nervous! I experienced a bit of tension in my playing, but not to the point of pain. No heating pad afterward, no pain killers, no 'ouch!' I haven't been able to say that in . . . decades? CONSTRUCTIVE THINKING REALLY WORKS! AAAAAAHHHHHH!"

Your Inner Wisdom and Your Body's Messages

Physical pain, despite being common, isn't the only kind of physical imbalance musicians face. In fact, barring an acute injury—breaking a wrist, for example—significant physical pain usually only rears its ugly head after plenty of less-painful advance-warning signs.

Common warning signs to pay attention to include:

- fatigue, lack of stamina and endurance
- excess muscular tension making it difficult to play quickly
- stiffness, tenderness, or soreness

- numbness, tingling, popping, clicking
- guarding a body part and altering your movements to compensate for discomfort
- trying to correct "poor posture" by moving around a lot
- a belief that you have a problem with a specific body part ("a bad back," "bad knees," "weak fingers," etc.)
- negative emotions that carry a heavy, down, compressing feeling or energy
- forcing your sound in an effort to project
- overfocusing on what your body is doing when working on your technique

What happens if you don't notice these warning signs, or if you deny, ignore, or push through them? Well, sooner or later, you're likely to feel worse.

Consider this quote from F.M. Alexander for a moment: "Pain is your friend."

You might wonder how that can be—after all, friends aren't supposed to hurt each other, right?

Well, actually, our best friend is the one who dares—even when it hurts—to tell us the truth. First, she will speak gently and quietly . . . but if we ignore her and keep doing something hurtful, our friend's voice will strengthen, getting louder, to help us become aware of *what we need to change.*

It's time to *wake up and become your own best friend, which means listening to your body (which is YOU!)* when it's trying to get your attention. And guess what? *Your body is innocent—it simply reflects what's happening in your mind.*

A vast, friendly source of wisdom within you is working for you 24/7, organizing every aspect of your life, including your thoughts and actions. This "Inner Wisdom" coordinates your breath, your internal organs, the thoughts in your mind, how you talk, walk, and move about.

But you're probably not used to tapping into this with your conscious awareness.

When you experience pain, this is your Inner Wisdom sending you a very clear message through your body, in an attempt to get you to pay attention to your thoughts and change certain behaviors. These behaviors block your energy, cause overall compression, and generally take you in the direction of dis-ease and possible injury.

Once you realize that pain is simply the voice of your own Inner Wisdom—your very best friend—instead of blaming your body for hurting you, you can actually start to appreciate the messages your body is sending you via physical aches, pains, a down mood, or fatigue.

Think of pain like a fussy toddler pulling at your pants legs, trying to get your attention. If you listen, give it a little loving attention, and appreciate what it's trying to tell you with sincerity and gratitude, everything starts to shift.

On the other hand, if you don't listen, the messages will get louder and stronger. Your discomfort will increase and over time may very well escalate into a full-blown tantrum, possibly even resulting in injury.

Three related types of physical disturbances

The three types of disturbances that can cause physical discomfort, pain, and/or injury to your body are listed below:

1. Misuse

I define "misuse" here as using the whole mind-body-self in a way that goes against and interferes with your natural design, thereby disturbing the easy flow of energy, breath, and movement.

Sadly, misuse of the self is nearly universal, although it doesn't always result in noticeable discomfort. In fact, I've met many musicians who are clearly severely misusing themselves, but they aren't experiencing any physical pain at all.

I remember working with a well-known violinist who when playing his instrument put a tremendous amount of pressure on his lumbar spine (and other parts of his body), yet he experienced no pain and was convinced he was creating no excess tension when playing. He had no idea that the reason he saw only limited improvement in his intonation, despite highly disciplined, targeted practice over many years, was directly related to the tension caused by the misuse of himself as a whole.

An interesting thing about the body is that there isn't a predictable timeline for misuse to show itself. Sometimes, all it takes is a few moments to manifest as pain; other times, all kinds of things happening under the surface remain undetectable for years, but suddenly flare up as excruciating pain, injury, or serious disease.

Since it's not always obvious how your system will handle misuse, it's a very good idea to learn how to improve your "use" by thinking and moving in healthy ways that will prevent problems from developing later.

2. Overuse

"Overuse Syndrome," also known as cumulative trauma disorder (CTD) or repetitive strain injury (RSI), results from chronic irritation to a particular body part. An overuse injury can occur when you ask your body to function at a higher level than it can safely deliver at that time.

Most professional musicians are familiar with discomfort stemming from overuse, whether it's in overpracticing, extra-long rehearsals, or too many back-to-back performances without enough rest in between.

Simple overuse discomfort can normally be eased by disengaging from your instrument for a while, whether that means resting a few hours, days, or weeks.

Unfortunately, most overuse problems are much more complex and can't be so simply resolved. Instead of sensing when your body is being stressed or stretched beyond what it is capable of bearing with ease, and instead of heeding its signals to stop the harmful movement, you ignore your body's whispers and end up hurting yourself. This kind of overuse is really a form of misuse.

When F. M. Alexander went to his doctor for help with hoarseness from speaking onstage, the doctor suggested he not speak at all for a couple of weeks—take a "rest cure." This is still a common first step recommended to alleviate vocal problems. When he did this, he felt better at first; however, as soon as he got on stage to perform again, the hoarseness came right back.

This shows us that his problem was not one of overuse but one of misuse—or both. To resolve his performance problem, Alexander had one choice: to learn how to restore the healthy balance and functioning of *his whole system*.

3. Underuse

In professional musicians, this is the least common of the three types of physical disturbances, since to maintain their skills and perform on a regular basis, professionals rarely take more than a day or two away from their instruments.

However, it's always advisable, after a time away, to go slowly and ease back into playing your instrument with simple movements because there is always a risk of injury when the body hasn't been engaged in a complex, demanding task for a while.

Personally, I'm very familiar with the type of discomfort that can arise from underuse, since I typically spend unusually long periods away from my instrument when I don't have an event to practice for.

I spent nearly three months away from my violin after I finished recording my solo album in September 2021. Consequently, certain muscles in my left arm were fatiguing more quickly than usual and feeling uncomfortable just from holding up the instrument when I finally picked it up again. So over a couple weeks, playing for only five to ten minutes per day at first, and gradually building up to my desired length of practice, I gently eased back into my routine.

Musicians need to be cautious, aware of the need to plan ahead for a period of reacclimatization to the psychophysical demands of playing their instrument if they'll be spending time away. This is necessary in order to prevent an overuse injury resulting from underuse, especially when there's general misuse involved.

Things you may have tried to relieve physical discomfort

If you've ever experienced pain or chronic discomfort from your playing, you've probably tried one or more of the approaches listed below:

Self-care:

- Rest and take time away from your instrument
- Try to fix your posture or change your technique
- Study anatomy to try to figure out what you're doing wrong
- Do preventive or remedial stretches/exercises, including yoga
- Apply heat or cold to the painful area
- Change basic habits such as diet and sleep patterns
- Take supplements

Traditional Medicine:

- Visit a medical practitioner for diagnosis and possible treatment, including surgery
- Take prescribed or over-the-counter drugs
- Seek out physical or occupational therapy; do prescribed exercises

Alternative Therapies:

- Massage
- Chiropractic

- Acupuncture
- Energy medicine, such as Reiki or Healing Touch
- Rolfing

Depending on your presenting problem, history, and the quality of your self-use, some of the above approaches, when skillfully applied, may improve or resolve the physical issue and ease your discomfort.

However, since nearly all physical problems stem from misuse of the self overall, none of these solutions can get at the root cause.

The only approach to healing I'm aware of that covers it all, helping you get to the fundamental root cause of systemic misuse—thus, preventing a problem from recurring or showing up elsewhere in your body—allowing you to relieve physical discomfort, recover more quickly from injury, overcome performance anxiety, improve your relationships, live a more healthy and balanced life, AND dramatically improve your technique and musical expression . . . is the Alexander Technique, especially The Art of Freedom Method, which teaches Primal Alexander. I'll be discussing Primal Alexander and how to apply it to your music-making in more detail in Part 2 and Part 3 of this book.

How is your posture?

Most of us think we have "bad" posture. But without being clear about what that really means beyond the obvious—slumped shoulders or a swayback, etc.—how helpful is it merely to say you have bad posture and judge yourself for it?

You may have been thinking for many years that you should improve your posture. So why hasn't it happened yet?

And what exactly *is* "good" posture, anyway—if it even exists? You may have a picture in your mind, but what does it actually involve?

When I ask my students what they mean by "posture," a typical answer is "the particular way you *hold* your body in a position, usually while standing or sitting. Or while holding your instrument." Rarely are the mind, emotions, or creative spirit considered a factor.

In The Art of Freedom, we consider the whole mind-body-self to be our primary instrument, so our approach to posture includes the whole self. If posture is the way you hold your whole self, then it would be a good idea to start considering how to do this.

How do you hold yourself?

Take a moment to ask yourself the following questions:

Do you generally hold and honor yourself with softness, flexibility, and ease? With loving-kindness and compassion? Or—filled with stiffness and fear—do you hold yourself up to rigorous scrutiny and judgment?

Do you try to "pull yourself together," "get a grip on yourself," or try not to "lose your head" when things go wrong? Or can you let yourself feel, "fall apart," and "lose it" when the going gets tough?

Do you hold yourself accountable for your thoughts and actions? Or do you neglect the self-holding and hand over your autonomy, letting circumstances have a "stronghold" on you, letting others dictate how you think and behave?

How does the whole self (mind? body? emotions?) respond to the way we *hold* ourselves? Does our holding allow us to expand with loving ease? *Or do we react by compressing ourselves?* Do we open up in generosity of spirit? Or do we shut down in fear?

As living, changing, thinking beings in constant motion, we need to pay attention to how we treat ourselves, and observe how we respond to our self-treatment. *Posture improves naturally when we pay attention to the quality of our self-holding.*

People often assume that the Alexander Technique is about improving posture and physical alignment. Even though this isn't at all true, it makes sense that people perceive the Technique in this way because improved posture is a common beneficial side effect. Also, our body posture and alignment are visible and obvious, whereas this is not always the case with the whole-person effects of the Technique, such as improved mood, less reactivity, or better relationships. They are visible but not necessarily traced back to the Technique as source.

The Art of Freedom Method teaches the Alexander Technique in a way that is all-encompassing, explicitly promoting authenticity of being—the opposite of posturing or pretending to be somebody you're not.

Like it or not, your musical sound reflects your state of being.

As a musician, you probably are convinced that to play your instrument well, "good posture" is necessary. True, in a sense, because how you hold yourself absolutely does affect the way you hold your musical instrument, and therefore the quality of the sounds you produce.

When your body is stiff and your mind is not present, your sound will suffer. Your head, neck, back, hands, fingers, and other parts of your body will be either too tight or collapsed, and the lack of balanced muscle tone will affect your musical sound—negatively influencing your tone quality.

The excess tension will block your ability to pick up the feedback you need (through your sense of touch, hearing, sight) to make the appropriate adjustments in your musculature necessary to get the precise sounds you want. Because you'll be relying on a compromised/blocked sensory feedback system, you will not be the best or most accurate judge of what you produce, you'll be able to only approximate your wishes, and the effects are likely to be inconsistent.

When your mind is present and your body flexible and free to move, you will find yourself more sensitive to what is actually happening in the moment—both within your mind-body-self and externally—and you'll be better equipped to be objective about the process and its results.

More often, you will start to notice how you are interfering with your technique and musicality by thinking thoughts that create unnecessary tension, and that increased sensitivity will give you abundant opportunities to stop and choose a new, better way to hold yourself and your instrument. Your enhanced ability to respond with sensitivity is 100 percent guaranteed to bring you closer to what you want, every time you do it!

Next Steps

If you're currently experiencing pain or having difficulty recovering from an injury, it's a good idea to get an accurate diagnosis of your presenting issues from a qualified medical professional so you don't inadvertently worsen your problem from a lack of information.

That said, whether you know exactly what the problem is or not, it's never too early to start (and it definitely can't hurt!) exploring how your overall self-use may be causing or contributing to the problem.

The way you think, feel, and move is either supporting your healing or keeping you stuck in a cycle of dis-ease. In every moment, either you are allowing your energy to flow and support your healing, as designed, or you are blocking it, and in so doing, preventing your body's natural healing mechanisms from doing their job.

This book is here to teach you how to let the body's natural healing mechanisms work *for* you! And this is exactly what I teach in-depth in my private coaching and group programs online.

If you're willing to consider that the body is beautifully designed with the ever-present potential to live and move free of pain, and that the key to getting back to an easier way of being lies in how you use your whole mind-body-self, I encourage you to reach out to me sooner rather than later, so that I can help. You can contact me through my website at www.ArtofFreedom.me.

"For twenty-five years, I had suffered from severe chronic pain on a daily basis which was caused by what doctors told me were permanent, incurable health disorders and injuries. Sometimes the pain was so bad it hurt to wear clothing; other times, I could barely get out of bed. Now that pain is just the tiniest whisper. Not only is the pain all but gone, I am a far better musician now and a much happier person in every way. What Jennifer teaches is life transforming! I learned what I think affects how my body feels and to change my thinking in a way that helped my body release the excess tension that leads to pain. In doing that, I now use (move) my body in a way that has much less tension.

"With Jennifer's guidance, my mindset has completely changed, giving me a new perspective on everything that is so much more positive, and filled with wonder and gratitude. I now have the skills to handle anything—musically or otherwise—in a new way that is so much easier and does not cause pain.

"My playing has also improved dramatically. I learn music faster, and my sound is so much better! Everything about it has become more open and free; it just flows. These skills have carried over into every aspect of my personal life, making it so much easier. Jennifer's teaching works for any musician (I play lever harp) who wants to invest the time and effort. Jennifer's teaching has its foundations in the Alexander Technique, but she takes it so much further. Not just my playing but my entire life is now better than I ever could have dreamed, thanks to The Art of Freedom."

~ Angèle, Harp

It's not about the body

Yes, sometimes
your body hurts.
And yes, it's hard
to play your instrument.

And YES, it is extremely worrisome when your pain won't leave,
and day after day, it's harder to believe!

. . . because you just don't know . . .
. . . precisely how . . .

To make it go away
and permanently fix it.

You try to change how you hold and play
You modify your technique, and work-around for comfort

You rest
You stretch
You wish
You breathe . . .

But no . . .
truly NO............

It's NOT
about your body.
Your body is simply reflecting YOU.

Just like your music—it reveals who you are.
Your body is a collection of residues and thoughts
Of past experience and future projections.

Are you present?
Aware?
Are you conscious of your thoughts?
Do you recognize their effect on how you feel?

Most of the musicians I work with: at first, they are not.
This is not a judgment, a criticism, or a plot.

It's just the way
We human beings are.

We regret the past, or hang back in nostalgia.
We fear the future, or grab for desire.
We strive towards goals, we push, and we shape . . .
We focus, we concentrate, we work, and we crave . . .

When we practice, we correct . . .
When we perform, we neglect . . .
Who we are
What we love

We forget to let go . . .
. . . and let our Love create...

Getting Physical

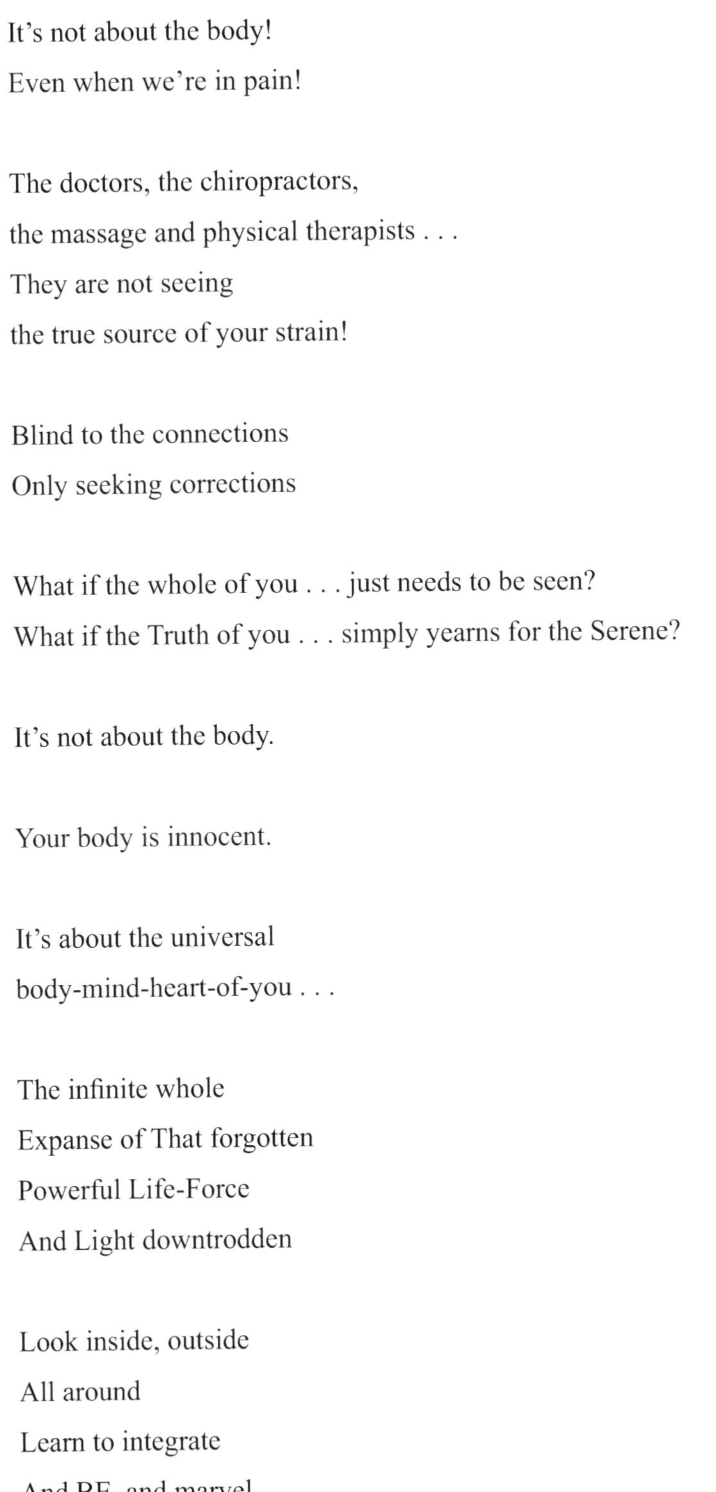

It's not about the body!
Even when we're in pain!

The doctors, the chiropractors,
the massage and physical therapists . . .
They are not seeing
the true source of your strain!

Blind to the connections
Only seeking corrections

What if the whole of you . . . just needs to be seen?
What if the Truth of you . . . simply yearns for the Serene?

It's not about the body.

Your body is innocent.

It's about the universal
body-mind-heart-of-you . . .

The infinite whole
Expanse of That forgotten
Powerful Life-Force
And Light downtrodden

Look inside, outside
All around
Learn to integrate
And BE, and marvel

At what seems impossible
But, with detached curiosity—is possible

Open up your mind
Your heart, and your Art
To EASE and delight!
Day and night!

Imagine and live and Be your SELF
Accept your pain, it's only illusion
Rise above your ego's ruses
Release the doubt, and be without

The habit of suffering
Protective buffering
From Truth—the pure Truth
Of what's happening NOW

Melting again, and again . . .

And . . . do you see?

oh YES . . .

. . . and wow............

RESOURCE:

A downloadable PDF of this poem is available from the Bonus Materials page:
https://www.artoffreedom.me/book/bonusmaterials

Feeling Your Emotions

Are your feelings sabotaging your success?

You can't have an emotion without your body.

~ *Mio Morales, Creator of Primal Alexander™*

When Kyle first came to me for coaching, he had a number of physical aches and pains, and he felt terribly dejected about his cello playing. Since he'd finished his university studies a few years before, he now felt aimless and "too old" to achieve his childhood dreams. He was even contemplating giving up pursuing a musical career altogether. Kyle was burned out.

As we worked together over the next months, I taught him about how our emotions are intricately connected through the mind and body, and I delicately suggested that he needed to learn to feel his emotions to free them up—first without his instrument, and then while playing.

This was an uncomfortable prospect for him since there were quite a few negative emotions lurking under the surface that he was used to ignoring. In addition, like most classical musicians and as an excellent professional cellist already, Kyle was very invested emotionally in playing correctly, with technical accuracy and a consistently beautiful sound.

But here I was, suggesting that he needed to practice letting go, going wild, and permitting ALL of his emotions to run loose through his music—the good, the bad, and the ugly. I encouraged him to give himself free rein with an infinite range of emotions and total permission to sound messy, uncontrolled—even horrible—*on purpose*! By allowing himself to feel more and pour his heart into his music without worrying about the sound he was producing, he would need to sacrifice his need for perfection.

By doing this, Kyle would be diving into new territory with The Art of Freedom Method. Gone would be his tight discipline, to be replaced by the wonders of self-exploration and a new discipline of moment-by-moment awareness that I knew would paradoxically yield even more precision to his playing down the road, but with more exquisitely meaningful and beautiful results than he could ever imagine.

Determined to make the most of our work together, he agreed to experiment with the ideas and did his Primal Alexander Awareness Etudes twice a day. Primal Alexander is the revolutionary touch-free method of learning the Alexander Technique developed by master teacher Mio Morales, which offers a powerfully effective system for increasing conscious awareness and effortless ease in living. Primal Alexander is delivered mainly through the exploration and practice of structured "Awareness Etudes," which I have my students practice every day as a key component in The Art of Freedom Method.

Awareness Etudes are invaluable. They are short, simple movement studies that help us pay attention to what's happening to ourselves as we engage in any activity and enjoy the ease that arises from a specific way of using the mind called ConstructiveThinking.

When you practice a series of Awareness Etudes (about five minutes twice a day for beginners in my coaching programs), as Kyle did, you very quickly find that your mind holds quite a lot of power to influence your experience in your body.

You become more sensitive to your inner experience, and it gets easier to discern whether you're using your mind-body-self in a way that is positive, healthy, and efficient or whether you're interfering and making things harder for yourself.

If you catch yourself interfering by no longer being present to your experience (through mind-wandering, negative thoughts, etc.), you can bring yourself instantly back to yourself, with the result that your movements become easier, more fluid, flexible, responsive.

On the contrary, when you move in the mindless way you normally move based on habit, without paying attention to what's actually happening within you from moment to moment, you'll start to notice more and more often that your movements are constricted, stiffer, less fluid, and use more effort. (See Chapter 20 for more specifics about Primal Alexander Awareness Etudes.)

Applying my mindset and movement suggestions to his cello practice, Kyle showed up regularly to his private coaching sessions and my group classes to learn along with other musicians facing similar challenges.

After a few months he revealed to me that something unexpected was happening to him. Not only was his cello sound becoming richer and more open, but he was pleasantly surprised to find that his moods were stabilizing, and he was happier in general.

Kyle shared with me that he had previously been prone to extreme mood swings, periodically falling into negative, dark periods that could last for weeks at a time or longer.

He noted that the dark periods were now happening less frequently, and he was able to come up out of them sooner. He was less reactive in general, and things that would normally have thrown him off and caused his mood to spiral downward weren't bothering him nearly as much. Not only that, but he wasn't having any of those prolonged periods of unhappiness anymore.

Of course, he still had his emotional ups and downs like anyone else, but he was able to quickly bring himself back to a healthier way of thinking and feel better within minutes instead of weeks.

In addition, Kyle's physical pains (including extreme jaw and back pain) were gone, and his powerful new practice skills were steadily improving his cello playing, both technically and musically.

In fact, Kyle was so inspired by the changes he experienced that he decided to learn how to teach Primal Alexander himself (more on this technique ahead).

"It would be an understatement to say that I was struggling before I joined Jennifer's program. I was suffering from jaw and back issues that I knew were related to playing the cello. I was not enjoying my practice most of the time, and I felt like I was banging my head against a wall, getting nowhere. I did not enjoy my sound and just felt so uncomfortable with my instrument.

"That all started to change very soon after I joined. The first thing I noticed was that the jaw pain that had left me almost completely unable to eat without tremendous suffering for many months disappeared within a few days. I almost couldn't believe it!

"Over the past year or so, my playing has changed in ways that I only dreamed were possible and my relationship to my instrument and my enjoyment of it are improving steadily and consistently. Those magical times when everything just clicks happen much more often now, and I have a much better understanding of what conditions allow that to happen. It is no longer just a happy accident that only happens once in a while.

"Lessons and classes with Jennifer are always eye-opening and never boring. She is always playing around with different ways of looking at things and sharing those ideas with her students, and she asks great questions, which often lead you to look at areas for improvement that you may not have even considered otherwise. And she's highly skilled at catching really subtle habits that are causing things to not work as well as they could.

"Her commitment to this work and to her students has inspired me to become an Alexander Technique teacher myself, and I have already had so many wonderful experiences sharing what I have learned with my students."

~ Kyle, Cellist and Educator

The "suffering, starving artist"

Now let's dig into that syndrome I introduced earlier: the suffering artist stereotype which promotes the idea that suffering is necessary to make great art. To me, this is not a necessity but a deeply ingrained belief system. I spoke of artists like Van Gogh, Beethoven, and Melville, since examples of the starving or unrecognized artist are present in every artistic field. Deep in the psyche, consequently, many musicians believe that to make great art they must suffer, whether that belief is conscious or unconscious. Sadly, that puts them in an impossible situation.

Do you believe that you need to "suffer for art's sake"? That every great artist does? (Or even in extreme cases starve!)

The reality is that many musicians tend to earn less than people in other fields with a comparative level of education. They are systematically undervalued and underpaid relative to the large amount of time, dedication, and money they put into their education, daily practice, and equipment.

Even worse, all too often the musicians themselves, buying into the belief that great art requires suffering, have subconsciously adopted corresponding attitudes, which lead to general negativity and low self-esteem, perpetuating the cycle of being undervalued and underpaid.

Furthermore, the average musician makes less than half of what the average American worker makes per year. For example, the average starting salary for the college graduating class of 2022 in the USA is $55,260[8]; the typical early career salary for someone with a bachelor's degree in music is currently $23,029.[9]

---

8 Abby McCain, Zippia, the Career Expert, "35+ College Grad Earnings Statistics [2023]: Average Starting Salary out of College," https://bit.ly/438qd3X.

9 Andy Kiersz, "Here's What the Typical American Worker Earns at Each Age," updated Nov. 20, 2018, Here's the Typical Salary of Americans at Every Age (businessinsider.com). Also, Sokanu, Career Explorer, "How Much Money Can You Make with a Music Degree?" https://www.careerexplorer.com/degrees/music-degree/salary/.

While money doesn't buy true happiness, and income is not an accurate measure of overall success, there is certainly a minimum amount needed. Obviously, having the ability to buy enough food prevents a "starving artist" syndrome!

Of course, ultimately, true wealth comes from the richness of our inner experience and personal fulfillment. Being an artist, with the potential for creative expression and meaningful connection with others, is potentially one of the most rewarding occupations on the planet.

Even so, studies have shown that large percentages of musicians suffer from emotional disturbances such as depression and anxiety, in addition to physical pain.[10] So, if musicians are chronically undersupported and undervalued by mainstream society, it makes sense that it would require a great deal of mental strength, determination, and resilience to rise above these unhelpful environmental conditions in order to stay true to your original dreams.

This is one reason why my coaching programs typically offer community support. It's so important that musicians be surrounded by others like them who understand, love, and encourage them, and who validate the pursuit of their artistic passion. But even within highly supportive environments, it can still be tough to break through the deeply imbedded belief that great art can only be born of suffering.

As the Buddhists have long instructed, suffering is an inevitable fact of life. Everybody suffers. We're born, we suffer, we die . . .

Do you think that belief is true or false? Pessimistic or realistic? And what about happiness?

I believe the answer depends on how you choose to look at life, in any given moment. The way I see it, joy and suffering are always available, but we need to consciously decide which we want to experience more.

If we have the freedom to choose how we respond to our experiences and how we interpret them—that means we have as much freedom to rise above our suffering as we do to stay focused on that suffering. And therefore, we can also choose to be happy, regardless of how painful our circumstances are.

As the Indian satguru Mata Amritanandamayi, whose retreats I have participated in, says, "Happiness is a choice."

---

10 Jonas Vaag, Ottar Bjerkeset, and Børge Sivertsen, "Anxiety and Depression Symptom Level and Psychotherapy Use among Music and Art Students Compared to the General Student Population," Frontiers in Psychology 12: 607927 (2021), https://doi.org/10.3389%2Ffpsyg.2021.607927.

For in the instant that we become present and aware of our immediate experience, we have the ability to choose our next thought, which has the power to take us closer to what we want or further away. Our choice of thoughts dramatically influences our experience of reality, creating our point of view. In fact, research shows that happier people and those with a positive mindset about stress are more successful.[11]

The problem is, because of how our brains are hardwired to respond to potential danger, choosing to think positively in the face of what *feels* decidedly negative, problematic, or painful can be very difficult and even seem utterly impossible.

We are designed for survival

In some strange way, suffering when things are hard can paradoxically seem easier and feel like exactly the right thing to do, even when it takes you further away from what you really want deep down, which is simply to be happy.

The reason is largely biological since noticing things that are out of the ordinary, unexpected, and potentially harmful is absolutely necessary to your survival. In fact, the human brain has a built-in negativity bias which causes us to pay more attention to what our subconscious flags as negative or potentially dangerous than to positive or neutral events, which aren't perceived as a threat to our survival.[12]

Everything we experience through our senses serves as a stimulus to our human organism, including our proprioceptive sense (body awareness), which allows us to feel things happening within us and gives us information about our movements and position in space.

When something happens to trigger a fear response in you, your autonomic nervous system goes into high arousal. This reaction prepares your system to respond by getting ready to fight an enemy, flee from danger, or freeze like an animal playing dead ("Maybe if I don't move or breathe, that lion won't see me and I'll soon be safe, once he's gone!").

There is also a less commonly known fourth possible reaction seen primarily in females, which is the psychological instinct to "fawn" (submit) or "tend-and-befriend," which elicits behavior to protect the self and offspring, and to seek connection and support from community.

---

11 "Stress, Mindsets, and Success in Navy SEALs Special Warfare Training," Frontiers in Psychology 15 (Jan. 2020), https://doi.org/10.3389/fpsyg.2019.02962, and Paul B. Lester, Emily P. Stewart, Loryana L. Vie, Douglas G. Bonett, Martin E. P. Seligman, and Ed Diener, "Happiest Soldiers Are Highest Performers," Journal of Happiness Studies 23 (2022): 1099–1120, https://doi.org/10.1007/s10902-021-00441-x. Also see Clifton B. Parker, "Embracing Stress Is More Important Than Reducing Stress, Stanford Psychologist Says," Stanford News.

12 John Lazarus, "Negativity Bias: an Evolutionary Hypothesis and an Empirical Programme," https://www.sciencedirect.com/science/article/pii/S0023969021000254#bib0045.

For example, a physically weaker animal, meeting a larger animal, if it is not bent on food, may know that its only chance for survival is to adopt an attitude of submission to the stronger animal by accepting its dominance and showing that it doesn't pose a threat. As a result, possibly the stronger animal will decide to pass the weaker one by—again, if it is not hunting for food—leaving it and its offspring in peace. If you've ever seen a tiny dachshund crouch low to the ground, lying with front paws out, as a strange German shepherd charges toward it, this is the underlying instinct. And it works.

All humans experience the above-described fear-based response—also known as a "startle" pattern—exhibiting some or all of the following characteristics to one degree or another:

- The head is pulled down onto the spine, while the jaw juts forward in an effort to protect the vulnerable neck from harm.
- Overall muscular tension increases as the spine compresses, and the whole body goes into a generally compressed state.
- Less blood flow is delivered to the thinking brain, more to the musculature.
- The chest collapses, and breathing becomes shallow and restricted.
- Limbs tighten, including hands and feet, and the hips and knees lock up.
- Stress hormones are released.
- The heart rate increases.
- The palms become sweaty.
- There is an urge for elimination (urination or defecation).
- The stomach is upset.

One of F. M. Alexander's most important discoveries was the dynamic relationship between the head and neck/spine/body that governs our overall coordination and movements. He called that dynamic "head-neck" relationship the "Primary Control."

Alexander went on to discover that "unduly excited fear reflexes" are the root cause of interference with the workings of our Primary Control; fear is the main thing that gets in the way of naturally well-coordinated movements and ease in living. When we don't let go of our instinctual fear-based reactions, we end up living on high alert, in a state of near constant anxiety, much like a hunted animal.

Imagine for a moment that you're a primitive human, walking through the jungle, your senses on high alert as you look around, listening for any signs of potential predators. You really need to pay attention; if there's a lion in your vicinity, you may have very little time to escape with your life. If you miss the warning sights and sounds or if you don't take them seriously, within seconds you might be dead!

On the other hand, if you notice a few berries or a rabbit along your path, it won't be urgent for you to take action on your find. Your system won't go into a fight-flight-freeze response, and your brain won't flag these benign events as anything very important. Not only are these events not a threat to your survival, but you've got plenty of time to gather the berries or kill an animal to feed yourself and your family (my apologies to the vegans reading this!).

Even though humans have evolved over hundreds of thousands of years, and living in our "civilized world" is naturally quite different from being an early human in the jungle, our biological organism hasn't really changed that much. Our environments definitely have changed, but this facet of how the mind-body-self functions in relation to the world around us essentially hasn't. We still pay more attention to things that are unexpected or seen as a potential threat, and we give less importance and pay less attention to whatever seems benign.

Unfortunately, much of what happens in our modern lives the human organism isn't designed to recognize. From the asphalt of our streets to the speed of our cars and airplanes, the height and fluorescent lights of our buildings, and the whistles of trains, blaring car alarms, and incessant notifications from electronic devices . . . so much of our modern lives is unnatural.

So we end up going into a startle pattern much more frequently than when, long ago, we knew the types of things we were likely to encounter on our walks through the jungle, and we had a limited number of possible options to choose from.

So, what are you to do if you're surrounded by unnatural stimuli that are constantly triggering your innate fear reflexes, which are innocently designed to keep you safe?

Oh, and . . . what does all this have to do with being a musician?

Performance anxiety is an evolutionary (and very common) problem

One of the most common reasons musicians come to me for coaching is their difficulty in overcoming nerves triggered by the unnatural situation of performing in public. Stage fright can cause many of the symptoms listed above. It's like a modern version of the kind of reaction our ancestors had to unknown potential dangers in the jungle.

Imagine that a human being—an animal without claws or sharp teeth—is placed in the middle of a stage. As she stands there, exposed and highly visible under a direct spotlight, hundreds of unfamiliar eyes watch her every move, waiting to see what she's made of. The space is hushed—nobody else moving—and she has no idea whether the animals out there in the audience are friends or foes.

To this lone animal, vulnerable, surrounded by potential predators, it could be a highly dangerous situation! So, it's only natural that her instinctive survival mechanisms are triggered, and her startle pattern kicks in.

Finding herself in such a situation, she will either gear up for a fight, make a beeline for the exit, freeze and try to look invisible, or hunker down into submission, hoping to avoid an unpleasant outcome.

Of course, this human animal is not thinking rationally but is simply reacting as her biology is designed to, to protect her under these types of circumstances.

The problem is . . . if you suffer from stage fright . . . that human animal is YOU.

The part of you that reacts to being seen and heard in front of an audience by going into a startle pattern starts in a part of your brain known as the reptilian brain. It's that part of you that is made to keep you alive when circumstances suggest that your survival is threatened.

Happily, even though we have a reptilian brain, we also have a prefrontal cortex, the newest part of our brains, evolutionarily speaking. This is the part of the brain where conscious thinking such as planning and decision-making takes place. Think of it as the throne room or command-control tower of your body, from where you can see the rest of yourself as if from above, observing your situation more objectively. This is the part of the brain that allows you to pause and consider your options before choosing to act.

Although being triggered into a startle pattern is an instinctual, animal reaction that happens quickly and below the level of consciousness, often too quickly for us to prevent it, once we notice that we've been triggered, we have the ability to override our animal instincts (for better or for worse) and behave differently from how our instinctual nature would have us react.

What you need to know about stress and fear

We can, in fact, respond to stress in two ways. The fear-based way I've described above is natural, instinctive, unconscious, and reactive, arising from our reptilian brain.

The other way uses the prefrontal cortex to refrain from acting for a split second, which allows us to assess the situation and think intentionally (not necessarily verbally), choosing a different response that rises above the reptilian brain and is hopefully based on a more accurate interpretation of the situation. All of this can take place with lightning speed. Alexander called it "quickening the conscious mind."

This is really good news for musicians with performance anxiety since it's obvious when you stop and think about it that performing in front of an audience is NOT in fact a life-or-death situation, no matter what your reptilian brain causes you to feel. It's hopeful news because it means you can overcome your fear and respond to the situation with more ease, presence, and creativity instead of mechanically going through the motions, just to get through the performance alive!

By learning how to take charge of your thinking mind, you can redirect your thoughts and actually prevent your body from secreting more stress hormones—in that way influencing how you feel in your body and emotionally.

Emotions are simply chemicals coursing through your bloodstream that alter how you feel in your body, and it's your mind that interprets those feelings and gives them meaning. It is entirely possible to change not only how you feel emotionally, but also how you react physically to certain circumstances, by changing the way you think and assign meaning to what's happening.

Consider this: you can actually only know you're "nervous" if you're experiencing certain physical symptoms that you label as "nervous" and undesirable. When you're nervous, you might experience anything from an increased heart rate, "butterflies" in your stomach, dry mouth, cold extremities, to shaking hands or legs, etc.

If you don't have any physical symptoms, then you won't have the experience of being "nervous." As Mio Morales says, "You can't have an emotion without your body."

One of our biggest problems as human beings is that the unconscious brain doesn't know the difference between what we see as reality happening outside of ourselves and what we visualize in our minds and what we interpret these images to mean. This might seem outrageous, but it's been tested. It's true. This is why the vivid memory of traumatic events that did not happen to us (even violent images on a TV screen) can trigger us in much the same way as thinking about those events later. The unconscious doesn't see a difference between something real and something imagined. It's easy to whip up groups by focusing enough on scary dramatic scenes.

The reality is, what we fear more than anything is our own thoughts, and we especially don't want to trigger any painful emotions, either by hearing about a current event or resurfacing a memory long hidden.

Ultimately, we are afraid to know ourselves. We are afraid of what we might find buried deep within our psyche, and we fear taking responsibility for our own state of being, our reactions, our choices, our behavior. Imagine what could happen, we tell ourselves, if we tapped into the unknown. We are afraid of something that does not actually exist.

That said, instinctual fear is human, and I am not suggesting we get rid of it. The "startle pattern," which is vital to our survival, is on our side—ever ready to help us fight, run away, freeze, or surrender in the face of a true threat.

Instead, what we need to learn is how to (1) detect the early signs of "startle"; and (2) recognize that we have the ability to respond differently to stress by drawing on our human specialty: consciously directed thought. We can pause for a split second, discern, and consciously choose what would be the best course of action. This, in turn, may actually take us right up and out of our fear response.

Most of the stimuli that modern life presents us with are in fact *not* life-or-death threats. If we regularly practice close observation, pausing more often to check in with how we're feeling, we'll get a better sense of whether the startle-related tension we unconsciously carry around with us throughout the day is necessary.

We can then realize our human—not animal—ability to overcome "unduly excited fear reflexes"; also, we can experiment with a new way of thinking not bound by those reflexes that helps us find more ease, calm, and creativity in our activities.

Some typical ways musicians deal with performance anxiety

Even though they may have been performing for many years, many musicians still get nervous to play in front of others; they can't seem to get rid of the discomfort, and they feel like the anxiety is getting worse over time.

By the time my students seek me out for help with this, they've usually already tried one or more of the following things to get rid of their performance anxiety, but they've found that these methods haven't worked, haven't worked well enough, or they've worked but the musician doesn't feel good about the method (for example, not wanting to depend on drugs as a long-term solution).

Two big reasons for this are that most musicians have a basic lack of understanding about:

1) the fundamental unity of the mind, body, and emotions;

2) how to use the prefrontal cortex—our conscious, thinking mind—to respond differently to perceived threats, in a way that takes you out of a startle pattern and calms down the nervous system.

By the way, lest you suspect that stage fright is related to a musician's skill level and that more accomplished musicians don't get nervous, this is not at all the case. Even famous, legendary musicians can experience a high degree of stage fright. A few notable examples are Barbra Streisand, Adele, Luciano Pavarotti, Nathan Milstein, Vladimir Horowitz, Cher, and Renee Fleming.

These are some typical ways musicians try to overcome stage fright:

- overpreparation: practice more and work harder
- meditation or breath-control techniques
- positive thinking, affirmations, and visualization
- psychological counseling, therapy, or psychiatric treatment
- prescription drugs, such as beta blockers
- recreational drugs, such as alcohol, marijuana, or nicotine
- distraction, including movements such as pacing or talking
- eating certain foods, like bananas

Some of the above methods might have merit, and can be at times extremely useful, though rarely do they deliver consistent results you can count on when you're under a lot of stress and your mind feels out of control.

In my Art of Freedom programs and sprinkled throughout this book, I offer a foolproof—drug-free—way to comprehensively and systematically overcome performance anxiety by taking conscious, constructive control over your mind, body, and emotions. For more detailed information and a practical way to deal with performance anxiety, visit the Bonus Materials page here: https://www.artoffreedom.me/book/bonusmaterials

We need to feel our emotions if we want to express them musically

Up to this point, I've discussed suffering mainly in terms of fear, as manifested by our biologically programmed startle pattern, and I've proposed how we can overcome this instinctive, animal-like response by activating the prefrontal cortex and consciously choosing to create a different, more positive, creative experience.

But what about when you're playing a piece of music that is fraught with emotion, and you actually *want* to feel the depths of those scary, painful, heart-wrenching feelings so that you can express the composer's (or your own) intentions and share authentic, deeply moving communication heart-to-heart with your audience?

We wouldn't be musicians if we weren't aware that music has a mysterious ability to instantly change how we feel.

The magical and wondrous thing about music is that it is an alchemical cauldron for anything and everything contained in our human experience. We all know how powerful music is—it has been used for anything from inciting warriors into battle and lulling fussy babies into sleep, to calming manic patients in Ancient Greece and celebrating marriages all over the world.

There's a certain magic to the vibrations of organized sound that pulls on our "heartstrings," triggering thoughts and feelings within us that can be either healing or destructive, depending on the types of vibrations, the meaning we ascribe to what we feel, and how we choose to respond—either consciously or unconsciously.

I'd venture to guess that most artists become artists because they have a heightened sensitivity to the depth of human emotions. We musicians feel, and we feel deeply. Not only this, but we assign an infinite variety of meanings to what we feel, so that there is an infinite variety of musical expression open to us.

As musicians, we have the incredible opportunity to feel and be moved by deep emotions, we can transmit our feelings to others, our listeners can receive those feelings, and we can choose to process those feelings in a way that either causes us to keep suffering or allows us to transcend them in a way that heals emotional wounds.

The problem is, when we're caught up in our own emotions and we don't know HOW to feel them fully, process them, transmit them, and respond to them in a healthy way, we can actually make ourselves feel worse.

We musicians often haven't been taught the following, which can get us in trouble, and prevents us from becoming truly great artists. Great musicians need to learn how to . . .

- respect the double-edged sword in the emotional power of music
- dare to feel the full depth, breadth, and intensity of an emotion
- process emotions quickly
- transcend emotions in a way that increases bliss and overall well-being

An emotion that is not allowed to be fully felt and processed is blocked—either suppressed (intentionally and consciously not felt) or repressed (unconsciously not felt). Blocked emotions not only reduce the quality, emotional impact, and expressiveness of a performance, but stuck emotions can actually cause more suffering in the musician—even to the point of physical pain.

So, to come back to the idea of suffering I presented earlier in this chapter, suffering IS inevitable to be a great artist. And yet, so is JOY.

We need to be able to feel fully, let go, and express the full range of human emotions in order to transmit and share an authentic human experience with our audience. However, staying stuck in our emotional suffering without transcending and transforming those emotions into JOY is what ultimately sabotages our art—and ourselves.

Students typically begin working with me because they want to improve their musical skills, or they want to overcome pain or performance anxiety. But they are always surprised to find that one of the biggest benefits of our work was something they didn't anticipate at all: my students get happier!

Some common yet uncomfortable emotional tendencies in musicians

Admitting the truth about yourself—even to yourself—can feel uncomfortable, not to mention scary. On the other hand, change requires self-reflection and self-honesty. If you turn a blind eye to your inner experience and you don't know your habits and emotional tendencies, you can't do much about them. That will keep you stuck indefinitely with whatever degree of happiness or unhappiness you're used to.

A list of emotional issues follows. These are the ones that tend to come up for my students from time to time. Of course, none of these issues is unique to musicians—they're simply part of the human condition! Everyone has the potential to experience any of them to a greater or lesser degree, so please don't judge yourself if you recognize any of these tendencies within yourself.

As I always tell my students, if you notice anything at all happening inside of you, this awareness in itself is cause for celebration!

- social anxiety, performance anxiety
- perfectionism, hypercriticism of yourself, fear of criticism from others
- judgmentalism
- fear of failure, fear of success
- chronic feeling of "not-good-enough," imposter syndrome
- lack of self-confidence, low self-esteem
- lack of curiosity and motivation, burnout
- procrastination
- caring too much about what others think
- people-pleasing, overfocusing on others' needs and denying your own
- self-centeredness, lack of gratitude, lack of generosity
- not assuming full responsibility for your own feelings and well-being
- self-pity, blaming others and circumstances for your lack of personal or professional success
- excessive self-blame; putting yourself down and making yourself feel bad
- erratic mood swings, depression, general anxiety
- inability to fully feel, accept, and process emotions
- lack of ability to communicate freely and authentically with others

Learning The Art of Freedom Method can go a long way towards helping you overcome any of the above issues. If you are experiencing extreme discomfort or any other psychological disturbances not listed, and it's difficult for you to function or feel positively about yourself, I recommend that you consult a medical professional or experienced counselor to help you move forward with expert support.

In the next chapter, we'll look at some of the ways your spiritual life can influence your musical life.

Making Music with Spirit

Do you let your music flow with Inspiration?

There are more things in heaven and earth, Horatio, than are dreamt of in your philosophy.

~ *William Shakespeare*

When somebody who plays a musical instrument tells me, "I don't think of myself as a musician"—or a professional musician tells me, "I don't feel like a *real* musician,"—to me, that indicates a fundamental misunderstanding of what being a musician actually is. Inevitably, it turns out, such people don't feel worthy of expressing the music inside of them, which I believe is everyone's human birthright.

To me, a "musician" is simply "somebody who makes music." Since music is natural to the human experience, everyone is born a musician!

Babies gurgle and coo . . . Isn't this music to a parent's ears?

Toddlers hum and play with rhythm . . . Children sing when they play.

We use rhythm and/or pitch to express our emotions, and we call it music. Expressing our emotional energy through movement and sound vibrations is a universal and entirely natural human experience.

I believe that all human beings have an enormous variety of emotional energy vibrating inside them, and those vibrations can be expressed outwardly by the body to create sound, with a greater or lesser degree of intentional organization. Everyone has this natural ability—unless something (including injury or disease) blocks that freedom of expression.

Sadly, all too often an external event causes a person to react in a way that stifles their emotions and silences their music. Sometimes, the event is obviously traumatic, but often the trauma is subtle—its effects revealing themselves gradually over a long period of time. Every time a person's inner song is stifled is a trauma to the soul.

Just one thoughtless comment ("Oh, you shouldn't sing—you have a terrible voice!" or, "You're wasting my time with that noise!") can be enough for a person's inner voice—her soul—to be silenced and her musical light to be dimmed for years.

Even professionals who make music at a very high level can suffer from early traumatic experiences that made them question their self-worth and ability to produce art that is worth listening to. Here's Chloe's story . . .

When Chloe found me online and we began discussing options for study with me, she sent me a wonderful video of herself playing jazz violin. I thoroughly enjoyed her performance. It lifted my spirits as I listened to it throughout the day, and I wrote her, "What fun!" Sadly, my heartfelt comment triggered her, and she shrank back into self-criticism, thinking that her jazz fiddling was somehow frivolous, inferior to that of classical musicians.

This was easy to understand when, after we were working together later, she shared with me how her classical violin teacher (when she was a young teenager) was not a kind or patient man, but, highly critical, he rarely had an encouraging word as she struggled to please him and live up to his unrealistic standards. She worked hard, but her teacher discouraged her bluntly, telling her she had almost zero chance to become a professional musician.

Knowing her history, I marveled at Chloe's determination to pursue music as a career. When I asked her what had motivated her to keep playing in the face of such strong external and internal criticism, she admitted that she had never really experienced joy while playing the violin, but she did have a powerful experience as a child that she will never forget.

One night, Chloe moved her bed into the middle of her room and turned on some music she loved. She lay there, relaxing on the bed as she let the music wash over her. She became filled by the beauty of this music and felt as if she were being transported—as if she were rising above her own physical body. She experienced such ecstasy through the music that she knew beyond a doubt THIS was what she wanted to do with her life—be a participant in creating this beauty so she could experience it again and again, and share this ecstatic experience with others.

Chloe was *inspired* through music, and this Inspiration carried her through a very difficult situation with her teacher in her teen years. Lacking good instruction, she struggled greatly with poor technique and unhelpful habits, and a tremendous amount of self-doubt.

After a few months in my private coaching program, Chloe revealed to me that she was still playing on a student violin purchased for approximately 100 British pounds ($100 US)! What a miracle that she was still playing the violin, against all the odds!

At first, coming to me, Chloe was completely unable to recognize that her playing was already quite stellar. She felt stiff and constrained while performing and had internalized all the harsh criticism she'd received from her teacher. The result was she suffered from imposter syndrome, unable to consider herself a "real musician." No matter what style she played—whether Bach or jazz—it was never good enough.

Although she yearned to feel free and express the love of music that was ready to burst from her heart, she found herself completely unable to let go. Her mind wandering, getting distracted while she played, there was a constant inner chatter of self-criticism, second-guessing her choices, trying too hard to sound good and play with accurate technique. And worrying about what her audiences might think.

Her deep love of music was still in there, but she didn't know how to surrender to that. She had no idea how to get out of her own way and allow her creative spirit free rein to flow through her.

As she began learning The Art of Freedom Method and applying Primal Alexander (explained in detail up ahead) to her daily practice, I encouraged Chloe to make some short videos, playing, and to share them with my online studio of musicians working on similar issues. She was understandably nervous at first.

But through our work together, and as her mind-body coordination kept improving, she saw her playing more objectively. finding that she could slowly let down her defenses, relax, and open up her soul to express herself fully and authentically. Her playing improved the more she did this, and as making the videos got easier with practice, she started to enjoy her music a lot—as did, naturally, her audience!

In Chloe's words . . .

"Building a career in music is tough when you're constantly second guessing how your music is being perceived, and over-analysing the reactions you get from audiences, whilst also spending all your time in the practise room beating yourself up about not sounding good enough. I should know—that was my reality before working with Jennifer! And choosing to dive right into a six-month coaching programme was the best thing I could have done when at a professional crossroads due to these psychological challenges two years ago.

"I was just about ready to give up—the violin was only making me suffer, and my obsessive thoughts about not being good enough were eating me up. But Jennifer's teachings gently brought me around to my own power and freedom in this moment, and the next, and the next, to direct my physical, emotional and musical bodies in a whole new way, free from niggling worries and the weight of the past.

"I'm free to be able to live the music I play and free to get real satisfaction from sharing it whole-heartedly with others. Jennifer's work is truly transformative. I'm so glad I chose to work with her."

~ Chloe, Classical and Jazz Violinist

The process of Inspiration is healing

Performance anxiety, perfectionism, persistent physical pain . . . we can often trace these back to core soul wounds triggered by events that caused us, deep down, to fear for our personal safety. If we want the music hidden inside us to shine, soar, and be heard in all its radiant, flowering beauty, then we need to ask how these deep fears and wounds can be healed.

The first step to healing is to recognize that something is amiss. Something's out of balance within us that is worth paying attention to, listening to, and learning more about.

Once we realize that something's wrong and we have a desire to heal, we need to open to the possibility that our subconscious mind, our innermost heart, and our body's wisdom carry all the keys to our pain, our healing, and our freedom. The miracle of conscious awareness gives us the power to choose our thoughts and therefore shape our experience in the next moment.

By taking full responsibility for our own well-being and taking intentional, mindful action to change our lives right now, we can create a future more in alignment with our truest nature and desires. Seeing that we have a hand in shaping our future builds our confidence, which is what allows us to create inspired art.

The best art, healing us by bringing us back to the beautiful integrity of our wholeness, reflects the ultimate truth of who we are.

When a musician is inspired, she is tapping into the source of Inspiration, which is the deep, vibrant Love within and everywhere around us. In the moment that she connects to this loving Source, her ego begins to soften and melt, and the true, innermost Self is allowed to shine through, like the ever-present sun suddenly revealed when the clouds part.

In this magical moment, grace and beauty are transmitted . . . souls are touched, moved, seen, heard, and transported. As Plato put it, "Beauty is the splendor of the True."

Real Inspiration enables a deep and natural healing process, in which our energy or 'life force' is allowed to flow with greater ease, and our biochemical and neuromuscular healing mechanisms are freed up to do their jobs of caring for us from within.

When a musician becomes a clear channel for the transmission of a musical idea, she has the potential, indeed the beautiful divine birthright, to convey profound meaning and the full richness of the human experience through an elixir of sound.

When skilled in the art of Inspiration, the artist knows how to tap into creative flow and play with Spirit in such a way that her own emotions are awakened, which causes the emotions of the receptive listener to resonate with those vibrations. This in turn awakens emotions within the listener, who then assigns his own meaning to the experience.

During inspired music-making, both musician and listener have the potential to wake up more fully to who we already are, while realizing our freedom to choose who we wish to become in the future—beginning in this very next, fresh moment that is now.

This process has the potential to be profoundly healing and uplifting for everyone who is open to being moved by what comes through. The process is uncommon and profound, even though it's entirely natural to the way human beings are designed to function and share experience with others.

The problem is, most people think and move in ways that block the free expression of musical ideas, and they don't understand how to let the endless streams of their emotions flow into rivers of inspired creativity.

Instead, fear and performance anxiety are allowed to run the show, and unhelpful thoughts get in the way . . .

Wondering what other people will think of you gets in the way . . .

Perfectionism, self-criticism, and self-doubt get in the way . . .

Physical pain gets in the way . . .

Technical problems get in the way . . .

You get the idea.

Freely receiving and transmitting musical ideas with creative spirit is natural. But being able to ignite, draw on, and develop inspired creative flow at will, with conscious intention, is a rare skill. Some people are naturally more available to this process than others, but this skill can be learned by just about anyone who has the sincere desire.

To learn the skill of tapping into inspired creative flow requires:

- Courage and humility, along with a willingness to not know, be wrong, and risk making mistakes
- A willingness to let go of old beliefs and habits and open up to fresh new ideas that might work better—even if they feel unfamiliar or wrong at first
- A willingness to learn by observing yourself and others as objectively as possible, and enough healthy curiosity to experiment with new ideas
- Patience and trust in your inherent ability to improve your overall coordination and move with increasing ease as you realign with your natural design
- The ability to use your mind well: first, to formulate clear intentions; next, to intercept and redirect any thinking that gets in the way of the best use of your whole self. I'll be describing how we do this with Primal Alexander ConstructiveThinking further on.

In the Alexander Technique, "constructive thinking" is a term that describes a very particular way of using thought that shifts your awareness to allow the whole mind-body-self to rebalance naturally and with ease. Marjory Barstow, the first person to graduate from Alexander's teacher-training course in England, in 1934, coined the term; it is not to be confused with what is currently known in psychology as "constructive thinking," which is defined as simply an enhanced ability to solve problems.[13]

Mio Morales, who studied with Marj for more than twenty years and in the mid-'80s assisted her at her summer workshops in Nebraska, has his own take on the concept of constructive thinking. Mio's ConstructiveThinking™ puts a big emphasis on curiosity and experimentation.

13 Anat Drach-Zahavy and Anit Somech, "Constructive Thinking: A Complex Coping Variable That Distinctively Influences the Effectiveness of Specific Difficult Goals," Personality and Individual Differences 27, issue 5 (Nov. 1999): 969–84, https://doi.org/10.1016/S0191-8869(99)00041-0.

I first got a demonstration of Primal Alexander ConstructiveThinking from Mio at the International Congress for the Alexander Technique in Limerick, Ireland, in the summer of 2015. It seemed a bit strange at first when he started teaching a few of us who were lounging around a dining table how to do something he called "TheCyCle™," which entailed cradling our own fingers, counting to four, and doing something he called "ConstructiveThinking." I felt a bit self-conscious doing this meditative experiment in the middle of a bustling dining area, but I found the practice calming and pleasant. My curiosity was piqued. I will explain this core teaching to you in detail coming up. (You can get your first taste of ConstructiveThinking and learn TheCyCle in this book's companion video training which you can access here: https://www.artoffreedom.me/book/training.)

Learning to access creative Inspiration using ConstructiveThinking is at the core of what I teach. The process is profound, potentially life-changing, healing, and dramatically helpful for your whole self as well as your musical skills.

The best part: it's so simple . . . and so EASY to tap into! All you need to do is learn how to stop doing what's blocking the natural ease within you and, as F. M. Alexander said, "Let the right thing do itself."

Is tapping into Inspiration a spiritual practice?

Well, no . . . and maybe yes. . . if you want it to be!

As always, it depends how you think about things, and how you do them. I firmly believe that all human beings are creative, spiritual beings, so anything we do can be taken as a spiritual practice if we're practicing it with good intention, conscious awareness, and in harmony with our creative spirit, or universal Love. (See the Introduction of this book for more thoughts on different words for "spirit.")

When I was nineteen, I became interested in practicing meditation more deeply.

Learning about the contemplative practices at the heart of many of the world's religions led me to a very personal discovery: what I had been experiencing while communing with music alone in my heart as a child was the same thing found at the core of all the world's spiritual traditions. This deeply personal and unifying experience, a primordial "religion of the heart," is accessible to every human being. It is none other than the practice of pure, true, unconditional Love.

I'm talking about Love with a capital "L," which is transcendent, lofty, and impersonal while also subjective, deeply personal, and profoundly intimate: the kind of Love that's a connector, uniting everything through the very stuff of life—the universal Substance, Energy, and

Joyful vibration that unites all things, all beings, all of nature; indeed, the entire Universe. There isn't any ego attachment in spiritual Love.

Personally, I use the word "Spirit" in addition to the word "Love," for the following reasons:

1) I grew up in a non-religious household that didn't use the word at all, so I had very few preconceived or religious ideas about this word.

2) Outside of a religious context, I mostly heard people use the word "spirit" in relation to creativity, energy, and enthusiasm, so I had many positive associations with it.

3) In my sheet music, as mentioned, I often saw the phrase *con spirito* (meaning to play with an elevated energy, brightness, and "spirited" liveliness). Naturally, as a child I liked playing *con spirito*—this was fun!

One day one of my teachers in college called me a "free spirit." What did he mean? I didn't know, but I liked the idea and never forgot it. When the great violinist Yehudi Menuhin praised the passionate fire within me, I think he was saying the same thing. Somehow, these encouraging words validated my personal experience and motivated me to stay connected to what I felt was at the core of my best music-making. I knew I wanted more of that musical "spirit"!

And yet, at that time my understanding of how to consciously integrate my sense of spirit with my musical experience was still very vague, requiring me to go through a long period of largely rejecting music in favor of spirituality until I learned that these two subjects are absolutely compatible and essentially the same.

Eventually, I learned specific ways of integrating these seemingly different aspects of my life, which are now an important part of what I teach. (Part 2 will share more of my personal story, what led to finding that spiritual-musical integration.)

Tapping into the creative spirit of Love—mostly through music, in my case—I discovered a blissful flow that connects all things; being separate and disconnected is only an appearance. We dissolve into nothingness as we simultaneously merge with everything else and are delivered into the lap of oneness.

Finally, we can relax when we experience everything as a whole, free of separation and conflict. We can let go of the small ego defined by fears, anxieties, negativities, and worry and identify instead with something much greater—something Infinite and Absolute in its unicity—and much smaller since it's also the stuff of the tiniest atoms within us.

Because this is such a universal experience, which includes everything and excludes nothing, I firmly believe that the process of becoming inspired—tapping into this creative, flowing presence—is innate, perfectly natural, always accessible to everyone. Inspiration is how we tap into the source of creativity, and it is also how we realize the true Self of who we are; it is pure Love, or Being-Consciousness-Bliss.

All we need do is to accept that we do not and cannot know everything, surrender the ego, get out of the illusion that we can control a world made up of separate things, and—in opening up—"let the spirit blow where it listeth."

But how do we get out of the way of what is natural, universal, and filled with the spirit of Love? Is it easy or difficult? How do we stand aside, freed from the grips of fear, and let Inspiration flow through us to communicate the "splendor of the True" from heart to heart?

Could anything be more desirable than this?

So . . . can we put these ideas to practical use for musicians?

Good question!

Here are three reasons I believe it is vital to approach music from a universal perspective of Love, playing *with* our creative spirit instead of without it:

- When the spirit of Love is not included in your music, though it might leave your audiences dazzled by your acrobatic skill, it will lack a certain depth, spaciousness, and vitality that has very little to do with technical skill. Even beginners can transmit this special quality when inspired.
- Whether you like it or not, your sound reflects your state of being and transmits who you are, in any given moment. Even if you're nervous, if you choose communing with Love over being driven by fear, this choice will be transmitted to your audience. But if you prioritize the separate over the whole and your egoic desires over your inner wisdom, the quality of your sound will reflect these choices, too. When your mind, body, and heart are open—so will your sound be. If your mind is narrow and your body tight, your heart closed . . . your sound will reflect that. So . . . will you choose to move towards Love or hold back out of fear? We will sense what you choose through your sound—like it or not.
- You might be surprised to realize that you can practice this process any time and all of the time, even when you're away from your instrument. In fact, when you start living with this spirited depth of awareness, your whole life "counts" as practice time! Part 3

of this book provides more reflections on this practice (which I call Primary Practice) of developing the whole musician and using your daily life to improve your musical skills.

The process of creative Inspiration

To summarize . . . the process of creative Inspiration—or playing "with spirit"—is simple, natural, and easy. It is our normal, uncorrupted state of being. However, we get in the way of this open, free state of being when we think in ways that cause us to forget how we are connected and integrally united with everything in this universe.

When we forget about the oneness of reality, we fall into the illusion of separation, and we lose awareness of our connection to Spirit. As we become afraid, our egos inflate to try to make up for what we feel we have lost. We puff ourselves up—in the mistaken attempt to make ourselves and others believe we are bigger than the small individual we believe ourselves to be.

We forget our infinitude, our possibilities, our potential, our true Self.

We become competitive. We try to prove our greatness, or we try to hide our smallness.

All along, all we really need is to realize we are already perfect and whole as we are in this very moment—because we are, in fact, one with everything. We are made of the Love that is inseparable from the source of all creation.

I recommend taking time to contemplate these ideas. Be curious and wonder about them. Don't take them on "blind faith"—rather, experiment with them in your daily activities. What happens when you choose to think that you are whole, connected, and one with a creative spirit that is endlessly flowing Love?

Contrast that with the thought that you are separate from others . . . worse or better than others . . . and consequently that you need to try hard to connect with others . . . that you are flawed or imperfect . . . just a small ego in a wild jumble of competitive and judging souls.

How do you feel when you think one way, and then the other?

What happens to your mood? To your body, your breath, your movements?

Which way do you prefer? Which path would you rather choose to explore further: Love or fear?

You can always change your mind, of course.

For now, I propose that you open up to the possibility that you have everything you need inside of you and all around you . . . that loving is easy because it is your true nature . . .and there is nothing to do, prove, or show . . . you can just rest in being your true Self in this ripe, creative moment.

And then . . . let yourself make music and see where the flow of Inspiration will carry you next!

If you'd like to learn more about Inspiration for musicians, you can access a video on the topic from the Bonus Materials page here: https://www.artoffreedom.me/book/bonusmaterials.

When things get difficult, let the tears flow and let the ego die a little

Sometimes, you're able to rise above challenges, overcoming them quickly. At other times, you're caught by surprise and knocked off balance by an unexpected tsunami of feelings before you even know what hit you.

At times, life can seem overwhelmingly complicated, painful, or even meaningless, and that may feel like a burden too heavy to bear. Your soul may be tossed down a rocky river of tears before you can access the joyful, creative ripples of ease that are always there waiting for you just beyond those times of suffering.

A difficult situation can become a valuable opportunity to humble yourself and prune your personality of what no longer serves you, which can then be used as raw material for creating powerful art.

As long as we're alive, Life calls us to keep shedding the old ego-skins of habit and reach into ever deeper reserves of the creative spirit within.

A crisis can serve as a powerful and undeniable demonstration that you're human, far from invincible. A crisis can force you to face yourself and the reality of your life as a whole in a dramatic way that in everyday life doesn't seem quite as urgent.

Challenges are designed to wake you up to what's ultimately most meaningful and important, and to motivate you to take positive actions with spirit. Ironically, when you choose growth, Love and Life, there's always a kind of ego-death to make way for the beautiful transformation of your personality.

During difficult times, you have the option to rise up, use all the strength of mind, heart, and body you can muster, and make lemonade out of lemons . . . or great art out of tears.

In fact, you're being asked to make an unequivocal choice between going in the direction of more growth and life . . . or sliding into the direction of increasing decay and death . . . and the choice is right NOW.

Don't miss the treasures hidden in terrible things!

If you don't learn from your difficulties, you can be sure that Life will serve up another opportunity for you to learn from, because Life is kind; it will always give you another chance to let go of your habitual ego and make a better choice.

Every time you deny the wise inner truth of who you really are, the challenges you face are likely to grow in intensity so as to capture more of your attention. Perhaps they give rise to a painful yet healthy disillusionment as to what you previously believed about yourself and the world. Resisting the truth that is revealed to you will just prolong your pain and postpone healing and joy.

The old way of seeing things must be replaced by a shift in perspective, a shattering of the familiar order so you can step into a new paradigm.

There is nothing more painful than the existential suffering that takes hold of a soul brought low, exposed to herself as helpless as a newborn baby. And no soil more primed to nurture the soul than the rich, black soil found in the depths of despair. I know, as you will see later on in the book.

But this is where the soul's treasures are buried, so don't be afraid to feel; to be the hero who ventures to the center of the earth, seeking the treasure that only you know is there.

Falling into despair without hope is a path to self-destruction. That is NOT the purpose of a crisis.

We artists are extremely susceptible, at risk of drowning into the vortex of feeling that floods us when unexpected shocks occur, because to be an artist means being sensitive, open to a wide range of feelings—everything from blissful elation to icy loss of hope.

Art is made of everything in the universe, and feelings are the life-stuff that spins through it, holds it together, gives it meaning, and transports the one who wishes to experience it.

But it's not enough to get sucked into the world of feeling and express them, which is what most good artists do. That kind of art can be entertaining, moving, and even uplifting, but without a bigger purpose and a means for the artist to use those feelings to serve that purpose, getting carried away by endless feelings is a surefire recipe for getting lost.

The true artist lives the truth of her creative spirit in everyday life

It takes tremendous courage to allow yourself to feel and move through the depths of suffering that can arise within you as an artist. To face the darkness, feel the terror, and hold fast to the faith that you WILL survive; to trust that you *will* be able to pick yourself up and dare to take another step forward after you've been knocked down and life no longer seems to have any meaning.

You need to *want* to see the bigger universal picture, put things into context with a wise sense of priorities, to bring the important things forward and let the unessential fall away. You need to learn how to discern what is blocking your path, so you can move forward full of hope, no matter what.

Being a creative artist is a vocation, but it is not apart from our common vocation of being human. To be fully human is to be an artist practicing the art of living.

We can all choose to turn the moments of our lives into true and meaningful art . . . or not.

To do this means paying just as much attention to how you lift a pen or pour tea as when you lift a violin bow or touch a keyboard.

The true artist is willing to shed illusions in favor of the reality revealed in the moment. The true artist has the ability to carry her audience on a wave of feelings rooted in the truth of the present moment, and she never loses touch with her real, central presence for long.

The true artist practices art as a way of being, healing, and transformation, which is completely integrated with everyday life. A purification and transmutation of soul can occur when the ego surrenders to uphold the deeper meaning of your art.

When your art and life are integrated in light of this purpose, the creative spirit can lead you with grace on a straight path through the ups and downs of life and all the way to the welcoming doors of death.

There is an old German saying: "Those who die before they die, do not die when they die."

To deepen your artistic sensitivity and practice this kind of presence requires total commitment to discovering your purpose and knowing yourself, much like the commitment of a renunciate monk or Japanese samurai who devotes his life to serving a greater cause with unflinching discipline.

I've written this book to help you see through the surface layers of the music on the page and hear beyond the vibrations that reach your ears . . . *so you can realize that your whole life is a musical mystery waiting to be played into existence through the instrument of your body every day.*

Each fresh moment of your life offers the opportunity for a new expression of your creative spirit to rise up from the divine, omnipresent silence that is pregnant with the inner music of your soul.

Part 2

Discovering a Holistic Solution

In Part 2, I share how I struggled over many years to understand how to be myself and how my discoveries of spirituality, the Alexander Technique, and Primal Alexander all influenced my own experience of being a musician and a teacher of musicians. I also share the epiphany that led me to create The Art of Freedom® Method, which integrates all aspects of the self with Love, true concentration, and the pursuit of great artistry.

Know Your Heart's Desire

What do you really want?

You are the embodiment of want.

~ *Mata Amritanandamayi*

One of the best things about being an artist is that you can pour all of your personal longings, wishes, dreams, and desires into your art, where they can be transcended and transmuted into something sublime and healing for yourself and the world.

What the specifics of your longing are, nobody even needs to know because your feelings are shared wordlessly, straight from your heart.

When your emotions are fully embodied—freely expressed—at their core they represent the pure existential longing of the human soul for love and unification: something everyone can feel and identify with.

Sharing your longings and desires openly with abandon and vulnerability, however, is often easier said than done! One of the problems of many musicians is that we have endless contradictory thoughts that cloud and confuse our minds, and conflicting desires that create excess tension in our bodies and spread anxiety through our systems.

Some of our conflicting desires come from wishing to please others who are directly or indirectly involved in our music-making. Voices from the present, such as fellow musicians, jurors, or audience members, and old voices echoing from the past, such as former teachers, family members, or friends; all clamor for our attention in our minds, telling us how they think we should feel and how they think we should play.

When you try to please others in a way that runs contrary to what you truly desire and believe deep within your own heart, you're setting yourself up for an internal conflict that blocks the free and easy expression of your music.

For example, if you play in an orchestra, it's normally not acceptable to question the conductor's interpretation, resist the rehearsal schedule, or go against the dress code. The same in a ballet corps.

If you have a teaching job, you may have to follow a curriculum and teach some classes you don't enjoy or students who aren't interested in learning. With most employers, you may not have much say in raising your salary, and you certainly can't just pack up and go on a vacation in the middle of the semester or concert season!

Of course, it's important to be able to find freedom and happiness within any structure we wind up in. Attaining internal freedom while accepting full responsibility for our choices and accountability for our actions is one of the most important things I help my coaching students with, and it's something I've worked on for much of my own life, in both musical and nonmusical contexts. Let me share an example.

I learned a tremendous amount from playing with a well-known music ensemble for many years. I had many wonderful experiences, as I appreciated my colleagues and very much enjoyed the music we made together. As with any group, though, not everything was smooth sailing.

I became quite uncomfortable at one point, when we were asked to have certain expressions on our faces and to move our bodies in prescribed ways, sometimes literally following choreographies, so that as a group we would "look like" we were enjoying ourselves and feeling musical passion together.

It seemed to me that we were effectively being asked to perform not only as musicians, but as actors and dancers, as well. Even in complying, internally I struggled with the request and at times felt indignant; I found it difficult to feel the movements authentically, coming naturally from within. Had I been hired to play my instrument well and sound good, or to look good, too?

Being put in a position that required me to submit to an external authority while going against my own convictions about musical performance caused me to ask myself things like, *Why am I here? Why am I doing this? What does it mean to have both an audible and visual component to a performance? What is entertainment? How can I do what is being asked of me in full integrity, play my best for the group and my audiences, and enjoy myself to boot?*

Especially since I had the luxury of not needing the money from that job at the time, it was important to me that I enjoyed playing in the ensemble; otherwise, what was the compelling reason to stay?

My uncomfortable inner resistance to this situation lasted for some time, causing me to reflect deeply on my own values. I learned a great deal about myself. By staying open, being willing to change my perspective over time, I received important teachings that extended far beyond the specifics of that work environment.

I finally did make peace with that situation while staying true to myself as I worked on integrating my own needs along with those of the ensemble. I was able, for instance, to effectively apply the words of one of my most influential Alexander teachers, Helen Hobbs of Cleveland, Ohio, who used to tell me, "Poise is the best visual," as I learned to bring more external movement into my performance without at the same time sacrificing my Self-Use, internal ease and flow.

It wasn't until years later that I would finally curtail my involvement in that ensemble when new conflicts arose. Interestingly, the pandemic hit within weeks of making that decision. I filled the new time and space created by those circumstances by recording and producing my first solo violin album.

I'm sharing this story because it's such a good example of how important it is to use every situation we find ourselves in as a crucible for personal and artistic growth. I learned so much from working through that situation.

As I struggled to overcome the various challenges presented by playing with that ensemble, I deepened my understanding of what it takes for an artist to feel deeply, communicate clearly, and share herself fully and authentically from the heart—to the ultimate benefit of everyone involved.

I also learned how important it is to be clear about what we want. How can we balance our needs with those of others if we aren't even aware of our own?

Life is continually presenting us with new challenges that compel us to face the truth about ourselves and live with more authenticity if we choose to.

Having wishes, dreams, and goals in life is normal.

To want things and to desire experiences is human. To begin with, we all have an animal instinct to meet our basic needs for growth and survival. Yet, from a very young age the world teaches us to want more than that, as our uniquely human ability to think and make conscious choices allows us to have endless desires that go far beyond fulfilling our basic needs.

All day long, we superimpose an infinite variety of goals, wishes, dreams, and desires on top of the primal urge to keep on living, and sometimes our conscious choices can even override and go against our best interests for self-care and survival.

Many of the desires we have didn't actually originate with us; they were impressed upon us by those with influence in our lives, such as early caregivers, family members, teachers, and friends—even bigger-than-life movie stars, politicians, and magazine models. For better or for worse, our entire culture has a profound effect on what we want and the choices we make.

We've been taught to put things into two categories: things that are worth desiring, and things that are not. Pleasures and comforts are generally considered to be good and desirable, while pain and discomfort are not.

One of the strongest lessons we've received since babyhood is that prioritizing *somebody else's* desires is good and desirable. Plenty of positive feedback, attention, or love reinforced those desires; conversely, loving attention would often be withdrawn when we broke spoken or unspoken rules.

"Smile! Wave bye-bye!"

"Go to sleep! Eat! Sit up! Say 'Momma!' Walk!"

"Good boy! Good girl!"

Babies, toddlers, and young children learn quickly that obedience guarantees food, safety, shelter, and attention, while the opposite attracts negative feedback—at worst, even abuse.

Most children quickly discover that it pays to "be good," and pleasing others is an easier path to feeling good than not.

Of course, this isn't necessarily a bad thing! Given that we have loving, caring caregivers, we learn how to safely navigate the jungle of the outside world, our culture, and institutions, and we can more easily fit into the molds that society has created, succeeding as a result according to the world's standards.

We learn how to fit in and belong to the groups we choose. All in all, we learn how to get what we think we want.

Sometimes, we even learn how to surpass expectations and stand out, so that we get more of the "good stuff" that everyone else seems to want: more pleasure, more praise, more money, more recognition, more success.

The problem is, when we prioritize our goals over our process, we automatically bring more tension than necessary to our actions, which actually makes everything we do more difficult than it needs to be.

What's worse, since we've been trained since birth to take on and prioritize the goals and desires of others, we are likely to lose sight along the way of what *WE* actually want underneath. In fact, it's not uncommon at all in our culture to be completely out of touch with our feelings and what we truly want for ourselves, independently of what others want and what others have trained us to want and feel.

When we learn the people-pleasing lessons too well, it's all too easy to deny that we have wishes of our own, perhaps in direct conflict with what others want. It can be very difficult for the well-trained people-pleaser to even admit to having any of her own desires because she was told that it was better to give than to receive, she should be content and happy with what she has, and she shouldn't want more.

In fact, it's not at all uncommon for a people-pleaser to believe it's impossible to both have desires of her own AND be a good person. What a double-bind!

Sometimes, the people-pleaser knows she's trapped, but she can't imagine another way to be, so she continues to put the needs of others ahead of hers, in a misguided belief that denying her own well-being is the only way to be and do good in the world.

On the other hand, sometimes the people-pleaser senses her entrapment, blaming others for how she feels, and decides to rebel. Instead of trying to please others, she decides to do whatever she wants, while ignoring others and trampling on their legitimate needs and desires. Of course, that's not real freedom, because the desires of others are still the reference point for her reactionary choices.

Used to denying their underlying feelings, it can be very hard for either compliant or rebellious people-pleasers to take full responsibility for their lives, own their desires, and claim their dreams by taking appropriate actions to achieve them. They haven't learned how to get in touch with their deepest, most true, and heartfelt desires. Those natural and authentic desires are, in fact, always full of empathy and in harmony with the authentic needs of others.

This may come as a surprise, but in my experience most people fit into either one or both of the above people-pleaser categories, whether they realize it or not.

To learn how to prioritize your own well-being, while staying sensitive and responsive to the well-being of others, requires a great deal of savvy discernment and practice.

This is absolutely necessary if you want to be truly happy AND help others experience true happiness, too. As a musician who wants to share music from your heart with your whole self, with ease and joy, you need to learn how to do this, one step at a time.

To know who you are and what you want . . . to be true to yourself and claim what you want . . . to shed the masks and throw off the costumes of the roles you've been cast in . . .

. . . to put on the robes YOU want because YOU want to wear them, not because somebody else implied that you're "bad" if you don't go along . . .

. . . to stand your ground despite strong opposition, grow a backbone (in everyday jargon), own your desires and just GO for what you want . . .

. . . these are not easy things for a people-pleaser to do, to say the least!

No, it's not easy to admit and go for your dreams. But this is the kind of self-love you need to develop if you want to be truly happy and fulfilled, *and it's also what you need to make truly great art.*

The unexpected way I learned about roles, purpose, and desires

I was nineteen years old when I met my husband (now ex-husband). We married when I was twenty, just before I graduated with a bachelor's degree in music and a Performer's Certificate from Indiana University. Before then, I'd lived with my family or a series of college roommates. Because I'd never lived alone, I was used to adapting to others. Even though my people-pleasing habit sometimes made me feel miserable, I still frequently gave in to things I didn't like or agree with while on the inside subtly rebelling. But I would "stuff" the rebellion.

I have to admit that by my forties I'd been feeling generally unhappy for quite a long time. I didn't feel free to be fully myself outside of the clearly defined roles I'd taken on throughout my life, finding it impossible to break the spoken and unspoken rules I'd agreed to follow. For many years, it just seemed too risky (even though I certainly tested the boundaries of my marriage in plenty of ways that I'm not proud of).

So, when my husband and I finally decided on a trial separation after nearly twenty-three years of marriage, I was quite excited to move away for a few months. I relished the thought of some time alone. My two boys were teenagers by then, old enough, I thought, for me to stay in a nearby house they could walk to from school. And they could stay over with me anytime.

I yearned to do some deep soul-searching. There were just too many ways I wanted to burst outside of my boxes!

The first couple of weeks on my own, I felt like a tremendous weight had been lifted off of me, leaving me, at last, plenty of quiet time to rest and think. But what happened next turned everything upside-down, bringing a very different—and much more difficult and profoundly rewarding—experience than I could have imagined.

No sooner was I on my own, than within two weeks, a serious case of pneumonia slammed into me like a truck in the middle of a recording session in Cleveland, knocking me down with fatigue and a sickness like nothing I had ever experienced. I kept coughing and could barely function to get through that session.

Somehow, I managed to drive myself back to Cincinnati the next morning with a high fever and went straight to my doctor, without even going home first. Unfortunately, my doctor misdiagnosed the pneumonia twice over the next ten days, and I suffered quite a lot without getting the antibiotics I wasn't aware that I desperately needed. When I finally got a chest X-ray on the advice of an old high-school doctor friend (thank you, Facebook!), it showed my left lung completely filled with fluid, and I'd been stripped of nearly all of my energy.

Thankfully, the antibiotics saved my life. I barely suffered anymore—even the coughing wasn't painful. For the first time in my life, I lay in bed, completely unable to do anything at all for many weeks. Without a shred of energy left, I barely had the strength to think!

Of course, all of my juicy plans for soul-searching, reading, and journaling went up in smoke. In the end, instead of having this trial-separation time alone to figure out what I truly wanted for my life, the pneumonia helped me discover much more about what I did NOT want. Because—to my great surprise—as my system was drained of all energy, all of my desires vanished.

I found this desire-less state very unfamiliar and quite fascinating! As I lay there for days on end, I observed myself as if from outside, quite aware that all of the goals and roles I'd assumed before then were suddenly inconsequential. Just GONE. GONE was my desire to do anything. GONE was the inclination to think, feel, move . . . even do much to stay alive.

Poof! My outer self disintegrated and seemed nonexistent. The parts of me that weren't my true self no longer had any scaffolding to hold them up.

Until then, I had wanted to be a good person, and I cared *a lot* about being good at everything I did: I was a "good daughter," a "good mother," a "good violinist," a "good student," a "good teacher," a "good friend," a "good neighbor" . . . even a "good spiritual seeker." It seemed, to all appearances, I was plenty "good enough," and yet, I put a tremendous amount of energy into convincing myself this was true.

Pneumonia robbed me of so many of the thoughts and beliefs that had formed my habitual identity. There simply wasn't any energy left in me to *do anything* or try to *be anybody*; nor was there any energy left to care anymore.

So, I watched the woman—myself—lying there for days and days . . .

I watched her stop thinking, stop moving, stop doing, stop striving . . . and even stop praying (that one was shocking!) . . . but I just . . . didn't . . . care. I didn't feel like soul-searching, meditating, contemplating, praying, or doing anything at all other just than being.

How strange, I thought! *Surely, this isn't OK?!?*

Well, whether it's OK or not . . . I just . . . don't . . . care.

So, I just kept being and watching . . .

Until, one day, I suddenly realized that I wasn't very happy in this limbo state of nonactivity and nondesire. Somehow, it wasn't bringing me peace. The emptiness I was experiencing wasn't a bright void pregnant with possibilities but was simply a bleak nothingness getting darker by the day.

As I experienced, lying there, an increasingly heavy, downward energy slowly taking over me, I observed that I didn't much like the direction I was going in. I didn't like feeling listless, aimless, joyless, lethargic.

Hmmm . . . how interesting, I thought! I was fascinated by this realization.

That's when I had the simple, yet very profound realization I had no direction in my life: that I wanted—or needed—it because just lying there doing nothing, I was unhappy. Slowly, the thought hit me that it was important to have a desire . . . a goal . . . something to aim towards—even the simplest wish to be happy.

At that point, I guess I'd recovered enough energy to get curious and start thinking again, because I began doing little experiments with wanting and aiming, slowly allowing myself to have desires and goals again.

The first new desire that arose was the pure desire for desire. I wanted to want something. I wanted energetic upward movement, purpose, direction. I wanted to be at peace and happy again, I discovered.

I began thinking a little bit about what might make me happy . . . like, sitting outside on the porch, enjoying the balmy fall breeze, enjoying the warm flavor of a nourishing soup, or sharing an experience with a friend on the phone.

I started with little goals since I only had enough energy to do one thing each day: I could either do laundry OR make a meal.

These were survival needs. Happiness goals. Energetic goals. Goals that felt like me, like clearly what I wanted.

Going through this process was truly fascinating and utterly life-changing! Once all of the old masks and desires had dropped away, I discovered that many of the goals I'd had before weren't actually mine at all.

I'm not sure I ever could have discovered this if I hadn't been alone with this pneumonia that knocked me out for so many weeks, and I'm deeply grateful for that experience.

Even though I didn't come to any conclusions about my marriage at the time, and it wasn't until more than a year later that the marriage ended for good, in hindsight I know that I received all the important answers to the deeper questions I wasn't even aware I'd been asking when I left home.

That experience changed something essential in my perspective. It was the beginning of learning how to live and think for myself, on my own terms.

At first glance, it might look like I adopted a new, selfish attitude. But I believe it was anything but that.

Magnanimous selfishness

Over the next few years, I had to work consciously to get in touch with my own desires and beliefs, because whenever I asked myself point blank, "Jennifer, what do you *REALLY* want? What do you *REALLY* believe?" I could hardly answer the question.

I just didn't know. It had been far too long since I'd asked myself these questions with deep sincerity, free of any expectation, or any threat of punishment for believing, wanting, or doing the "wrong" things.

It wasn't easy because I'd never looked at life this way. I was so used to measuring my thoughts and actions against old programming, societal conditioning, and others' expectations, that I barely even knew what I wanted beyond my immediate survival or comfort goals of the moment.

It took quite a while to figure out who I was, as separate from everyone else in my life and history. To this day, it helps to regularly ask myself what I want, and to reaffirm the beliefs that are mine.

Going through that experience of being deathly ill was an essential step towards learning and embodying "magnanimous selfishness," a phrase coined by Mio Morales.

The principle of magnanimous selfishness is actually a spiritual principle shared by all the world's religions that, when applied, assures that everyone benefits from your choices directly or indirectly, sooner or later.

As it says in the Bible: "You hypocrite, first take the log out of your own eye, and then you will see clearly to take the speck out of your brother's," Matthew 7:5 ESV.

A rule on airplanes is to "put your own oxygen mask on first before helping others."

The point is, if you're not taking care of yourself first, making sure that you are fully aligned with your own highest and best interests, you can't bring your best, whole, integrated self to relate with someone else. So, whatever you offer anyone else will be limited and less effectual than it could be; and sometimes even harmful in that you won't be as sensitive to their subtle needs and under-the-surface feelings. You may even end up hurting people when all you're doing is trying to help them.

If you want to give your best to an activity, you need to do that activity with as much awareness as possible—with your whole self—the best you can. You simply cannot do that if your mind-body-self is scattered, splintered, distracted, not fully attentive to your own being first.

In order to be fully present to your own experience, you need to bring yourself back to the present moment, become recollected, centered, unified in mind-body-spirit, and be as conscious and aware as fully as you possibly can.

As a musician, that's the only way you can bring your best, highest, most authentic and whole self to your musical instrument, your performance, and your audience.

Learning how to live and give in this way is "selfish" or "self-centered" only in the sense that we put our attention on the SELF first, others second; rather than being outward-directed, we become primarily inward-focused and heart-led.

This way of functioning is "magnanimous" in the sense that you cannot help but be kind, compassionate, and generous to the world around you when you are centered and good to yourself first. This is when you can finally realize the truth that you and the world are not separate; we are all in this together; we are all one.

Taking care of yourself IS caring for others; and caring for others from the center of your heart IS caring for yourself. There is no longer any distinction between "me" and "them," "mine or yours or theirs" . . . Because there is just one integrated world of universal Being-ness, in which everything is interconnected, interdependent, and in constant flow of giving-receiving LOVE.

Your heart's truest desires can be found through music

This unification, this sense of loving interconnectedness is what every human being yearns for at the core of their being.

Unifying Love is what I want, what you want, what everyone wants. It's what drives everyone and everything we do, from the depths of our hearts.

It's what turns the animal drive to survive into the human desire to connect and belong; and when realized, it becomes a Divine desire to transcend both the animal urge and our terrestrial human need.

What makes music so special is that it gives us a natural opening into the world of the soul as our emotions are stirred, deeply buried longings of the heart are awakened, and we become moved by Love. Music carries us wordlessly on the wings of time beyond the world of forms, into a deeper dimension where thoughts and everyday desires can be safely left behind.

Once your thinking mind slumbers and the heart awakens, animal and human desires fall away, and only the desires to BE and to LOVE remain. Things become simple, and we are momentarily satisfied within every cell and vibration of our being. The humdrum of daily life is transformed into something electric and REAL . . . and we touch the Divine, whether we know it or not.

Again and again, we are drawn to come back to music. We practice for hours, strive to improve our music, even aim for that elusive ideal of "Perfection," not knowing that what we are really striving for is Being-Consciousness-Bliss, the true essence of who we already are.

In fact, all of our problems as people and artists stem from a profound lack of self-knowledge, a misunderstanding of who we are in relation to the world, and a general lack of awareness in the moment.

Even when we do have some sense of who we are and what we want, our chaotic minds and wounded egos block much of our ability to experience meaningful connection and joy.

No matter how hard we might try, we are not always able to transmit the strong love we have within us through our music. We don't really know HOW. And yet, we can sense in our bones the transformative and transcendent power of music, so we keep yearning, searching, and practicing the best we can.

Sometimes, we succeed. Connection is made, passion is communicated, and our shared musical experience is sublime! Sometimes, nothing special happens, our performance falls flat.

All too often, our fingers fall onto the wrong places, and passages that were easy to play at home are suddenly out of control. We tremble with nerves. We worry about what people will think. And we can't stop thinking about what might happen—or already did.

When you don't have control over yourself and your reactions, your playing lacks consistency, and your performance is less than reliable. It can be terribly frustrating and downright demoralizing to put yourself out there and have things turn out differently from how you planned.

There's nothing more frustrating to a musician than having practiced a piece for many hours, days, weeks, or months . . . feeling ready to perform it . . . and then—for no apparent reason—you get onstage and nothing works.

Or . . . you prepare your orchestral excerpts for months or years before a big audition. You're as ready as you'll ever be. You've played your excerpts for others. You nail them every time . . . then pay hundreds of dollars to fly out to an audition. But in the moment when everything needs to come together, you hit a wrong note or the tempo is off . . . and what happens? The jury won't even listen to you past the first few lines of music.

So, why is it so hard sometimes?!?!?!

The good news is, it's not your fault.

Because nobody taught you *how* to really get to know yourself, how to take charge of your own mind and body—to claim your own desires and achieve your goals in a healthy way, with effortless ease.

Nobody taught you *how* to put yourself first so that you could play your instrument for others with magnanimous selfishness, with your WHOLE SELF.

Nobody taught you *how* to question your thoughts, your beliefs, and your programming.

This is what this book and my coaching programs are all about. I want you to learn exactly how to do these things so you can stop referring everything in your life to what others want *for* you, or have cajoled you into believing or doing for them.

The Art of Freedom Method is about having a center. Knowing your true heart's desire as well as your personal secondary goals, and how to achieve all of it with JOY.

If you want to bring your whole self past the finish line in one piece, there are some fundamental things you'll need to know and do. I'll be discussing these things in greater detail throughout this book.

To get what you want and achieve your true Heart's Desire, you'll need to learn how to . . .

- Recognize your people-pleasing and rebellious tendencies, and decide to rise above them
- Know your mind and clarify your intentions. Get clear about what YOU want, and WHY
- Develop a vision. See the big picture AND the itty-bitty baby picture of the next step and the next . . . to manifest your dreams
- Be curious and willing to learn through experimentation; have the humility and the courage to be wrong before you can be right
- Identify conflicting intentions, and beliefs that no longer serve you
- Do less of what is unnecessary and let go of old habits that get in your way
- Be present to your own experience in the moment
- Act without hesitation and keep moving towards your goal, free of hurry or worry
- Trust that your mind-body-self knows exactly how to get you where you're going, even when your thinking mind doesn't have a clue
- Catch yourself whenever you veer off-course
- Commit to choosing Love and Truth over fear and ego
- Cultivate an attitude of gratitude, joy, and magnanimous selfishness, every step of the way
- Remember that patience and faith are everything!

As a musician, if you want to learn how to get what you want with maximum ease and efficiency, you'll also need two more things:

1) a guide who has first-hand experience of this process and understands in depth and breadth what musicians need to go through in order to achieve their goals, and . . .

2) a proven system with crystal clear, simple steps to follow, which will guarantee your progress and get you where you want to go as quickly and effortlessly as possible.

This book is here to fulfill all of the above. I am here to offer guidance along your way, and I can guarantee your progress when you follow the steps I'm going to share with you, in the precise ways that I will describe later in this book and teach to my students.

If at any point you'd like more personalized guidance on how to apply these ideas to your unique situation even more quickly and easily, feel free to reach out to me through my website at www.ArtofFreedom.me or use this form to inquire about my private coaching and group programs: www.ArtofFreedom.me/apply. I look forward to connecting with you!

The Freedom to Be Yourself

Self-mastery is the key to artistic mastery

I was a Hidden Treasure; I loved to be known, so I created the creation in order to be known.
~ *Sufi mystical tradition*

As a child, I was painfully shy. When my mother took me to music classes for toddlers, I was always the little girl on the outside of the circle, watching from a distance, not daring to join in.

There's actually a video of my mother and me on the Mr. Rogers television show when I was just three years old. She had been invited to the show to talk about the lovely wooden toys she was making for children, but I could barely answer Mr. Rogers's questions as he held me and I shyly fiddled with my hands behind my back!

Things got a little easier once I was in school. I didn't have any trouble participating in group games or communicating with adults close to me, but how to have good conversations with other children continued to perplex me.

I didn't have any performance anxiety playing the violin, though. I could play the violin fearlessly as a soloist with the Berlin Symphony Orchestra, with the famous Jesus Lopez-Cobos conducting, in front of an audience that wrapped 360 degrees around the stage. But speak to a few people in public? *No way!*

Whenever I was asked to speak from a stage at a concert, I would flat out refuse; someone else would have to do it. Around age eleven, interviewed for a newspaper, I still remember how terrified I felt! My mother had to make phone calls for me, or they just wouldn't happen.

I'm not exactly sure why I found expressing myself verbally so challenging, but since I didn't feel understood, I must have decided it was easier to stay quiet much of the time.

Just be yourself.

My father to the rescue. He would tell me, "Just be yourself."

What good advice it sounded like, so I would try . . . and try . . . and try . . . to "be myself." But being myself in social situations often felt truly impossible, and I was mystified about how to go about doing that. What did it mean to "be myself"? And who was "myself," anyway?

It didn't make any sense to me. "Myself" wanted all kinds of things, wanted all sorts of feelings and experiences that she couldn't seem to have. Even though "myself" wanted to connect with others, she felt nervous, small, and scared. "Myself" wanted to run away and hide, and "myself" certainly did not want to expose herself by speaking!

My experience of myself was constantly changing, too. One day, I'd feel happy and free, and the next day lonely and miserable. One day, I would play my heart out on stage in front of hundreds of people with ease, and the next day, shrink in front of a camera or a microphone.

My father's words "Just be yourself" became something like a Zen koan—a sort of riddle or puzzle designed for meditation. I used to contemplate this idea and think about it a lot, wonderingly. I tried to figure it out, but I didn't understand it at all.

Besides my father's wise words and a very real Mr. Rogers telling the young me every day on television that I was "special," I was influenced by a popular children's LP my parents gave me: "Free to be You and Me."

As celebrities sang and read songs and poems targeted at gender neutrality and emphasizing individuality, tolerance, and ease of identity, I got more insight into what "being myself" might mean. It proposed that I could wear whatever I wanted, think whatever I wanted, or become whoever I wanted to be when I grew up.

I loved these ideas! And I pondered them all the time . . . at home, at school, and while playing my violin. The idea of being free to be myself was very enticing to a girl who much of the time certainly did NOT feel free to be herself!

I gathered that there must be people out there who had already solved the riddle; they seemed so at ease in being themselves. If these people were telling me it was possible to be free and be myself, I was determined to learn how.

This mystery of how to be myself has served as a signpost for me of my higher purpose—a kind of quest for the "Holy Grail"—through every stage of my life. I fully expect this quest for Self-realization to continue for as long as I live because any other purpose pales in comparison to fully and unabashedly realizing who I am!

My violin was my best friend

In addition to my weekly violin lessons with an outside teacher, my mother (an excellent Suzuki cello teacher) taught me at home, practicing with me every day until around the age of ten. My mother knew how to motivate me positively, and she knew how to help me improve through smart and systematic practice.

I will be forever grateful to my mother for teaching me without pushing me—she certainly wasn't a "pushy stage mom"—and she never forced me to play the violin. I always knew I was playing for me, and I never had any doubt that's what I wanted. Becoming a successful solo violinist was my only tangible goal in life.

On the other hand, I do remember some very tearful practice sessions that ended up with us arguing and me running to my room, sobbing in frustration. No! I did not want to play that passage AGAIN (!!), having been asked to play it many times in a row correctly.

Once, after a painful practice session like that, my mother took away my violin, put it by the front door, and said she was returning it to the shop. I was very young and I don't remember that episode very well, but she tells me that the next morning she found the violin had been quietly removed from the doorway and put back in its usual place. I wanted that violin more than anything, so I was ready to practice again.

As I grew older, music kept me sane and healed my heart many times when life felt too painful or overwhelming. When I didn't know how to be myself in this world, at least my violin would still be there for me, waiting for me to show up and reconnect to my inner dreamworld.

Everything I shared with my violin was acceptable. My violin listened to me, responded, and validated all of my thoughts and feelings. My violin was a perfect mirror of everything that was going on inside of myself.

I loved that I could pour my heart and soul into that violin; that it didn't need me to use words that could become twisted or used against me; it simply accepted everything I gave it. I loved this "me" that was being expressed through sound.

Of course, not everything came out beautifully when I played the violin, and not every practice session was joyful, to say the least. In fact, most of the time I didn't really like practicing much at all, unless I was playing through my pieces to express my emotions or for my own enjoyment.

Practice your Primary Instrument—YOU!

If you want to master your art, you need to master your instrument, and the only way to do that is to practice.

It's challenging to have someone else with you in the practice room, keeping you on track, but it can be even more challenging when you don't get outside support to help you stay accountable.

Sadly, many children don't get much musical support from their parents as they're growing up, and I really admire those that keep working on their own and eventually become professional musicians, despite having the odds stacked against them!

No matter how much or little help we may have gotten when we were young, in the end we all end up alone with ourselves in the practice room. This means we need to learn how to become our own best teachers as soon as possible! And that means learning how to discipline ourselves by mastering our thoughts, moods, and movements with plenty of kindness and self-compassion.

After all, who wants to practice with an impatient, angry teacher forcing you to do things you don't want to do? The only way to practice well, with ease and joy, is to be self-motivated in a way that you actually WANT to practice because you're ENJOYING what you're learning.

Besides being self-motivated and enjoying your practice sessions, there's another really important piece that's completely missing from most people's concept of practicing, which makes all the difference to the quality and effectiveness of your practice.

People have the mistaken idea that practicing is all about practicing your musical instrument, but they forget that musical instruments are completely silent and have nothing to say without YOU!

The only way to truly master your art is to recognize that your musical instrument is only a mirroring extension of YOU. If you want to have good control over your musical instrument, it's only logical that you first need to have some degree of conscious, constructive control over your own mind-body-self.

That's why I encourage you to think of *yourself* as your primary instrument—your "Self-Instrument"—and your musical instrument as your secondary instrument.

I discovered early on that my violin was simply a tool, and music was a means for expressing myself. My violin was a box that amplified my thoughts and feelings, making them audible for the world to hear when I stroked its strings with a bow.

If I felt passionately angry or sad and got carried away by my feelings, my sound would suffer, reflecting my own suffering.

If I was feeling calm, open, peaceful, or loving, my sound would grow and shine, reflecting the happiness in my heart.

The quality of the music you produce is a direct reflection of the quality of your ability to feel what you're feeling without letting those feelings knock you off-balance and bog you down. That means knowing how to direct your mind and your whole self with open awareness and a high degree of mind-body coordination. Your ability to think clearly and integrate your being with what you're doing will reveal the degree to which you have constructive, conscious control (Alexander's words) of your whole self.

Artistic mastery requires self-mastery

Without practicing your Self-Instrument (what I call Primary Practice, discussed more fully later in this book), you can still make music, of course. But you will never be able to produce truly great art because there will always be something lacking as you unconsciously block the free flow of who you truly are, from both yourself and your audience.

Until you dare to start knowing, being, and sharing your true self with honesty and vulnerability, your music will suffer—just like you. Mastery of your Self-Instrument is what will allow you to both "be yourself" and master your art with ease.

After many years of wondering and trying hard to be myself, feeling like I just couldn't do it, I now know that there is nothing easier in the world. In fact, the answer is so simple you might scoff at it, thinking it can't be that easy!

The key to being yourself is simply knowing and accepting that there's nobody else you could be.

You are *already* you. And you're already sharing who you are without even trying! If you feel unable to be yourself, then that's just an indicator that you might not know yourself very well, and you're not really OK with who you are.

If that's the case, then you're probably not giving yourself full permission or freedom to be and express yourself without hiding behind a mask of who you think you *should* be.

As a human being traveling through time on this planet called Earth, I want you to know that you are the hero of your own life story. This is a role nobody can take from you, and paying attention to your Self-Instrument is the way to embody the unique character of YOU in this story.

Your musical instrument, whether it's a violin, trombone, voice, or conductor's baton, is a vital tool on your unique musical journey, but it is only your *secondary* instrument. What is happening to your primary instrument from moment to moment is *always* of primary importance; everything else is merely secondary.

As you travel the path of artistic mastery, it's absolutely essential to grasp that your musical instrument and what you do with it are less important than embracing the essence of who you are and attending to what you do with your whole self—in the presence or absence of your musical instrument.

Since YOU are your primary instrument, you need to become the #1 expert on how to use (think, move, control, or direct) your own mind-body-self in the most efficient and effective ways possible if you sincerely wish to experience success and fulfillment as a musician AND as a human being.

If you want to play notes that are in tune, with good timing, and accurately reflect the emotions of the music, you need to know how to tune your Self-Instrument first. THIS is what needs to be practiced, above all.

Without forgetting, of course, the master Alexander Teacher Marjorie Barstow's wonderful words, referring to the Alexander Technique: "This is much too serious to get too serious about!" Marj may as well have been talking about music or life itself!

NOW is the time to tune yourSelf, practice yourSelf, and be yourSelf with ease . . . by waking up your curiosity, being present, and patiently holding space for the whole person you are to shine.

Sadly, our modern musical culture doesn't typically acknowledge the primacy of the whole person, and it focuses almost exclusively on what a musician is doing with the musical instrument, to the exclusion of the Being he brings to it and the rest of his life—as if making music were done in isolation, unrelated to anything else. Pretty much everything about how the mind and body work together as a synergistic, interdependent system is ignored.

As performers and educators, we usually direct our focus towards specific musical challenges, desires, and problems that need to be addressed, prioritizing immediate solutions by manipulating the specific body parts involved in executing particular skills or those that appear to be directly responsible for technical limitations. In the process, we overlook systemic issues and their underlying, indirect, and longer-lasting solutions. It is completely forgotten that the state of the whole person influences *everything* we do with the musical instrument.

That said, even if this fact isn't acknowledged, it's still possible to be highly successful as a musician. However, without this holistic awareness and without carrying this awareness into practical action, an artist's full potential simply cannot be fully realized. There will always be something blocking the full expression of his creative soul, and that lack will be reflected by the reduced quality of his sound and depth of musical expression.

So, how *DO* you "be yourself"?

In truth, you don't "DO" being yourself—you simply "BE" being yourself.

As a child, there were many times when I would lie on my bedroom floor and "just BE"—especially if listening to Indian music and meditating without realizing it. I remember knowing with the core of my being, deep in my heart, that this "BE-ing" was in fact the real Me—my true Self. Everything else seemed superimposed, egotistical, and selfish.

It was this Me that could so easily and fearlessly express herself through music. But it was another matter altogether to "just be" this true Self, feeling at ease, free, and fearless under any circumstance!

Even though I had the intuition and experience of my true Self within my heart, and I could express this well through music, I still held the strong belief that I couldn't really "be myself," and I didn't understand how to get there.

I was under the fundamental misunderstanding that there was always something wrong to fix, something missing, or something that wasn't "good enough"—beginning with "myself."

If "myself" wasn't good enough, then it seemed logical that I must have to DO something to rectify that! It's easy to see where I got that idea; after all, everybody in my life was DOING things to try to improve or correct things—from home to school to music lessons to rehearsals to performances.

It seemed to me that violin practicing was by definition about looking for, finding, and fixing what was "wrong" by DOING something different and working hard to get it "right." Learning how to make better music was rarely about being fully present with my experience and learning how to enjoy myself and the process of making music, independently of any goals to be achieved.

Everyone around me, including many of the spiritual teachings I found through books and conversations, seemed to be teaching that we always need to be *doing* something to change or improve ourselves, and I accepted this belief as true.

The concepts of letting go of negative thoughts and practicing virtues such as patience and detachment—ideas which are in fact more about "undoing" than "doing"—made sense, but I was somehow quite unable to connect my intellectual understanding of those ideas with my everyday experience of living in my body.

Spiritual writings the world over teach that we need to transcend the body and give up our attachment to feelings, desires, and things . . . but the only way I could imagine doing that was to try separating my mind from my body, which was a futile exercise that just caused me more suffering and discomfort. Letting go felt difficult; being patient often felt like pulling hard on a horse's reins; detachment felt cold and disconnected from myself, separated from the rest of the world. Consequently, all of these resulted in an increase in muscular tension instead of relief from my habits.

At the same time, spirituality stresses the importance of cultivating happiness, love, and joy—but how could I feel those things while also feeling detached and disconnected from my body? I didn't understand. What was the secret to *feeling* joy while simultaneously trying to negate my feelings? How could I escape from a body that seemed like a prison?

Spiritual life, the way I understood it, was wonderful in theory, but nearly impossible in practice. It wasn't until I discovered the Alexander Technique that I realized I'd been trying to do multiple contradictory things at the same time and I was making things much more complicated than necessary!

The Alexander Technique is not a "spiritual practice," per se. But it has shown me indirectly how to live my spiritual life more fully, deeply, and authentically by *embodying and applying* paradoxical ideas with awareness of my whole, undivided self. This is well-represented by the Chinese Taoist symbol of the Yin-Yang, which contains the balance of everything and its opposite, all in one:

When I discovered the Alexander Technique, I finally understood much better how the spiritual saying, "if there is a heaven on earth, it is here" could be true—and that it applies as much to living in this physical human form as to walking on this planet. This was when I first understood in a very practical way that I truly AM free—already—to be myself. Right here, right now. I don't have to do anything to be myself, because I already am and always will be ME.

The Alexander Technique has given me powerful new insights into how to transcend the body while simultaneously accepting and being completely within and aware of it. The Technique empowers me to more effectively take charge of my own mind and thoughts, body and movement, heart and feelings.

Even my experience of space and time is now more fully under my control. It also shows me how to do that while making music. I don't have to rush in life, and I don't have to rush in music.

The true Self is universal, common to all, shared by all, fundamentally loved by all, yet—sadly—it is not recognized by all. Even though being and expressing yourself is the easiest thing in the world in principle, in reality it may be the biggest challenge you can ever take on.

Being yourself means identifying the ego habits you've taken on that hide the real YOU, like clouds blocking the ever-present sunshine. It means getting to know how you think, how you feel, how you react to things, how you move, how you live . . . so that you can let go of what is unnecessary and rest in the bliss of your Being.

It means getting really curious about yourself, being willing to let go of illusions and see through the ego-masks you've taken on to hide your true Self from the world, in the mistaken belief that you are separate from that world, and that the world can hurt your true Self.

The Indian sage Sri Ramana Maharshi said, "The only thing preventing you from self-realization is the belief that your self is not yet realized."

In other words, the only thing keeping you from feeling free to be yourself is the belief that you are something or someone other than who you already are, and therefore you need to DO something to change; that being isn't enough.

Once you realize that being yourself means you don't have to do anything extra, you can simply let go and BE, and in that moment you realize that you are—and always were—free to be you. You realize who you are.

And your true Self is glorious, perfect, beautiful, light, free, and JOYOUS! You have all the time and space in the world to live, be, and delight in who you are, *right now.*

A few years after I discovered the Alexander Technique, The Art of Freedom Method for conscious living and masterful artistry was born of my own hints of understanding and little personal tastes of these realizations.

An epiphany in my kitchen

Many years ago, when I first started teaching hands-on Alexander Technique, Daniella and her sister Adrianna used to come to my house for weekly Alexander lessons. We'd have so much fun together in those lessons that my former husband used to poke his head into my studio and say, "Is there really a lesson going on in here? It sounds more like a party!" which would make us laugh even harder!

So, when, about a year after moving away, Daniella came back to visit me, looking very unhappy, I was worried. For a while, she and I sat together on the deck in my backyard, having tea and cake, making small talk about our lives. For some unknown reason, I didn't want to ask her why she looked so sad.

I was worried, and I felt that I couldn't let her leave without at least offering her a mini-Alexander lesson, right there in my kitchen! She took me up on it, and we positioned ourselves, standing closer to each other so I could easily reach my hands up to let them rest gently on her head and neck.

I was just about to place my palm on the back of her neck, when I suddenly heard a firm voice inside of me saying sternly, *"No! Not like that! She is FREE!"*

This clear internal voice stopped me in my tracks, and there was nothing to do but lower my hand again. Obviously, something within me was adamant that I not touch her the way I was about to touch her.

In that instant, I had a flash of an epiphany. All of a sudden, I understood that I was going about it all wrong!

There was Daniella, looking sad. And there I was, worrying about her, thinking there was something wrong with her that needed to be fixed, and I needed to help fix her.

"No! Not like that! She is FREE!"

In that moment, I realized that Daniella, indeed each and every one of us, is FREE to be exactly as we are right now.

She is free to be down and sad, just as she is free to be up and happy.

She is free to be herself, just as she is.

She is already perfect, free to express the infinitude of human experience through an infinite variety of changing moods, expressions, feelings, desires . . . EVERYTHING.

Who am I to contradict her experience, try to change her, or think something needs to be fixed?

Who am I to think there's something wrong with how she is being and expressing herself in this world?

"No! Not like that! She is FREE!"

Once I saw all of this, I allowed my hand to float back up to the back of her neck, and there was an entirely different purpose, quality, and meaning to my touch when my palm landed softly on her skin.

This touch was simply the Self in me meeting the Self in Daniella. Sharing in her experience. Willing to go there with her, meet her where she was, feel along with her, and accept her completely in the moment.

I never found out what was making her sad, but it was clear that this meeting of souls with compassion, acceptance, and empathy was exactly what she needed. Her body slowly melted, responding to my touch with trust and recognition, and her heavy energy lifted, coming up out of her slump.

Daniella is a singer, and she knows she is free to be and express her true Self through song. What could be more beautiful than that?

"I had the joy of studying the Alexander Technique with Jennifer for a few years while I lived in Cincinnati. I had just graduated from an intense, five-year bachelor's program and was pretty burned out and exhausted. I didn't know what I wanted to do with my musical career—only that I wanted to have one—and was taking some time off to recover and discover my next steps. I wondered if AT could help alleviate the vocal fatigue and performance anxiety that I often experienced.

"Jennifer and I hit it off almost instantly and as both of our personalities tend towards humor, we were almost always laughing during my lessons. I loved our sessions and I would leave them feeling more open and nearly always needing to re-adjust the seat in my car to accommodate the apparent inches I would gain in height!

"Under Jennifer's guidance, I continued to strengthen my body-mind awareness, helping me to observe without judgment when I was creating tension and to release it—not only in my singing, but also in my daily life. As lessons went on, I gradually began to release many years of tension, overdoing, and stress that I had come to associate with my instrument. I was gradually able to let go of the tension in my tongue, jaw, and neck (and even less-thought-of places like my shoulders, arms, and feet!) while using my voice. It became easier to sing as I felt my voice becoming freer and more confident.

"I now enjoy a diverse musical career, both as a performer and a private teacher of voice and piano. I strive to incorporate body-mind awareness in my students as well, although I have yet to put them on top of a saddle, reading jokes like Jennifer had me do! I am forever grateful to Jennifer for her guidance and support as a mentor, her kindness as a friend, and for her living example of incorporating Alexander Technique into her own musical performances."

~ Daniella, Vocalist, Pianist, and Educator

Witnessing and allowing the Self to be Itself

The epiphany I had, working with Daniella in my kitchen, didn't just change how I taught the Alexander Technique; it changed my entire life. It made me rethink and question everything I had ever been taught about life, spirituality, and music.

What I learned in a very practical and immediate way about the power of prioritizing Being over doing has become central to the way I teach, although I've learned since then that touch isn't at all essential to that deep sharing of experience.

The universal Self is infinitely rich and at all times making constant ripples in the vibrant river of the life-force within us. We are free to play hide-and-seek with our authentic Self, free to put on ego-masks, free to let them fall away to reveal the innate treasure of Being-Consciousness-Bliss that we are.

Our sensitive souls are so desperate for the infinitude of the Self within us to be recognized and fully accepted that this recognition in itself can be enough to bring about a growing sense of healing, peace, and loving unity.

The moment in which I heard that strong inner voice say, *"No! Not like that! She is FREE!"* was the precise moment when The Art of Freedom Method was born. My Freedom Directions and Three Magic Phrases were a direct outgrowth of that singular experience. I will share more about these practices in Chapter 18.

The Art of Freedom Method is all about realizing our freedom to be, live, and let the universal Self shine, allowing Love and Light be fully and freely expressed through the creation of our music.

Being your authentic Self with freedom and ease means that you need to . . .

- dare to aim inward, look deeply within yourself, and be as objective and honest about yourself as possible
- be willing to face and accept the truth of what you discover about yourself . . . the clear and the murky . . . the known and the Unknown
- discern between what's real and positive in your heart and what's actually a hard, protective shield, trying to keep you safe by separating and hiding the true Self from others
- learn what will be constructive to share and what may be destructive, depending on the context
- consciously choose how much and when to share yourself with others, for the benefit of all.

It can take a lifetime to learn these things well since everything is always changing within and around us. We need to be adaptable, resilient, able to respond in a healthy way to whatever comes our way, in the infinite variety of situations we encounter through life.

This learning process can be brutally hard and painful, but only by learning to accept and let go of what opposes our innate freedom can we turn our life into one that fully expresses it. In the next chapter, I will share the pivotal moment in my life when, in despairing of ever feeling free to be myself, I was finally led to the doorstep of my first Alexander Technique teacher, whose teachings changed my life completely.

My dad, Philip Kennedy Wion, a retired English professor, specialized in the writings of Shakespeare. Since he's the one who sparked my desire to be true to myself in the first place, I'd like to close this chapter with this famous quote from *Hamlet*:

This above all: to thine own self be true

And it must follow, as the night the day

Thou canst not then be false to any man.

Wake Up Your Awareness!

Great art requires your whole self

I will no longer act on the outside in a way that contradicts the truth that I hold deeply inside. I will no longer act as if I were less than the whole person I know myself inwardly to be.

~ *Rosa Parks*

I admit it . . . I was one of the "lucky ones."

I was born into a musical family, surrounded by music even before birth. As a child, I had a strong drive to make music and plenty of natural talent, which loving parents, teachers, and community nurtured well. I received abundant praise from every direction, ever since I began playing the violin at age four.

Undoubtedly, in my mind, I would become an international soloist when I grew up—just like the famous violinists on the LPs I fell asleep listening to. My idols included, but were not limited to, Milstein, Kreisler, Rabin, Kremer, Menuhin, Grumiaux, Grappelli, Perlman, Heifetz, Oistrakh, Szeryng, and Kogan.

Also, excellent teachers encouraged my musical ambitions, including violinists Kypros Markou, also a conductor; Dr. Shinichi Suzuki, a Japanese National Treasure, founder of the Suzuki method of education; David Cerone, former professor of violin at the Curtis Institute and retired President of the Cleveland Institute of Music; and my teachers at Indiana University, Josef Gingold and Stanley Ritchie, the latter of whom introduced me to the Baroque violin.

I began entering and winning competitions at a very young age, and I was accepted to participate in virtuoso violinist Nathan Milstein's international masterclass at age twelve, where I studied for five summers.

When I was a teenager, Mr. Milstein suggested to the Zurich Tonhalle Symphony that I replace him as soloist when he injured his finger and was unable to play (a suggestion rejected by the orchestra board, which is why I call that my lucky break that never happened!). In 1986, the conductor-pianist Dennis Russell Davies wrote on his jury comments after I won the prestigious Y Passamaneck competition in my hometown of Pittsburgh, Pennsylvania, that I had "the possibility of a major career."

By eighteen, I had performed at Carnegie Hall twice (once as soloist), been featured in *TIME* magazine as well as in newspapers and on radio stations, and won second prize at the Stulberg International String Competition, for artists under age twenty.

Despite all of these successes, however, the more I pursued a solo career, the more strongly I sensed that there was something holding me back—something essential missing from my violin playing, and without it I couldn't fully realize my artistic potential.

Though playing musically came easy to me, my violin technique often fell short of my own high expectations. It frustrated me that there were so many gaps in my technique, still too many things I was unable to play, and my progress felt slow, even though I was "doing everything right."

What disturbed me the most was that I had an uneasy suspicion that no amount of violin practice could ever resolve my problem. Somewhere deep down, I had the intuition that I must discover this elusive missing "something" that kept me feeling perpetually dissatisfied. I sensed that what was lacking in my music-making was only a little scratch on the surface of my whole self, like a skin rash indicating a disease much deeper.

I never voiced my misgivings to my violin teachers—in fact, I hardly even dared to think these doubts to myself. My teachers didn't seem to think anything was wrong with my violin playing, so they just kept teaching me the way they'd always taught.

As a student of Josef Gingold at Indiana University, I'd bring a new sonata or concerto to my lessons nearly every week. After playing through the week's selection, Mr. Gingold would give me a few musical pointers, warmly praise my talent, then for the rest of the lesson sit me down in an armchair to share engaging, colorful stories from his illustrious past as Concertmaster of the Cleveland Orchestra under George Szell. I have wonderful memories of our time together—Mr. Gingold was a loving bear of a man—but I didn't find the answer to my dilemma there.

Since I didn't really comprehend what was missing, I had no idea what to ask for or where to look, but it was clear to me that whatever I was seeking wasn't to be found in any of the places I'd looked before.

Besides wishing for help from my teachers, some other examples of where I'd looked for relief from my malaise but found only partial solutions (or none at all) included:

- music: practice, performance, and competitions
- people: relationships with family, friends, lovers
- study: academic success
- books: time spent reading poetry and fiction—anything from Shakespeare and Tolstoy . . . to Agatha Christie and Stephen King
- food: just about anything sweet!
- movement: yoga, swimming, hiking
- art: crafts, writing poetry, journaling, drawing, painting
- New Age thought and psychism: ESP? Astral projection? Mind control?
- substances: alcohol in college, a year of beta blockers for performance nerves later
- nature and travel: in the USA, Asia, and much of Europe
- alternative treatments: homeopathy, acupuncture, chiropractic, massage, essential oils, Ayurveda, special diets, etc.

All of the above were more or less interesting to me and either helpful or, in some cases, harmful. But none filled the void in my life or satisfied my deep longing to figure out what was preventing me from fully realizing my potential.

I finally caught my first glimpse of the real underlying problem and solution to all of it when—introduced to a universal, spiritual perspective on life—I became interested in comparative religions and mysticism at age nineteen.

The more I learned about spirituality, the more I realized that there is a meaningful common experience that unites all of humanity: a loving, universal, perennial religion of the heart. You might call it a "religion of Love," accessible to every human being, which lies at the intersection of all religions. Forgetting and becoming disconnected from it causes tremendous suffering and gets in the way of everything we try to accomplish.

Once this spiritual wisdom began to awaken within me, I very quickly recognized that here was what had been missing from my life for as long as I could remember, and suddenly I didn't care anymore about my problems with my violin. Or anything else.

Now I had words to put to my early childhood intuitions and soulful experiences of music. I realized that my lifelong love of music had been my personal way to seek and find that universal Love, as the mind-body-self becomes a willing instrument giving full expression to Love/Self/Spirit/God in this world.

In a sense, music had been my personal religion, my doorway to the universal Heart. Paradoxically, once I realized this had been my way of connecting with God without knowing it, I felt it had served its purpose and I no longer needed music the way I had before.

Spirituality itself now became the focal point of my life. Nothing else—not even my beloved violin—had much meaning anymore, apart from experiencing this new universal Love I felt so strongly within. I knew that realizing this Love in our everyday experience is what allows us to transcend suffering and experience real joy; and it's what gives our lives and our art meaning, depth, and purpose.

THIS perennial religion of the heart was what I'd always longed for as a child and teenager, and I knew it beyond a shred of a doubt.

But there was still one problem . . .

Soon after I was introduced to a spiritual way of life that allowed for a personal experience of universal Love, I got married at age twenty, devoting all of my time and energy to spiritual study, meditation, and learning how to take care of a household. I loved my new life, in which music took on a much smaller role than ever before.

However, as the years passed, I slowly—very reluctantly—had to admit that something was STILL missing from my life, which became more and more disconcerting to me.

To the outside observer, everything in my life looked normal, even better than normal. By all accounts, I "should" have been perfectly happy. After all, I had everything I needed plus talent, good looks, a kind and successful husband, wonderful healthy kids, a beautiful house in a great neighborhood, fantastic vacations, coveted gigs, enough students, and extra money to buy special things I wanted.

The problem was, I still felt fundamentally unhappy. And this general sense of dis-ease and imbalance was slowly increasing over time instead of diminishing, which worried me greatly.

How could this be?

If the sages were right, and "The Kingdom of God is within you" . . .

. . . "If there is a heaven on earth, it is here, now". . . and . . .

. . . "Being-Consciousness-Bliss" is our true nature . . .

Given that I was *trying really hard* to be a good person and do everything right, just the way I thought I was supposed to . . . well, then how could I still be so unhappy?!?

It just didn't make sense, and I was ashamed. My increasing lack of joy just made me feel more and more frustrated, guilty, and bad about myself . . . as if there were something deeply and fundamentally wrong with me that I would never be able to overcome.

You should practice contentment and gratitude! You have so much! You should be happy with what you have! These thoughts were a constant refrain that echoed throughout my psyche. It's not that I wasn't grateful (I truly was—every single day!), but I still felt so unsettled and couldn't figure out why. For a few fleeting moments, it even crossed my mind one day to worry for my sanity!

I vividly remember the day I found myself alone in my dining room, fallen to my knees, sobbing with tears of helpless desperation. I just couldn't take it anymore, and I didn't know what to do. I cried from the bottom of my heart and begged a Greater Power to help me. I had no idea what kind of help I needed, but I knew I needed help!

To my great relief and amazement, my desperate prayer was answered extremely quickly. Within days of that "dark night of my soul," I found myself on the doorstep of a local Alexander Technique teacher's home. When Erik Bendix opened the door to welcome me inside, I had a very strong intuition that *this was going to work.*

I was right.

But before I share what happened next, let's back up a bit so I can give you some more background and insight into the problems that finally led me to those Alexander lessons.

Thinking of the mind, body, and emotions as separate is bound to cause problems

When I was a kid, if it had been possible to become a disembodied mind drawing a bow across my violin strings, I probably would have figured out a way to do it, in an unconscious, misguided attempt to keep my body out of the whole experience! As I wrote earlier, I'd always thought of music as a mental activity.

I didn't start out with such a strong mind-body split. Most little children love bringing their whole self to everything they do, and I was no different. Wanting me to be balanced and "well-rounded," my parents encouraged me to engage in all kinds of games and activities. When I was four, my mother took me to ballet lessons because I loved to dance, and violin lessons because I loved music. I also loved playing catch with my dad and hitting balls in our front yard with a little pink plastic bat—and I was pretty good!

I quickly quit my ballet lessons, though, when the teacher had us push and stretch our bodies in ways I found painful. I was no longer interested in dancing if it was going to hurt! Also, my violin group lessons were at the same time as baseball practice on Saturdays, and I didn't hesitate to choose my bow over my bat.

Pretty soon, I was one of the best young violinists in my little world, and I was excelling academically in school. Thanks to my mother's early reading lessons I skipped first grade . . . and much later, my senior year of high school, as well.

Playing the violin, reading books for hours on end, and doing well in school made me feel smart and in control of my life, and I received plenty of praise from every direction. It felt good to feel like I was one of the best at everything I did, even while also the youngest.

I'm embarrassed to say, however, that this did go to my head a bit, and I also developed a tendency to look down on people who were more interested in sports and social activities than intellectual pursuits. Since pride was strongly discouraged, though, my feelings of superiority just made me feel bad about myself and guilty much of the time. On top of that, my natural shyness fed my desire to be alone and retreat into my music and books even more, which didn't exactly help balance out this tendency to prioritize the mind over the body.

I now realize that my habit of escaping into music and books was just my innocent, albeit unhealthy, way of using my strengths to shield me from things that felt too difficult. Since I hadn't yet developed the social skills to speak freely and navigate relationship conflicts with ease, and I didn't have the desire or discipline to overcome the normal physical discomforts that often go with physical effort (like sore muscles and sweat), I took the easy way out and played it safe by escaping into my mental dreamworlds, where I felt inwardly strong and more in control.

The problem was, being caught "up in my head" all the time was not a balanced way of living at all. Ignoring my body, thinking it was something separate from and of less value than my mind, created quite a lot of overall tension in me since it was not consistent with the reality that the self is one indivisible whole.

The truth is, it's not possible to separate ourselves into independent, unrelated parts. Even though the way we use language contradicts this, there is no such thing as a "mental" activity, a "physical" activity, or even an "emotional" state. All parts are interdependent; every activity and every problem includes the whole self and affects the whole self.

The mind's thoughts cannot exist without a physical brain made up of neurons. We can't have our body carry out our intentions without the conscious direction of the mind. And it's not possible to feel and sustain emotions without the chemical secretions of body, the thoughts and desires of the mind, and the subtle energies of the heart.

We bring the whole self to everything we do, and the quality of our actions in any area of our life influences the quality of our experience in every other area.

The quality of your presence (your conscious awareness of how you think, feel, and move in the moment) that you bring to walking your dog, doing the dishes, or practicing yoga directly influences the quality of being that you bring to your musical practice and performance . . . and vice versa.

The only way we can experience overall balance—as a whole and in our specific activities—is to acknowledge this unity of self, practicing bringing this awareness to every activity we engage in. Having what Alexander Technique teacher Frank Pierce Jones called a "unified field of attention" is essential to developing true musical mastery.

My lack of self-integration and lack of awareness influenced my self-esteem, affected my relationships, and contributed in my twenties to my first experiences of performance anxiety (when I suddenly found myself trying to be inconspicuous and fit into the job I'd won in the back of the second violin section of the Rochester Philharmonic Orchestra after my husband got a job teaching music theory at the Eastman School of Music). Worst of all, it caused me to doubt myself and my abilities. It made me feel weak, unmotivated, and unhappy much of the time.

As a musician, my emphasis on the mind and my under-appreciation of the body caused many diverse difficulties in my practicing and my performance. For example . . . my technique was limited and my musical expression and rhythm were erratic. I never really enjoyed practicing, and I was completely uninterested in teaching violin.

As a young teen at the Meadowmount School of Music in upstate New York, where five hours of daily practice were enforced by adults patrolling the hallways, listening at bedroom doors, I would sometimes lie on my bed and listen to a recording, pretending to be following along with a score in case I got caught not practicing—because I would end up feeling exhausted and sore if I practiced more than two hours at a time.

Like it or not . . . you get better at what you practice

Here's an example of how I unwittingly reinforced my mind-body split.

As a young teenager, if I didn't feel like practicing, sometimes I would close my door and read a magazine on my music stand while playing my violin concertos on autopilot, so my mother would think I was practicing! Thankfully, I stopped doing this pretty quickly when I got caught (my mother says she could tell something sounded wrong!).

This little anecdote demonstrates how good I was at splitting my awareness of my mind's activity from my body's movements, to the point that I could even go through the complex motions of playing the violin without having any conscious awareness of what I was doing.

This ability to split my attention might seem like an amazing feat, but I learned years later that it was a skill I might have been better off not developing!

In my early twenties, when I was the concertmaster of an orchestra in Chicago, I was invited to perform the Chausson Poème, a very demanding piece for solo violin.

I was in the middle of playing the first page, which is technically quite challenging, when I suddenly "came to" and realized that I had been playing without any conscious awareness of what I was doing up to that moment. I had absolutely no idea where my mind had been, but it was certainly anywhere but in that concert hall!

When my mind suddenly came "back into my body," and I became aware of the fact that I was performing this technically challenging piece before the eyes and ears of hundreds of people, I had a brief moment of panic.

I kept playing without skipping a beat or missing a note, and nobody was the wiser. But *I* was absolutely mortified! Stricken with terror, I worried that I might lose my spot or mess up in some way, and I had a terrible time throughout the rest of the piece.

If a repeat performance hadn't been scheduled for the next night, I might never again have dared to perform solo. In fact, I was afraid to play anything from memory for many years after that, just in case I might dissociate and fall apart onstage.

My belief that my mind was separate from—and somehow better than—my body also contributed to my habit of frequently ignoring my deeper emotions. Instead of noticing and honoring my general unhappiness, inquiring within and realizing that my emotions and body were just as important as my mind, I would just escape further into my mind. Of course, denying our emotions just makes them stronger, like weeds that keep spreading because they never get pulled up by their roots.

Since I was externally successful in pretty much everything I tried to do, this mode of living seemed to be working well enough. I kept it up until things finally deteriorated far enough that I had no alternative but to reach out for help when I found myself experiencing a toxic stew of emotional anguish, mental confusion, professional disappointment, and physical pain.

When I finally broke down that day in my dining room and I realized I needed outside help, I found it in the Alexander Technique. In the next chapter, I'll describe what those first lessons were like and how they dramatically altered my entire life for the better.

Finding "The Missing Link"

The discovery that made everything easier

Don't be afraid of ideas.

~ *Erik Bendix*

Before I describe my first Alexander Technique lessons and the far-reaching impact they had on my life, let me introduce the originator of the Technique, Frederick Matthias Alexander, and give you a very brief history of its evolution.

Born in Tasmania in 1869, Alexander was an aspiring young Shakespearean actor who moved to the mainland of Australia in 1889 to pursue a performance career. After some time, however, he began to develop hoarseness in his voice whenever he went onstage to recite.

When Alexander's doctors and voice specialists weren't able to find anything physically wrong with his vocal mechanism, taking matters into his own hands, Alexander decided to figure out for himself what was the matter. His desire to act being very strong, he was highly motivated to find a solution; otherwise, he would have had to give up his dream.

After a long period of time (multiple years) of observing himself in mirrors and experimenting with how he was thinking, moving, and speaking, he cured his vocal-performance problem and went on to enjoy a successful acting career.

As a result of his methodical process of self-observation and experimentation, Alexander made some stunning and revolutionary discoveries about how the human mind and body work together for optimum functioning, which were far ahead of his time. Much of what he discovered is now supported by scientific research, including studies done specifically on the Alexander Technique, in addition to cutting-edge neuroscience research.

In fact, in 2010, I designed a successful pilot study on the Alexander Technique to help surgeons while performing laparoscopic surgery at Cincinnati Children's Hospital Medical

Center. Our research paper won a prize at the American Academy of Pediatrics, was presented at two national medical conferences, and was published in the top journal for urology in the world.[14]

Lucky for all of us, Alexander described his entire process of discovery in great detail years later in his 1932 classic, *The Use of the Self* (newly released in 2019) in a chapter entitled "Evolution of a Technique."

Once his acting career had taken off, Alexander began teaching others how to improve their vocal performance, and it was in teaching others that he began to realize the broader implications of his work. Not only were his methods highly effective for performance and skills improvement, but the results were also therapeutic in allowing all kinds of people to overcome myriad psychophysical ailments, ranging from asthma and emphysema to postural anomalies and mental disturbances.

As he and his students began to recognize how valuable his discoveries were, Alexander moved to England in 1904, where he later established his first training course for Alexander teachers in 1931. Alexander also wrote multiple books to help spread his ideas amongst a wider audience. In this way, he established a prominent place for himself in London society. Among his more illustrious students were the Archbishop of Canterbury, the writer Aldous Huxley; also John Dewey, founder of North American modern education; and the playwright George Bernard Shaw. But despite his popularity amongst London intelligentsia, very few people—if any—were able to learn his methods solely from his books.

In the early years, Alexander used some touch when teaching, much as any other vocal-performance coach might, but he later found that precise physical manipulation and postural adjustment of his students was a more expedient way to get his ideas across.

It wasn't until 1914, however, that he began to apply his unique manner of "inhibitory control" to his use of touch. (I'll be speaking more about Alexandrian inhibition later in this book.)

Reported to have had something of a temper, he would succumb to frustration at times when his students weren't able to follow his verbal instructions. Apparently, he even threw a book out the window at a student as he watched him, while walking down the street after his lesson, revert to his old movement patterns!

14 Pramod P. and Trisha P. Reddy, Jennifer Roig-Francoli, Lois Cone, Bezalel Sivan, W. Robert DeFoor, Krishnanath Gaitonde, and Paul H. Noh, "The Impact of the Alexander Technique on Improving Posture and Surgical Ergonomics during Minimally Invasive Surgery: Pilot Study," Journal of Urology 186, suppl. 4 (Oct. 2011):1658–62, doi: 10.1016/j.juro.2011.04.013. E-pub Aug. 19, 2011, PMID: 21855928.

Knowing that Alexander experienced ordinary impatience just like the rest of us, the following story of how he first came to use touch to manually prevent his students from falling back into their unhelpful habits makes perfect sense. Apparently, one day, one of his students just wasn't getting what Alexander was trying to teach. So, in frustration Alexander brought up his hands and placed them on the student's head/neck area to physically demonstrate what he meant, saying something like, "Not like that . . . *like THIS*." Instantly, the student got the message and was able to move in the way Alexander was indicating.

Events like this made Alexander realize that a highly specialized use of touch could make his job much easier, which led to the birth of the Alexander Technique as most people know it today: a hands-on method that mainly uses kinesthetic guidance to teach the student how to let go of habitual thought and movement patterns, leading the student into a better and healthier "use" of the self. As Alexander put it, "Mine is a method for the control of human reaction."

Alexander was able to bring about truly remarkable changes in his students through the use of touch. Since he never stopped teaching with his hands, the potential for effective touch-free transmission of his ideas was left largely untapped until recently. One of the reasons I've written this book is to help people see what can be possible in teaching and learning Alexander's methods with Primal Alexander, Mio Morales's touch-free evolution of Alexander's original discoveries.

Pain brought me to the Alexander Technique

By my early thirties, I'd already tried the Alexander Technique twice with two different teachers and dismissed it as unpleasant and "not for me." When I began experiencing neck pain that wouldn't go away with regular physician care, chiropractic, or massage, a friend urged me to try it just one more time, saying I only needed to find the "right teacher" for me. Pretty desperate by this point, I reluctantly decided to give it one more go.

The results of my first lessons with my new teacher, Erik Bendix, were nothing short of miraculous. Each forty-five-minute lesson consisted of a bit of talking at the beginning, then some gentle hands-on guidance in standing, sitting, walking, or playing the violin. This was followed by a period of "tablework," where I lay (fully clothed) on the table as my teacher gently moved my limbs to reeducate my system towards a more natural way of moving with greater freedom and less tension.

Not only did the neck pain and emotional distress I'd been feeling for weeks disappear completely within just a few lessons, but every aspect of my life suddenly felt lighter and brighter. I felt GREAT! This seemed to be the solution to all of my problems, and I wanted more!

Quickly obsessed with the Alexander Technique, I began taking two lessons per week for a total of thirty lessons. This marked an unforgettable period of personal transformation for me, as I opened myself up completely to learning whatever I could about this mysterious new process for self-integration. Much like a young toddler, I felt as if I were exploring the world for the first time.

Not only was my body quickly and completely freed of all physical pain, but my curiosity started waking up from a very long, deep slumber. Whereas I had previously been led to believe that curiosity and innovation were unhealthy ("Curiosity killed the cat!"), suddenly, bursting with questions, I felt wonderfully alive again! Everything felt fresh and exciting to me from this new perspective, which paradoxically felt utterly unfamiliar, yet at the same time as if I were returning home after a lifetime of absence from my own self.

I felt an enormous amount of gratitude towards my teacher, whose nonintrusive touch brought stillness to my mind and calm to my nervous system. After many years of unconsciously denying my body and my emotions in a misguided attempt to escape the limitations of my physical reality and become somebody different from who I was, I finally felt comfortable in my own skin.

As I stood there, gazing out the attic window of Erik's studio as he gently worked on me with "non-doing" hands, looking past the small crystal Buddha on the windowsill and down onto the street far below, a whole new world of possibility opened up to me. I learned that it was possible to fully embody so many of the things I already "thought" I knew, but didn't *really* know yet with my whole self.

Here's some of what I learned in those thirty magical lessons:

- I don't have to DO anything to prove my self-worth.
- I am valued, loved, worthy of attention, and good enough . . . simply by BEING myself.
- My true Self—my inner essence—is free, good, and beautiful, and nobody can diminish, deny, or take this away from me.
- I am free to think and believe whatever I want; I am in charge of my own mind.
- I can surrender, let go, trust, and be guided by someone else, while at the same time taking full responsibility for myself.
- I can trust myself and my intuitions.
- I don't need to be afraid of ideas.

- Less truly can be more.
- I can be a witness to my own experience of the moment.
- I can breathe freely and fearlessly, and I can allow my emotions to flow without fear or attachment.
- I don't need to fear love; it's safe to love and be loved.

Lessons on unconditional Love and authentic musical communication

For several weeks, my heart was on fire with joy and enthusiasm as I found myself falling completely in love with LOVE, with LIFE—my true SELF—again.

I discovered that it is in fact possible to feel, give, and receive pure Love simply by being open and present to the beauty of existence itself, free of any judgment, need, desire, attachment, or expectation—*and without doing anything at all.*

This surprising new sense of Love had a light and pure quality that was expansive, unconditional, and all-inclusive. At first, coming face to face with it scared and overwhelmed me because the experience was so strong and unfamiliar. But that fear quickly dissolved when I realized that this Love was simply my own true nature—and the same essence is in everyone and everything—indeed, it is the Divine "stuff" that connects us all.

Love is perfectly natural, good, and truly ever-present within us and everywhere, all the time. All we need do to experience it is to let the fears that prevent us from melting into it fall away. We need to be willing to allow Love's warm, glowing energy to move freely within us and around us, letting it flow in and letting it shine out. Just like the breath that goes in and out, Love flows constantly inwards and outwards, until there are no more barriers and there's simply One Love—completely impersonal, yet at the same time beautifully intimate because it carries you into the silent bliss of knowing your own Heart.

I remember going shopping after a lesson one day, pausing to marvel at the existence of a dirty snow pile in the parking lot, as if it were the most beautiful thing in the world. A few minutes later, I was laughing with abandon, smiling with Love into the friendly eyes of a butcher I'd never seen before and would likely never meet again!

Similarly, quite a few months later, when a visiting Alexander Technique teacher, Vivian Mackie, encouraged me in a workshop to look deeply into the eyes of my listeners as I played the violin, the idea of making myself that vulnerable and connecting that deeply with others in public absolutely terrified me. But what happened was quite unexpected.

As I played, looking into the eyes of one person after another, it seemed as if I could see and feel directly into their souls. It was a mutual, electric exchange of fear, surprise, resistance, love, childlikeness, and pure ecstasy. In just those few minutes of shared presence I witnessed and personally experienced a very wide range of human experience as my soul met the soul of each listener through the wordless sounds of music. I could see the music piercing their armor, waking them up just a little bit more to their own souls and the truth and beauty that lay dormant inside.

I could feel one woman's gripping fear and see one man's hesitation to connect, but I'll never forget the middle-aged man who looked simultaneously like he was falling in love and like an innocent six-year-old, wriggling in his seat with absolute delight!

I had a chance to experiment with this again just a few days later, while traveling through an airport. I'd arrived early, and there were about ten security guards standing around without much to do (this was before 9/11). When a guard joked with me about my violin and asked me to play for them, my first reaction was to laugh, ask her how much they'd pay me, and politely decline.

But on second thought, I unpacked my violin at a nearby gate and walked back. Since I knew I'd probably never see any of them again, I decided to take a risk and try what I'd done in the workshop. I poured my heart into my music while letting my eyes linger from one person to the next, looking deeply into their souls.

I learned so much about the nature of music, communication, and human beings by simply daring to give some time to connecting with these people in that harsh, cold, grey airport environment. They were clearly starved for beauty and authentic connection. I saw one woman's eyes fill with tears as she muttered over and over, "That's so beautiful . . . so beautiful . . ."

These experiences changed my life. These days, I don't necessarily look into people's eyes when playing, and I know that's not necessary in order to have the same kind of deep human connection with my listeners. But thanks to those experiences, I now understand the power of music to heal in a way that I never would have if I hadn't dared to play, looking into those strangers' eyes.

I brought my violin to my Alexander lessons only a handful of times (and not even once did I bring it to my Alexander teacher training, which began a year later). Each time I did, the experience was truly profound, and I had some mind-boggling revelations about my relationship with my violin and music. These were silent, mostly wordless teachings. Here are two significant things I learned:

- It is possible to have a completely different experience of time by thinking and moving with less habitual tension. I remember playing some of the "Méditation" from *Thais* by Jules Massenet towards the end of one lesson with Erik. I felt like I was in a time warp as I walked languidly towards my violin and everything I played felt like it was in super-slow motion. My teacher assured me that everything looked and sounded quite normal on the outside.

- It is possible to experience real Inspiration through making music in a way that connects directly with our creative spirit or Spirit (God, Source, Mystery . . .). Through our intention, sound can become a heartfelt prayer, contemplation, praise, surrender, bliss . . . or anything at all. One single note can pierce through all the darkness and heavy layers of materiality to touch the core of a heart. As I played just one long note like this in my lesson one day, quiet tears ran down my cheeks. It felt like something that had long ago hardened inside of me was finally being released to break apart and melt like an iceberg in the heat of summer. I felt reconnected to my true musical self again in a way that I hadn't for a very, very long time.

I think I already knew these things when I was a child, but the knowledge had become buried as I began striving to make music my profession. I'd taken on some beliefs that prevented me from fully enjoying myself and my music. Now that I was learning to let go of my fears and self-doubt, it felt like a rebirth as a musician; I could finally feel these things again with my whole self—mind, body, heart, and soul.

Daring to wonder . . .

Those early AT lessons woke me up from the dark limbo I'd become trapped in, caused by a lifetime of physical and mental habits that were tinged with layers of tension and subtle anxiety: blockages I hadn't even known were there until my teacher taught me how to notice them and slowly let go of them, bit by bit.

I remember one lesson in which I told my teacher I felt afraid to breathe, but I didn't know why. After some silence, he softly suggested that I would probably have a better understanding of why, once I stopped being afraid.

When I finally started letting go of some of the self-protective layers of muscular tension, and I stopped the constant mental gymnastics in which I tried to convince myself of things that were ultimately unconvincing . . .

. . . when I finally dared to begin questioning my beliefs about EVERYTHING…

. . . when I finally admitted that I REALLY didn't know, and that not knowing much of anything at all was actually OK . . .

. . . I very gradually began to feel more comfortable, safe enough to fully relax in someone else's presence. That's when I began to breathe more freely, as my whole body simultaneously began to loosen up and let go of the many burdens I'd been carrying around with me on a daily basis.

This was not a process to be forced; these were changes that were invited and gently given permission to unfold. Nevertheless, I was surprised by how quickly my energy returned, my heart felt light, and my mood was bright and shining.

One day, in my kitchen, marveling at how freely my arms were reaching up to get a glass from the cupboard, I watched in awe as they floated through space with a kind of effortless ease that was completely free of my habitual heaviness. They didn't even feel like my arms! I felt like I'd been transplanted into a new body, which I could move through my intentions and will alone, without identifying with it as "mine." This body appeared to be simply a tool or an instrument of the true, universal Self, the movements of which I was privileged to be a witness.

One of the biggest shifts I experienced from those early Alexander Technique lessons was an embodied understanding of how to balance my awareness of my inner world with my awareness of the world around me, and how to let the light of my creative spirit shine through my body.

As much as I'd tried to integrate every aspect of myself into a unified experience before, Oneness remained largely a theoretical idea in my head, one that only manifested into a real experience from time to time during meditation, or spontaneously when experiencing a particularly beautiful or joyful event.

Now I began to realize how to "be in the world but not of it" with my whole self, including my body, my mind, and all of my emotions, instead of splitting myself up into isolated fragments, shutting myself off from uncomfortable feelings, or trying to withdraw my senses by denying parts of myself in a futile attempt to reach the Divine.

Beyond any shred of a doubt . . . this process was giving me greater access to the self-integration of mind, body, and spirit that I'd been seeking for my whole life. This felt like an essential key to my happiness, the "missing link," "holy grail," and "fountain of everlasting youth"!

My rapid transformation felt truly miraculous. It was like a complete regeneration of my physical body, my questioning mind, my childlike playfulness, my loving heart, and my contemplative soul.

"Don't be afraid of ideas!"

With this new awakening, I slowly allowed myself to question everything about my life—including myself. I began to dare open up to all kinds of radical new ways of seeing things, even entertaining the frightening possibility that the ideas I'd accepted before might not be absolutely true; in fact, might some of them be destructive?

For example, adopting in a literal way the notion that I should not trust myself, across the board. Sometimes that's good advice (for example, I would miss most of my appointments if I relied on my memory without writing things down!). But it's only good advice up to a point, and only if the "self" that we're mistrusting is the ego, not our heart's intuition and personal Inner Wisdom.

At one point in time, I'd made a conscious decision to stop trusting myself, unknowingly throwing out the baby with the bathwater. Giving up so much trust in myself corroded my self-confidence and led to a corresponding increase in tension and anxiety.

When I began Alexander Technique lessons, my teacher encouraged me to pause and give myself a little time to get in touch with what was going on under the surface of my momentary experience. Instead of just telling me I should trust myself more, he encouraged me to cultivate a sense of healthy curiosity, awe, and childlike wonder—about myself and what was happening within my mind, body, emotions, and spirit; to give myself some time to be curious, to ask—and also to be OK with not knowing.

In Erik's quiet, nonjudgmental, accepting presence, it finally felt safe enough for me to take off the protective layers of ego-masks, to stop trying to control myself and the world around me, and to slowly reveal the truth of who I am.

When he proposed to me one day that I need not be afraid of ideas—that it was possible to have a thought and not react to it—I was astounded. That revelation changed everything. Suddenly, I was able to connect the tension, heaviness, and constriction I seemed to feel on every plane of my existence with the simple reactions I had to certain thoughts.

When I started examining my reactions, I soon found that I was creating tension in response to almost every idea I had, whether it was to move an arm, walk, or even breathe. I reacted to just about every idea related to making music, performing, playing my instrument . . . indeed, I even reacted with an increase of tension to the very thought of the violin itself! (I have since seen the same thing happen in the majority of my students.)

I recognized that I was the only one responsible for my own reactions since it was my own mind and body generating both the ideas and the resulting tension.

Of course, I may not have been responsible for putting those ideas into my mind in the first place, but once I became aware of how I was reacting to the ideas, I recognized that I had full responsibility for continuing to think them, and thereby react to them in a way that increased my overall tension, thus interfering with my experience of success and well-being.

Instead of being overwhelmed, I became overjoyed to make these discoveries about myself. It was mind-boggling to realize that the source of all my problems was simply that I was reacting to ideas, which were simply neurons in my brain, wiring and firing together into a particular pattern that I had the power to change.

The problem wasn't the ideas themselves, which is proven by the fact that each person can have a different response to the same idea. My only problem was that I was reacting instinctively, habitually, and immediately—without thought or consideration—to a simple idea.

It was like being afraid of a shadow, or an imaginary monster in a book. I realized that as a simple idea, it wasn't real. Why be afraid of a little thought? Ideas come and go, morph and change. If we don't fight them, hold onto them, deny them, or suppress them, they simply pass and cause no harm. Ideas in themselves don't hurt; it's what we do to ourselves and others in response to our thoughts that causes pain, suffering—even wars.

With this revelation, it gradually felt safe again to let myself have all kinds of new ideas.

Once I realized that I could have an idea and inhibit my reaction to it (over time and with lots of practice, depending on the idea), I dared to open up my mind again with curiosity. I was free to think, wonder, and ask questions. I could question my own thoughts, my beliefs, and my whole way of life . . . *with Love instead of fear.*

I was freeing myself to become like an innocent little child again, with an open mind and body, excited to explore the world of ideas and play without fear of getting hurt.

Thinking the unthinkable

I will never forget one particular exchange that took place during an early Alexander Technique lesson with Erik, back in 2003.

As usual, upon arrival, I presented my teacher with a long list of questions that had been bubbling up inside of me since my last lesson. I'd brought my violin that day. After we worked together for a while, with a little music and much silence, I dared to tell him I felt like quitting the violin.

After some more work in silence, my teacher indicated that quitting would be fine.

I was free to quit.

What an earth-shattering, liberating thought!

I'd asked my family for a violin when I was two, and I'd been playing the violin nearly every day since I was given one at age four; and the only time I'd ever voiced a desire to quit was in my early twenties. Those around me at the time discouraged the idea, telling me it wasn't good to give up an art that one had developed over time.

In hindsight, I'm very glad I didn't quit the violin. But, how much more healing it was for me all those years later, to finally have my forbidden desire to quit be brought out into the open and unconditionally accepted. In fact, what was being fully accepted was ME as a human being; it was of complete irrelevance whether I kept playing the violin or not.

As the lesson continued, I marveled at this radical acceptance. But when Erik proposed that I play "quitting" on my violin and I further contemplated the idea of no longer playing the violin, I suddenly became very sad. It was not joyful to play "quitting." I didn't want to feel "quitting." What came out of my mouth next was, "No . . . that would be too sad"; he responded, "That would be OK, too."

Rarely before had I ever felt as seen, heard, and accepted as in that timeless moment.

I no longer felt that my self-worth, or my sense of success in life, was tied to my thoughts, talent, skill, or performance. All at once, my entire being felt validated.

To me, this was a very real experience of unconditional Love, completely impersonal yet deeply personal at the same time. Completely detached, completely whole, and completely free.

Everything changed for me after this, as I was finally able to fearlessly assume 100 percent responsibility for my ideas, thoughts, feelings, emotions, desires, choices, and actions.

I finally understood that I was free to own my own thoughts and free to choose my response. Therefore, I was free to choose the direction of my next thoughts and actions, and thereby create a future for myself more aligned with my own inner Wisdom, free of what anybody outside of me might want me to think, feel, or do.

I could think for myself, choose for myself, create for myself, love and live for myself.

All of this meant that I had real control over my own life, not just the inconsistent and unreliable illusion of control, which I was all too often giving up to other people, external systems, and things.

I understood so much in a deep and visceral way in those early days of studying the Alexander Technique! And yet, to my enormous frustration, I felt quite helpless to put it all into practice without the support of a teacher's physical presence and frequent, hands-on guidance.

In the next chapter, I'll share how my strong desire for personal freedom, independence, and self-actualization led me first to become an Alexander Technique teacher myself, and then to stop using touch in my own teaching. I wanted to empower my students with the understanding and the ability to change, learn from and teach themselves, and improve on their own—just as I'd always wished I could do for myself.

A Simple Choice

Exploring touch-free Alexander Technique

Ask, and it shall be given you; seek, and ye shall find; knock, and it shall be opened unto you.

~ *(Matthew 7:7, KJV)*

Like most people who encounter the Alexander Technique, I was first introduced to Alexander's discoveries in a traditional format, in which a teacher uses gentle touch to guide the student through simple movements to help in letting go of excess tension and relieve all kinds of problems. Since this was the only learning format offered back then, I believed the only way to learn the Alexander Technique was to get that special hands-on experience in person from a teacher. In fact, many people—even teachers—still hold fast to that belief.

As I wrote in the previous chapter, my early Alexander Technique lessons were fantastic and completely life-changing, but they were also confusing because the good feelings I was experiencing were so new and I didn't have a clue about how the changes in me were coming about.

My teacher graciously answered my endless questions; otherwise, he was frequently quiet as he touched the back of my neck or my shoulders to gently guide my body from standing to sitting in a chair; briefly held my feet or grazed the backs of my knees as I played the violin; or slowly moved my limbs as I lay on a massage table.

The lessons felt wonderful as my mind became quieter, my body relaxed, my breath released, and my posture improved. My original neck pain quickly dissolved, I was able to move with much greater ease after every lesson, and my mood improved steadily over time.

I knew with my whole being that this experience of self-integration was exactly what I'd been longing for, and yet I had no idea how to recapture this calm and open state of being when I went back home and didn't have my teacher around to remind my system of what was possible.

Sadly, even though I would leave my Alexander lessons flying on cloud nine, the blissful, floaty feeling which is a hallmark of that modality would only last a couple days before fading. My old, habitual heaviness would slowly creep back into my body, leaving me longing for my next lesson so my teacher could "fix me" and "make me feel better" yet again. It really bothered me that I couldn't find relief on my own, and it was clear that the more lessons I took, the more dependent I was becoming on my teacher's presence and the special Alexandrian touch that felt like magic.

I now know that the main ingredient for the wonderful changes I experienced were in fact very subtle changes I was making myself in how I was thinking. But this wasn't evident to me until many years later, when I was already a certified Alexander Technique teacher and I began experimenting with helping my own students access the power of their own thoughts without the aid of my touch.

Seeking to understand the Alexander Technique

At the same time I was taking those early lessons in Cincinnati, I occasionally took some lessons with a teacher in my hometown of Pittsburgh, Pennsylvania. Maria Caruso had been my pianist as a child, playing the musical accompaniment for many of my recitals and competitions. I loved her dearly, with her beautiful, porcelain face and lovely waist-length hair. When I studied the Alexander Technique with her as an adult, even though her teaching style was quite different from Erik's, Maria's lessons gave me very much the same delightful sense of weightlessness and bliss; her explanations of what we were doing in the lessons had a marked effect on me, as well.

Having lessons with these two teachers who were polar opposites in many ways was very helpful in that it allowed me to see more clearly that the experiences I was having were unique neither to the teacher nor to the particular style of teaching, but thanks to the principles of the Alexander Technique itself.

Even so, as a new student it was hard for me to reconcile these two completely different approaches to learning the Technique. I became determined to get to the root of what was happening to me and finally figure out how to recreate those wonderful feelings for myself. Besides, even though I would have liked to, I knew I couldn't afford to keep taking AT lessons forever!

So, I brought all of F. M. Alexander's books home from the library and quickly devoured them. But I still couldn't really see how the ideas in the books corresponded to what I was experiencing. My new knowledge didn't seem to be getting me any closer to being able to recapture those heavenly feelings for myself.

In fact, it's notoriously difficult to take Alexander's writings and put them into practice without the help of a teacher, so I decided to embark upon a three-year teacher training course, even though at the time teaching was the furthest thing from my mind. Coming from a family of teachers, I had no desire whatsoever to teach!

The three years of my teacher training were some of the best—and most difficult—of my life. I emerged from that training with a much better understanding of the Technique, a surprising new passion for teaching (I thoroughly love it now!), and enough skills and confidence to launch a private Alexander Technique studio of my own.

But, to my great disappointment, even after completing the requisite three years (sixteen hundred hours) of formal training to become a certified Alexander Technique teacher, and even after taking plenty of extra lessons with excellent teachers I met outside of the training course, I was STILL unable to get the same results alone as when my teachers worked with me.

Not only that, but upon graduation, I was told I would learn more from the act of teaching itself and that I wouldn't really understand what I was doing until I had been teaching for at least ten years. That was highly unsatisfying for me! I'd been trying to understand this stuff and do it for myself for five years already—and now I was supposed to wait another ten?!?

No. *This was NOT OK.*

As I became even more determined to figure it out for myself, I kept reading and taking lessons from as many different Alexander teachers and from as many different schools and styles as possible. I founded an Alexander study group in Cincinnati so I could keep learning along with my colleagues, and I founded the Alexander Technique Guild of Ohio for the same purpose. I attended every national conference I could, in addition to several international congresses held overseas.

I was insatiable, and I had many fantastic experiences under the highly skilled hands of some of the best teachers in the world. There were the lessons that had me floating down the hallways afterwards, the ones that left me overflowing with love and joy in my heart, the ones that made me feel as if my head were filled with helium or my legs were stretched out three inches longer, and the ones that stunned me into silent awe as I marveled at the new fluidity in my limbs as I moved.

And yet, there seemed to be a shroud of mystery cast over everything I encountered in my quest to pin down clear, practical explanations and guidelines for practicing the Technique, and there were plenty of contradictions in the styles of these different teachers.

I found it rare for teachers to offer clear explanations, even in their descriptions of what the Alexander Technique was. To the point that the most common topic of discussion in the workshops and teacher's forums I attended was prompted by the question, "What is the Alexander Technique?" There were at least as many answers and new questions spawned by that question as there were participants!

Despite all the confusion I was encountering in the Alexander world, I still had the very strong intuition that the teaching and practice of the Alexander Technique ought to be something profoundly simple. It should be easily accessible, explainable, understandable, and consistently reproducible.

Yet for many years, nothing I encountered satisfied my need to be able to practice this Technique for myself and share it with my students in a way that was systematic and clear, quick and easy, simple and enjoyable.

Thankfully, I was given many opportunities to teach the Technique as I was searching, and it turned out to be true that the very best way to learn is to teach what you wish to learn!

Professional blessings in disguise

Shortly after I received my first Alexander teaching certification, I was hired by the dance division at the Cincinnati College-Conservatory of Music (CCM) at the University of Cincinnati to teach the Alexander Technique to dancers and musicians, both privately and in groups.

This was a wonderful opportunity, and I absolutely loved teaching these future performing artists. However, due to financial constraints at the conservatory, I was only authorized to teach my private students for one semester, at which point they would be on their own without any more input from me.

As they say, "Necessity is the mother of invention," and this restriction, which was very frustrating at the time, turned out to be a huge blessing in disguise. Since I would only have each student a few months, I felt a strong desire to teach my students in such a way that they would know what to do on their own to continue helping themselves at the end of the semester. That meant I needed to find a new way to teach because after a few months my students would no longer have access to the touch of my hands. How could they keep learning on their own without a teacher's hands if most of what they had been exposed to during the semester was delivered through my hands?

Considering that F.M. Alexander cured his vocal problem and established the foundations of his Technique without the benefit of another teacher's hands—simply by observing himself and learning to think differently—I deduced that this must be the key and I needed to explore more deeply what he had done for himself.

After all, Alexander said, "Anyone can do what I did . . . if they will only do what I did."

Hmmm . . . If he could do it—and he said anyone can do it—then why not me?

Thinking that way didn't seem arrogant to me; it was simply a logical conclusion to draw from Alexander's own words. The catch was, I didn't want to watch myself in mirrors for years to get results, like Alexander did, and I thought that's what I'd have to do if I wanted to do what Alexander did! So, I took what I thought was the easy (or lazy!) way out and kept trying to make things work based on what I'd read and been taught by other teachers, without realizing until years later that I'd completely missed his point.

When Alexander suggested that we do what he did, he didn't necessarily mean imitating his specific practice of observing himself visually with mirrors. Instead, the key to his discoveries lay in *learning to think differently to get different results*, which required a curious, self-reflective attitude and a willingness to observe oneself as objectively as possible (not necessarily just visually) and experiment, without having any expectation of results.

Through his daily practice of self-observation and experimentation, Alexander learned how to increase and expand his awareness and use his mind in a way that allowed his body to reflect that new openness, flexibility, and freedom. His disciplined practice also helped him become more sensitive to when he was interfering with ease of movement and to stop doing it, so he could eventually overcome his vocal performance problem and vastly improve his overall well-being and performance.

Once I understood better what led to Alexander's success, I figured that if I could learn how to think differently and work on myself as Alexander described, then I would be able to help my students do the same. That's when I started experimenting with my students to find quicker, easier ways to get results.

Venturing into new territory: experimenting with touch-free teaching

After the epiphany I had in my kitchen about freedom (see Chapter 9), when I realized that both my student and I are free to be exactly how we are in the moment, without the need to DO anything to change, I started realizing how powerful my own thoughts were to get different results for both myself and my students. I started experimenting with making my attitude, words, and ideas my primary teaching tools instead of my hands. *Lo and behold, it worked!*

My students were improving with much less input from my physical touch; emerging from their lessons, they felt better and played better, and they would come back with success stories to share from their week in between lessons. Their pain would often disappear or greatly diminish, their performance anxiety lessened, and their moods improved. Best of all, they felt empowered to continue exploring what I had taught them after the semester was over and they were on their own again. As a result, I gradually became more confident in teaching without touch, using my hands less and less as time went on.

I felt even more encouraged as I began meeting with a couple of colleagues online who were thinking along similar lines. They liked my ideas and began calling some of them "Freedom Directions." (More on Freedom Directions in Chapter 18.)

At that time, back in 2012, there were only a handful of AT teachers around the world who were interested in exploring online teaching, and it took a fair amount of guts to go against the prevailing culture. Even though Alexander made his own discoveries and solved his vocal issues without the benefit of a teacher's hands, and despite the fact that he himself taught without touch in his early teaching days, those of us who were curious to follow that line of inquiry were often criticized—even ostracized at times—by members of our profession who believed it was impossible to teach without touch and contrary to Alexander's teachings.

Naturally, all of that changed when the pandemic of 2020 hit, and suddenly most Alexander teachers could no longer earn a living using touch!

My explorations in touch-free teaching paid off long before the pandemic, though, when, to my great shock, my job and the entire Alexander Technique program at the university were eliminated in 2017, due to sweeping university-wide financial cuts. Losing my main source of income was terrifying (especially since I was going through a divorce at exactly the same time), but this turn of events proved to be another major blessing in disguise.

As I struggled to find local students, it wasn't long before the dearth of musicians in my area who wanted to learn the Alexander Technique caused me to turn to the internet, where I quickly realized it would be much easier to build a thriving teaching practice. Moving to online teaching required that I educate myself on how to market my practice in completely new ways, and I threw myself fully into the process, as I had very little choice!

Thankfully, by 2018, I'd successfully made the switch to teaching exclusively online and built a thriving virtual studio. I haven't looked back. I love teaching this way! The online medium pushes me to keep improving and refining my touch-free teaching skills, and now I know beyond a doubt that teaching this way works even better for me and my students than my lessons using touch ever could. The way I teach now is true to Alexander's original ideas and methods, and the results just keep getting better and better!

A serendipitous encounter in Ireland

Everything really started to come together, and my understanding of AT jumped up to a whole new level of effectiveness when I met Mio Morales at the International Congress for the Alexander Technique in Limerick, Ireland, in the summer of 2015. Mio is a master Alexander teacher who, at the time I'm writing this book, has been practicing AT for over fifty years and teaching it for nearly as long.

Mio's first Alexander teacher was Frank Pierce Jones, who studied with F.M. Alexander himself, and taught at Tufts University, where Mio was a student. Here, Mio developed his love for experimenting since Jones was the first person to begin doing scientific research to investigate the process and incredible results of the Technique.

When Mio asked Frank the quickest way to learn the Technique, he told Mio the best way would be to become a teacher, and he recommended that Mio go to Nebraska to study with his friend Marjorie Barstow. After graduating from Alexander's teacher-training course in England in 1934, Marj had moved back to her hometown of Lincoln, Nebraska, where she pioneered the practice of teaching the Technique to groups, holding summer workshops for students who often travelled great distances to study with her.

After meeting Marj, Mio began spending most of his summers in Nebraska, absorbing as much as he could from her over the next couple of decades, serving as one of her teaching assistants for many years. Mio spent the remainder of each year on his own, back in New York City, where he grew up and lived until moving out to Oregon to care for his aging parents in 2008.

Since his primary means of income at that time was as a composer, writing music for and touring with modern dance companies, Mio spent most of the year developing his ideas about the Alexander Technique entirely on his own, away from other teachers and free from the influence of other teaching styles.

Mio had the same kind of intense desire to understand what was happening under a teacher's hands that I'd had in the beginning; likewise, he wanted to be able to get the same kind of magical, uplifting experience for himself without depending on a teacher's hands. But Mio was much more self-reliant, fiercely independent, and obsessively dedicated to experimenting with Alexander's ideas on his own than I ever was!

Over the years, he found new ways to practice the Technique that worked better for him and his students than the more traditional ways of teaching that he'd been taught. He eventually stopped using the traditional Alexandrian procedures and verbal directions, for example, as he came up with his own teaching system through plenty of trial and error.

Mio and I had made a brief first contact a few months earlier, after I had been invited to teach some Alexander workshops in Japan. While I was there, people kept asking me if I knew Mio, but I'd never heard of him. Mio had been the guest teacher for the same Japanese workshops a couple years earlier, and I guess the students there thought we must know each other since our work had some similarities, and we were both from the USA.

After I left Japan, I reached out to Mio through Facebook to make a professional connection. We exchanged no more than a few words until we both showed up at the Alexander Congress a few months later and were formally introduced on the beautiful "Living Bridge" at the University of Limerick.

Mio and I hit it off right away, talking and sharing ideas about the Alexander Technique for hours on end. I was thrilled to find someone who had been exploring touch-free teaching for much longer than I and who was happy to discuss his ideas and share his process with me in depth. I knew right away that Mio's systematic approach was exactly what I needed to further flesh out and clarify my own ideas.

When I met Mio, he had been experimenting for decades. Over the years, Mio figured out what Alexander had actually done that allowed him to make his fantastic, healing discoveries, and he devised a brilliant system for how to teach others to do it for themselves (with or without touch), a system which he began teaching online in response to some of the Japanese students who wanted to keep studying with him after he left Japan. Mio continues to evolve and improve on this system (Primal Alexander) to this day.

Meeting another teacher like myself, who was interested in primarily teaching through the power of thought, was a complete game-changer. I attended several of his workshops in Limerick and was impressed by his ease of being, his sharp mind, and the simple clarity of his work. He would share his thoughts and work with anyone at the conference who wanted to learn—anytime, anywhere.

It was here, as previously mentioned, that Mio gave a few of us a casual after-dinner demonstration of something he called "TheCyCle," which entailed cradling our own fingers, counting to four, and doing a practice he called "ConstructiveThinking." Finding that it calmed me, felt meditative, I became curious. I knew that Mio based his studies on what Alexander had done for himself long ago, using the power of his own thinking along with self-observation and experimentation. What had he come up with? (Learn more about these concepts in Chapter 20, and in the companion video training here: https://www.artoffreedom.me/book/training.)

When we each returned to our respective homes in Ohio and Oregon, Mio and I stayed in touch, messaging each other every once in a while to compare notes, sharing a little Alexander observation or anecdote from our current teaching. Sometimes I'd ask him to share his perspective on a question I had, and I always found his suggestions enlightening and extremely helpful as I started incorporating them into my own teaching. He answered all the questions I had about the Alexander Technique that nobody else had been able to before, to my satisfaction, and practicing his system answered questions I wasn't even aware I had!

Just a few months after the Congress, Mio began meeting with a few of us Alexander teachers online to further explore what he had discovered, and that little seed group has gradually grown and evolved into multiple weekly classes for dozens of Alexander teachers who are enjoying the further flowering of his system.

It has been truly fascinating and a real privilege to witness the unfolding of this new process I'd had a first glimpse of in Limerick.

Primal Alexander turned out to be a real godsend for many Alexander Technique teachers around the world just a couple years later, when the pandemic struck. In March 2020, Mio and I teamed up to offer three weekends of free two-day workshops online, in which he taught nearly eight hundred Alexander teachers, all who suddenly needed to learn how to communicate Alexander's discoveries without touch.

Finally! A simple, easy way to get results!

For me, not only did Mio's novel, unique system allow me to experience much the same kind of wonders I'd experienced in my hands-on Alexander lessons, but Primal Alexander offered an extremely simple and repeatable step-by-step process by which I could better observe, experiment, and teach myself without feeling dependent on a teacher to get the results for me.

The cornerstone of the practice of Primal Alexander is the use of ConstructiveThinking, which I introduced in Chapter 7 as a very particular way to use the mind that instantly releases the overall level of excess tension, allowing inborn natural coordination to emerge with ease.

There are many ways to do ConstructiveThinking (CT), but in Mio's Primal Alexander, we begin learning CT by using a verbal thought in the form of a question. Asking a question in a way that opens us up to new possibilities automatically awakens a healthy sense of curiosity and natural movement within us. Usually, we start practicing ConstructiveThinking by asking "Where else do I seem to be easing a bit?"

"Where else do I seem to be easing a bit?"

This is just a whisper of a question that requires no immediate answer—and yet we are open to whatever possible answer(s) the body wishes to deliver up to the level of our conscious awareness.

The words in this question have been very carefully and thoughtfully chosen. To find the version that gives the best results for the most people, Mio tested them over time with hundreds of students. Let's take a closer look at the meaning of this question.

"Where else . . ." These words remind us that there is always ease (flow or release) within us, and the lively flow of easing is always happening under the surface.

". . . do I seem . . ." This reassures us that we don't have to know, or be sure, about what we're feeling. It's enough just to guess, have an intuition, or wonder. With practice, we become more sensitive and aware of what's actually happening inside, which builds our confidence over time.

". . . to be easing a bit?" Here, Mio uses the verb "easing" instead of the noun "ease" to emphasize the fluid, ever-changing and energetic nature of the letting go that easing represents within our bodies. Finally, the words "a bit" reassure us that the amount of ease is irrelevant; we don't have to notice a large change: what matters most is that the change is positive and makes us more open to the present moment.

This is key in Mio's work: *It's not about how much you change; it's about knowing in which direction and how you did it!*

This is one of the few areas in life where it's worth thinking in "black and white." Because we are living, breathing beings, our systems are in constant movement, and we move and change all at once, *as a whole*. Therefore, in any given moment of time, we are either going in the overall direction of greater ease, expansion, growth, life, consciousness, flow, and freedom, or we are going toward less ease, greater dis-ease, contraction, constriction, mindlessness, hardness, death and stagnation. The first direction takes us towards the good things we want with more ease; the second makes it harder to get there if we get there at all.

Once you realize the significance of your decision—which fundamentally amounts to a choice between love/life or fear/death—there's no debate: the choice becomes clear. The good news is that every split second gives you a new opportunity to make a fresh choice.

The reality is that the past doesn't exist anymore. All past choices disappear, and all regrets are erased by attending to the simple question, "What can I do NOW?" This is also a golden key to forgiveness, allowing us to move on after making mistakes.

Through the lens of Mio's system, I could finally understand what was happening in a lesson, what made things work or not, how to access more ease whenever I wanted to, and how to help my students do it for themselves, too.

I didn't always get the same dramatic "floaty effect" that I got from a great hands-on lesson (an experience I'm able to elicit on my own much more often these days from having practiced Primal Alexander for the last eight years), but I now understand that producing this feeling isn't the point. Besides, it's not actually possible to recreate an experience that two people have together with just one person! To me, knowing beyond a doubt when I'm making progress and knowing how I'm doing so is so much more interesting and valuable than the temporary "high" of a good hands-on AT lesson.

Now, the Alexander Technique wasn't shrouded in the same kind of mystery anymore; this was something clear, simple, and practical. Yet, at the same time, it appeared even more miraculous because I knew this process and its results represented what Alexander meant by the words "conscious, constructive, control of the individual." Those words were about the self—in the first person: my control over *me*; not somebody else's control. Primal Alexander highlights the student's ability to have better control over herself, independently of her teacher. This was delightfully free and self-empowering, and I relished it!

I just said the Technique was no longer a mystery to me, and yet, it brought me into an even closer relationship with the Great Mystery in a very beautiful way that keeps unfolding for me every day. Through my early, traditional Alexander Technique lessons, I learned how to consciously integrate and embody the spiritual intuitions I'd had as a child and in my early twenties. But Mio's system speeds up and deepens the whole process, allowing me to be more fully in tune with my true Self every day as I learn how to engage in all of my activities, including music-making, with more and more embodied awareness and grace.

Not only was Primal Alexander the simplest, clearest, and most immediately self-verifiable application of Alexander's discoveries that I'd ever come across, but it was extremely easy to help my students get instant results on their own, using his methods.

Mio's original teaching method filled in all the gaps, resolved many unanswered questions, and put doubts to rest.

He showed me the quickest, easiest way to free up my whole mind-body-self, and I was able to put it all into the context of music-making for my students so they could learn how to get great results for themselves, too. My students typically begin experiencing more ease in themselves right away—as early as DAY 1 of working with me.

Finally, it all makes sense . . .

The reason he calls it Primal Alexander

When I met Mio, he had been toying for a while with several possible names for his unique process of practicing and teaching Alexander's discoveries. I remember being in my house in Cincinnati, sitting around on the couch together one day, when Mio announced that he'd finally decided to call his work "Primal Alexander."

It's a very apt name for a method that goes back to the "primal" origins—the early beginnings—of the Alexander Technique: what Alexander did for himself that enabled him to solve his vocal-performance issues, and which he first introduced to others through the sharing of ideas and words, with minimal or no use of his hands.

Primal Alexander looks beyond all the diverse and sometimes contradictory schools of modern Alexander teaching, bringing everything back to their common denominator and indisputable roots, the fundamental principles of the Technique.

Primal Alexander could be considered essential, "pure" Alexander Technique, in the sense that it teaches us to do what Alexander did, and by doing that for ourselves, we can get the results and experience the same success Alexander did.

What is required is not necessarily to watch ourselves in the mirror, like I had originally assumed (although modern video technology is an incredibly useful tool that Alexander surely would have used!). To do what Alexander did for ourselves includes the following:

- Have a strong desire or goal that motivates us to do the work and stay the course
- Commit to taking personal responsibility for our own well-being
- Have faith in our innate freedom and our ability to change
- Trust our ability to think, learn, and problem-solve
- Wake up our curiosity to ask questions, form hypotheses, and create experiments to test them out

- Pay more attention to the process of discovery than achieving our goal
- Improve our self-observation skills
- Commit to discovering the truth about our own experience, moment by moment
- Open up to all possibilities, including the possibility that we and our habits might be taking us in the wrong direction even when they feel right
- Be willing to admit when we are wrong, and recommit to our process of discovery
- Show up, practice, stick to principle, and don't give up!

All of these points are prerequisites for anyone who wants to learn how to practice the Alexander Technique for themselves; therefore, they are also the prerequisites for practicing Primal Alexander. As Alexander himself emphasized, without the necessary mental attitude, no amount of Alexander Technique practice—Primal or otherwise—will yield the results we're seeking, and achievement of our goals will always fall short of what's possible.

Although the principles and prerequisites for the effectiveness of both traditional Alexander Technique and Primal Alexander are the same, Primal Alexander teaches these ideas explicitly through the precise and skilled use of words combined with the teacher's own modeling of the process—how he presents the ideas through his energetic presence, voice, and demeanor.

Since a Primal Alexander teacher doesn't usually use touch, there is far less confusion about whether the teacher or the student is the cause of any changes or improvements that may take place in the student.

There is no manipulation of the body; only a conversational exchange that encourages the student to experiment with different ways of thinking and moving (initially proposed by the teacher), and to actively engage in skillful self-observation and self-reflection. A teacher trained in Primal Alexander is able to detect extremely subtle and lightning-quick changes in the student that reflect the student's thought process, offering highly specific feedback to inform the next step in the experiment.

After each lesson, the student knows exactly what he did in the lesson that had a positive effect, and he knows exactly what to practice at home every day to keep improving on his own, without the immediate feedback of his teacher.

This is incredibly empowering for the student, who is taught from the very beginning to trust and take responsibility for himself, rather than depending on the teacher's hands to calm his nervous system through touch—something he cannot recreate on his own at home, no matter how he tries.

As mentioned before, over the years, Mio has developed dozens of "Awareness Etudes," which are short, simple thought-movement (mind-body) studies that cultivate a way of paying attention and thinking constructively during movement, which both calms the nervous system and allows our natural, healing energy to flow.

I've also created quite a few of my own Awareness Etudes, using Mio's framework, which are geared specifically towards helping musicians think and move with ease—with and without their instruments.

I don't think I'll ever stop practicing and teaching Primal Alexander because this self-teaching/learning process makes so much logical sense, and it works so quickly and beautifully for everyone who tries it with an open mind and a sincere desire to learn!

Where all of this has brought my music . . .

Even though I specialize in teaching musicians exclusively and I've spent quite a lot of time doing that over the years, the truth is that it was not until 2019 that I applied the Alexander Technique systematically and in depth to my own violin playing. In that year I decided it was time to make my own solo violin recording—one of the few things on my "bucket list" (another item on that list was writing this book!).

Until then, I had been applying AT to my everyday activities and my teaching, but only sporadically to my violin playing—normally when I was in a rehearsal or giving a performance, but not so much at home, practicing (since I barely ever practiced!).

Making up my mind to start practicing again regularly in order to make the recording, I knew that now was the moment to apply for myself in earnest what I was teaching others. Consistently using Primal Alexander in my everyday practicing skyrocketed my playing in a way that I'd witnessed time and again in my students. But to a much greater degree, which I had never experienced for myself.

I'll be talking in detail about how I help myself and other musicians improve, using Primal Alexander in practice and performance, in Part 3 of this book.

Give up the Illusion of Control

Ignite your curiosity and open up to All-Possibility

Out beyond ideas of wrongdoing and rightdoing, there is a field.
I'll meet you there.

~ *Rumi*

As I shared in the last chapter, one of the most notable changes in my life brought about by this strange new process of introspection and increased awareness with the Alexander Technique was a sudden reawakening of my long-dormant curiosity. As I became more open and able to notice more subtle things happening within me and around me, I slowly began to rebuild my trust in myself.

I adopted a more spiritual outlook on life at age nineteen and got married just after that at twenty, after which my innate curiosity slowly shut down, and gradually my self-trust eroded. Around that time, I had very little interest in practicing my violin or making music, which is no wonder since childlike curiosity is an essential ingredient for the creation of great art.

We humans are born with a healthy curiosity and are continually invited to participate in the creative process with the bright, lively spark of Inspiration. Rejecting this call and suppressing our creative spirit can cause a hardening of the heart, stifling confusion, and a terrible loss of joy and vitality.

We are all naturally creative artists, but we can only express our creativity with ease and carefree spontaneity when we are well-integrated, aligned, and listening to our Inner Wisdom—our unconditionally loving Inner Teacher, who resides in the heart.

We need to expand our capacity to draw from the creative wellspring of silence within, listening to the whisperings of deep truths present in Nature everywhere and in everything.

Listening with awareness, curiosity, and an open mind and body allows the soul to channel fresh, new ideas. That way, we participate in a creative process enlivened by the same awesome energy that flows through every living cell and supports every atom of the universe.

Imagine allowing that infinite, mysterious, loving energy to course through your veins, flow through your whole self and out your musical instrument, creating sound vibrations that emanate from the silent void like miracles! What could be more fantastic?!

Play it safe, or risk something new?

Opening ourselves up to All-Possibility in order to allow something completely new and magical to be created is risky; we have no idea what will happen—or how—and we can't control what we don't know! Taking that leap of faith into the Unknown can feel terrifying because it means making yourself vulnerable to the possibility of failure, of being wrong, of messing up—even giving up your old habitual identity as you abandon who you thought you were to become who you really are, as revealed moment by moment in the creative process.

As scary as it may be to let go of the old and familiar, it's even riskier to let perfectionism, self-doubt, and fear of what might go wrong take over and prevent you from surrendering to the mystery of All-Possibility and creative Inspiration.

But most of us have been trained to play it safe, not take too many risks, and follow the old familiar, rigid rules to stay within the bounds of what is acceptable. What's worse, all too often we surrender our curiosity and creative fire to those in authority, instead of making our own Inner Wisdom our ultimate guide.

When you submit to an external authority without honoring what's truly best for you, according to what you know to be true in your heart, you will slowly lose your joy, your love of music, and your passion for communicating beauty—what Plato called the "splendor of the true"—with others. Without realizing what's happened, you might end up wondering why you feel uninspired, unmotivated and bored, when the truth is that deep down, you are silently grieving the loss of connection with your true Self.

Of course, to fit into society and be outwardly successful, it's generally advisable to adopt the norms and do what is expected of you. For instance, it's commonly accepted that as a student, you should hold your instrument correctly and practice the exercises your teacher assigns; as a performer in an orchestra, you should show up at events on time, be prepared, and follow the conductor; as an educator, you must plan your lessons and deliver the quality teaching your students and administrators expect.

Even so, I've learned over the years that it's far *more* important to have a strong faith in yourself that comes from learning how to listen to your own heart and follow your inner guidance rather than blindly follow the culture and authority figures who dictate the rules of the outer game.

At the same time, it's essential to keep your inner world and outer world in balance, with a healthy dose of humility that always stays open to the possibility that you might be wrong—about anything. Learning how to balance your inner and outer worlds for deep peace, joy, and success is a lifelong process!

Not only does humility help protect you and others from some of the pain resulting from your inevitable mistakes, but having the willingness to believe that anyone can be wrong—including both yourself and those in positions of authority—means you're always open to discovering better, more natural and inspired ways of doing things that may not have been thought of before.

The flexibility and adaptability of an open mind-body-self is even more valuable than the laudable commitment to hold fast to something we've always been told or have even experienced to be right, but which might not actually be the best way—or even right at all.

When aspiring to create art, we need to be willing to let go of everything known—both what our own ego tells us and what we've received from outside—in order to be open to the mystery of Inspiration—something which often does NOT bend to established rules, but rises above them.

When we let that fiery spirit flow through us unhindered, something new, fresh, and pure can be created. Something as natural and unique as a leaf on a tree—both the same as, yet utterly different from, every other leaf ever produced before or after. That is how an inspired note sounds, too. So that even when it's out of tune or the phrase is lopsided, it can be admired as something imperfectly perfect when it stems from Inspiration. Just like we, ourselves.

Of course, listening to knowledgeable teachers, accepting good advice from trusted sources, and following rules that make sense is often the quickest route to learning what we need to know. After all, you need to have a general idea of the basics like how to hold your instrument, what needs to happen in order to make certain sounds and phrases, and how rhythm and intonation work before you can go much further. Being able to humbly submit to authorities outside of ourselves with integrity and imbibe new ideas is necessary and beneficial at every stage of our development!

But following even the best rules and most sincere guides can still stunt our growth and end up causing harm if we adopt a rigid moralistic attitude along the way. That attitude also makes it much harder to discern whether a rule is universally applicable, and whether it is personally helpful to you or not.

When you blindly adopt the belief that following those in positions of authority and accepting their rules is "good" and makes you a "good person" and if you don't follow the rules, that's "bad" and makes you a "bad person," you are giving up much of your own power and freedom of choice. Over time, you might forget to think for yourself, and it gets harder to see clearly and make choices based on more subtle information than what first met the eye.

My own belief in a worldview that divides our thoughts and actions into "right/good" vs. "wrong/bad" used to be very strong; for a long time I didn't question the value of this kind of black-and-white thinking.

In fact, as I got older, just asking certain kinds of questions with an unbridled or "unhealthy" curiosity, I firmly labeled as "wrong" behavior. Having a passionate desire to innovate, experience, or create something alternative to accepted norms also got relegated (by me) to the "wrong" box, as (supposedly) ego-driven, and of course that was also a "bad" thing.

Because I wanted desperately to be a "good" person and do things correctly, I resolved at that point to relinquish, along with my natural curiosity, my passions. I became the "arch conformist," determined to follow all the rules, make sure I did everything right, and accept as true whatever I was told by those I trusted in positions of authority. This may sound like rigidity in the extreme; true, I became a *temporary* slave to blind perfectionism. And perfectionism (the need to be correct and right in everything, to the extent possible) is the surest way to feed self-doubt and crush your creative spirit!

In fact, as I said, this conditioning is not really unusual. We've all been conditioned to accept without question the way of life we are born into, and to believe what we are told is worthy of our striving.

Being present and developing a loving, "unified field of attention"

Between the ages of two and six, our brainwaves are predominantly in a theta wave state, which, as very young children, is optimal for receiving and unquestioningly accepting whatever we are exposed to. We are designed to learn naturally, with ease and acceptance. And through imitation, we learn to behave in ways appropriate to our surroundings.[15]

15 Molly McElroy, "A First Step in Learning by Imitation, Baby Brains Respond to Another's Actions," University of Washington, Oct. 30, 2013, https://www.washington.edu/news/2013/10/30/a-first-step-in-learning-by-imitation-baby-brains-respond-to-anothers-actions/; Bruce Lipton, The Biology of Belief: Unleashing the Power of Consciousness, Matter and Miracles (Santa Cruz, CA: Mountain of Love Productions hardcover), 2008: 133.

In order to feel like we belong to the human network, and in order to survive when we are babies and small, helpless children, we automatically learn the rules of our culture, whether we ultimately choose to surrender and follow them, to bend them, or to fight them.

Sadly, much of what we pick up from those around us is not actually life-enhancing for us, even if we are conditioned to believe it is. Thankfully, something deeper within us than our rational, thinking mind actually *does* know what is constructive and beneficial for our whole self.

And yet, we have very rarely been taught that *how* we do the things we consider "good" makes all the difference in the world to their ultimate value. Whether something is "good" or "bad" for others and society is far less important than first knowing whether it is essentially beneficial or harmful to ourselves. Ideally, we learn to fulfill both goals—doing good for ourselves with "magnanimous selfishness" (see the previous chapter), while also doing good for others. We need to want what is best for both ourselves *and* the world.

The only way we can more objectively value both ourselves and the world is to develop what Frank Pierce Jones called a "unified field of attention," in which we expand our focus to be more universally inclusive. That is, become more aware of both our inner and outer worlds, with less and less distinction.

We can develop more conscious control over our attention by making what Mio Morales calls our "Primary Concern" to inquire and observe what's happening to us as we engage in the activity of the moment. We can do this easily, simply by asking "*What's happening to me as I ________?*"

Stop reading for just a moment to ask yourself this question, then wait a few moments for answers to reveal themselves. What's happening to you right now, in this present moment? Where is your attention? What are you feeling in your body? What are you thinking? How is your mood? What is the quality of your experiencing as you put everything else on hold and bring your attention back to yourself?

Redirecting your attention to this present moment by making your Primary Concern truly primary is the first step to adopting a less-reactive and less-judgmental attitude, and it makes it much easier for unconditional Love to blossom and learning to occur. With practice, the habitual sense of separateness that promotes fear and anxiety begins to fade away, our self-confidence increases, and healing takes place.

Performance anxiety and physical pain often stem from a lack of awareness of universal Love and goodness, and our habit of overfocusing on what feels "wrong" or "bad." These problems are exacerbated and we take a much longer time to heal when we judge anxiety or pain as "bad," and we make ourselves "wrong" or "bad" for experiencing them.

Since we want so much to be "good," we put a great deal of attention on trying to fix ourselves and correct what seems "wrong," which simply feeds our awareness of lack and separation and blinds us from the ease of Self-Love. This attempt at changing and controlling ourselves is misguided and only takes us further down the path of discomfort and dis-ease, even though we may believe strongly that we're doing the "right" thing by trying so hard to fix things.

The paradoxical first step to healing and solving all of the problems you may have as a musician, whether your problems present themselves as physical, mental, emotional, or spiritual, is to simply notice the problem without judging it or yourself, and NOT do something to try to fix it.

Instead . . . be present and get curious. Become a courageous adventurer-explorer of new territories within yourself.

Be curious and start listening to yourself with compassion instead of trying to change, improve, or fix yourself.

Just BE with yourself for a moment, open up to All-Possibility, and *listen*.

How well are you listening to your Self?

If you want to heal and recapture love, joy, and Inspiration in your life and music, start by learning to listen to your innermost Self with curiosity, patience, and steady determination.

Get curious about the silent workings of the wise Life-force within you that allows you to think, move, and create the next moment of your life in every waking moment.

Connect with the wisdom that courses through your blood with magnetic energy, travels through every single cell, and coordinates every element of your nervous system to reveal a miracle no one can fully understand; a miracle that takes place every time an idea is conceived and carried into action. Every time you think a thought, lift a finger, or walk down the street.

THIS Inner Wisdom is the entirely natural yet also sublimely mystical element that can transform an idea into a magical moment of artistic mastery—whether it's something as simple as the turn of a wrist during a Japanese Tea Ceremony, or the crossing of a violin bow from one string to another in a solo work by Bach.

In order to tap into the wealth of your own Inner Wisdom so you can realize your own potential for artistic mastery, you need to listen, learn, grow, and transcend your personal limitations. To do this, you need to develop the habit of asking for and *listening* to the guidance of your Inner Wisdom, the true source of inspired art.

Begin listening to this essential, core aspect of your Self in order to get your whole self in tune, just like you listen to the sound of the strings to get your violin in tune.

How well are you listening to the silent whisperings of your Inner Teacher in your heart that are gently prodding you take better care of every aspect of your primary instrument: YOU?

Nora is a professional cellist who came to me in the midst of multiple challenges in her life that were making it very difficult to stay balanced and effective, either emotionally or professionally. Her mother having recently passed away, Nora was charged with taking care of the estate (an emotional time indeed!); a bit of family strife was further complicating things; she was making multiple ten-hour car trips back and forth to the house to pack things up—all while trying to keep her private cello studio afloat, serve her students well, and learn music pieces for her upcoming performance gigs. At the same time, chronic physical pain made playing the cello hurt.

With all of this pressure, Nora felt she was barely able to keep it all together. Who *wouldn't* be struggling under such circumstances?

When Nora inquired about my coaching programs, she wasn't at all sure the timing was right for her, since it was nearly impossible to find time to take care of herself, let alone practice her instrument.

Nevertheless, it was clear to her that she needed the support—not just to deal with emotional stress, but to help her feel better physically and musically, since her cello playing was beginning to suffer from the excess tension caused by all the turmoil in her life.

Nora wrote this after her first two weeks in my program:

"It is said that when the student is ready, the teacher appears, and apparently I was more than ready. Even after two years of hands-on Alexander lessons and reading countless books, Feldenkrais lessons here and there, a near-daily yoga practice—and many years of performance experience—I have not felt so much ease in my body as I have in the last two weeks.

"Pain gone. Mind-set more optimistic, trapezius muscles released, back and shoulder pain, which I previously could only 'manage' but not eliminate, are GONE. These tools are simple but powerful. My only hope is that I can continue to learn and discover my own body/mind and that this newfound level of comfort and freedom doesn't go away!"

A few weeks after she began our work together, Nora played for an opera project that involved multiple long rehearsals and performances. She told me that, in the past, she would have fallen apart easily in those sessions due to the pain and emotional stress; but, to her amazement, with her new mind-body skills she was able to let go of her anxiety, tension, and perfectionism and actually ENJOY her performance pain-free.

Sometime after our work together concluded, Nora wrote this:

"It's now almost two years later, and I'm happy to report that I am thriving. I have a much better and healthier balance in my life and work, and I'm creating better relationships, as being a happier pain-free version of myself allows all my interactions to be far less stressful and fearful, and far more joyful.

"My daily practice of ConstructiveThinking continues in all areas of my life. CT helps me navigate everything from traffic jams to difficult interactions with studio parents, to performances with my trio, to orchestra and other gigs that often have a short preparation time. I am calmer, more focused, and yes, I'm still pain-free.

"The mind truly is our greatest friend and our greatest tool. Simple and brief daily exercises are a gateway to greater ease in everything I do. It is the most effective mindfulness training I have ever come across in all my years of seeking help. I am eternally grateful for Jennifer's teaching and for the work of F. M. Alexander as she teaches it. Life-changing!"

~ Nora, Cellist and Educator

Mastery requires taking better care of your primary instrument

It's pretty obvious that taking care of your musical instrument is necessary, right? You probably take good care of your musical instrument without thinking much about it.

You take care of routine instrument maintenance like repairing your bow, replacing old strings, fixing cracks, cleaning parts, etc. And, of course, you make sure your instrument is in tune before you play.

If this need is obvious, then it should be even more evident that you need to take excellent care of your Primary Instrument, the one that makes it possible to play any musical instrument at all.

And yet, we often take our mind-body-self and its healthy functioning for granted.

When we don't bring conscious awareness to what we're doing with the mind, body, and spirit, and if things don't work the way we want them to, we tend to blame our environment, our musical instrument, our past or current life circumstances, or someone else for our failings.

Or, we blame ourselves for coming up short, but without recognizing that our priorities are out of whack and we haven't set ourselves up sufficiently for success to begin with.

As illogical as it is, somehow it seems OK to settle for mediocrity in self-care, even though we yearn to step beyond mediocrity in our music-making.

Having our priorities and perspective skewed and bent out of shape by a culture that prizes doing over Being isn't anybody's fault. In fact, it's normal to forget about Being these days—dazzled by what we amazing human beings can DO. This is just human nature. *But that doesn't make this way of living our best or only choice!*

I believe that the best choice, which is always available to us and natural in its own right (Alexander called it "man's supreme inheritance"), is to rise above the default settings of our humdrum or self-destructive human nature and, instead, step into the awesome possibilities presented to us by virtue of that uniquely human capability that opens us up to the divine plane of All-Possibility. . . that is, *Consciousness.*

If we want our music to be as masterful and divine as humanly possible, then we must first believe it is, in fact, possible for us to rise above habitual mediocrity.

I'm not talking about skill levels here, because even a beginner musician on his first day with his instrument can be exceptionally above average in his approach—just as a seasoned professional can diminish the quality of his playing with an attitude that is below the standard required by a musical composition.

If we want to practice artistic mastery and create true art, as opposed to dabbling in mediocre craftsmanship (and I'm not saying there's anything wrong with that, if that's what you want!), then we need to become aware of and put our unconditional trust in that mysterious "something" that lives, breathes, and coordinates our whole self with the very existence of the universe.

This "Great Mystery" is the part of us that is also our best "Inner Teacher," "Higher Self," or "Inner Wisdom."

We need to make nurturing our relationship with our Inner Teacher our absolute top priority because this is what brings all of the seemingly separate parts of who we are (mind, body, emotions, creative spirit) into one unified whole, inseparable from the rest of the universe. This wonderful Inner Teacher is always giving us indications from inside, that teach us how to take better care of our Primary Instrument, so we can become better people and conduits for the music that wants to flow through us.

How you do one thing is how you do everything

How you use your mind-body-self in one activity represents a micro-view, or microcosm, of how you do everything in life.

For example, if you have a habit of clenching your jaw or hands when you get frustrated in a conflict with your friend, you're likely to engage in that same habit to some degree whenever you're about to do anything that frustrates you, such as tackling a technically demanding passage in a piece of music that's beyond your current ability.

Or, if you tend to get nervous and take shallow breaths when you think about performing for someone, you may fall into the same tension habits when thinking about approaching your boss to ask for a raise.

The way you move your legs when you walk or hold your hip joints when you bend is related to how you sit or stand when you play your instrument; and the way you sit at the computer and use your eyes is related to what happens with your eye and neck muscles when you're reading sheet music or watching the conductor.

How freely you feel and express your emotions on a daily basis is reflected in how freely you express them through music. Like myself when young, you may find expressing yourself through music is easier than speaking, but your creative self-expression will be hampered in both areas if you are preventing yourself from ever feeling anything deeply in any situation in your life.

If you have a habit of not giving yourself the time, space, or permission to acknowledge and feel your emotions deeply—with your whole heart, mind, body, and soul—then those restrictions will show up to prevent you from feeling and sharing those emotions fully through your music, as well.

The illusion of control

Alexander proposed that as we evolve as a species, human beings are meant to reclaim "man's supreme inheritance," namely, our distinctly human ability to develop "conscious constructive control" over ourselves.

Most of us do, in fact, feel a need to be more in control of ourselves and our environments, so we can feel more comfortable, safe, and secure in the world. We want to know that our actions have consequences; that our choices make a difference; and that our lives have an impact on the world and those around us. As musicians, we want to know and trust that our hard work in the practice room will deliver the results we want.

The key to developing conscious constructive control over ourselves is actually quite simple, and we can succeed at this very quickly, in the very instant that we allow ourselves to be present by shifting our attention to our Primary Concern, as described above.

Everyone knows it's better to "think before you speak" because this gives you better self-control over your words and actions, right?

Well, . . . yes and no!

Yes, it's wise to pause and consider your next thoughts and actions because you're more likely to make better choices than if you mindlessly, impulsively react to the situation at hand.

And yet, "he who hesitates is lost," and it's hard to deny that some of our most lucid moments and most ecstatic artistic experiences happen when there isn't any hesitation or any verbal thought at all!

So how can these two ideas—pausing to consider and acting without hesitation—co-exist?

The answer lies in what, in that critical moment of decision-making, we're doing with our consciousness. Rarely do we consider that our *manner of thinking*—not just the content of our thoughts—can either increase the relative ease and energetic flow within us and thus raise the vibration of our consciousness, thereby positively influencing those around us; or it can decrease our ease and lower our vibration, negatively influencing others, as well.

For example, it's probably a good idea to inhibit (not act on) your anger when hearing your student play the wrong note for the fifth time in a row; and instead, pause to carefully consider your next words so they sound less irritated; and speak with a softer, kinder voice.

However, if your entire system is filled with annoyance and resentment while you're pausing to consider what to say—and you're not actually letting go of that low-vibrational energy—then quietly holding onto your anger as you continue with the lesson won't help anyone, and your student will most certainly pick up on that negative energy. Consciously or unconsciously.

Beyond that, the word "control" is tricky, and it's easy to fall into the illusion trap of habitual ego- and fear-based thinking, believing that the small, thinking mind is the part of us that needs to be in control, when that control is entirely relative and often takes us unknowingly in the wrong direction.

What we really need to gain better control of is our attention. The idea that we can have real control over anything else is fundamentally just an illusion.

Masks of identity

The masks of identity we put on and the ego-personalities we grow over time in our attempt to protect ourselves from what we perceive as dangerous are an example of how we try to change ourselves to adapt to our environment, and also how we try to control our surroundings.

Because taking on these roles works well enough up to a point—we can even be quite successful in the world because of these roles—they contribute greatly to the illusion of our control. But at some point in our lives, we will come to realize that sticking to the roles we play is limiting our possibilities and preventing us from feeling the full range of human emotions.

In our attempt to control ourselves and our environment, we end up putting ourselves in a box. However safe or comfortable the box might be, it's still a box that limits our freedom and prevents us from realizing our full potential.

One of the worst things we can do to ourselves as artists is to put ourselves into a box of this kind, applying self-control and staying there, letting ourselves feel *some* emotions but not others, dampening the intensity of all of them out of a fear that expressing them might break the box. We might literally "fall apart."

Artists need to be able to express the full range of emotions, but you can only do that if you aren't afraid of them, because you trust that you can handle their intensity without dying! Instead of playing it safe with your emotions, you need to learn that *it's OK to actually feel them fully.*

And that's only possible when you have the tools of Self-Trust, Self-Love, and Self-Confidence. That is, trust, love, and confidence in your True Self. You need to know that your Inner Wisdom is always here—in your heart and in every cell of your being—taking care of you and offering whispers of guidance and reassurance through your intuitive faculties 24/7.

Your True Self—your Inner Wisdom and Inner Coordinator—or Consciousness itself, far beyond the ego's illusory masks—is what you really need to put your trust in because THIS is what is truly in control of every aspect of your life.

The Inner Coordinator (aptly named by a former student of mine) is what organizes every aspect of your mind and body, allowing you to live, breathe, think, and move. It allows all of your organs to function and take care of you from one moment to the next.

This subtle Director is what makes it possible for the heart to pump blood through your heart and whole body all day long, throughout your entire life. It brings ideas to your awareness, allows you to act on them, and coordinates your psychophysical response—with or without your conscious awareness.

It allows you to sleep and digest, taking care of your health and well-being. It keeps your feet on the ground and your head above water, your body balanced. It coordinates every muscle you need in order to walk down the street, talk to your friend, or play your musical instrument.

Only your Inner Coordinator knows exactly which muscles you need to use and how, in order to accomplish any activity.

How presumptuous of our thinking minds, with the very limited capacity of our brain's prefrontal cortex, to believe we know how to control this magical mind-body-self to manifest a pure idea into the reality of physical action!

Which muscles do you need to play a scale? What does each cell in your whole body need to do in order to allow your fingers to move in precisely the right way, with the least possible effort?

No anatomist, doctor, physical therapist, or yogi can answer these questions. Because the human being, which is in a state of constant flux, is a far too complex creature, and the human mind alone is far too limited to be able to control even the simplest of movements on its own.

Nobody can tell you exactly what needs to happen in your whole self even to lift one finger an inch.

So how *do* you do it? How do you play a scale? How do you finesse a bow stroke on a violin to produce a silky, lush, vibrant sound that makes your whole body thrill with energy, joy, and delight?

Your Inner Coordinator—your deepest, True Self—does it *for* you. Not your small ego-mind.

So, stop pretending you're in control, or that you can be. You're asking the impossible of yourself, and that is why you suffer.

Stop pushing yourself around!

It's time to give up!

Stop trying to be in control; stop trying to dominate your fingers and your sound; or to make things happen through your willpower alone.

You're just working against Nature, going against your natural design, like water trying to flow upstream.

Give up the reins. Hand them over to your true master: your True Self within.

Don't worry—your life isn't going to suddenly spin out of control because you no longer know how to do anything! Your Inner Coordinator generously shares the reins with you, inviting your conscious participation in ultimate self-control, through the intelligent use of your mind-body-instrument.

You are made for effortless ease of being, freely expressed when you play your instrument with less interference from your ego-mind. In the next chapter, let's look at how important it is to trust the natural ease, the Inner Teacher, within you.

Trust Your Inner Teacher

Effortless mastery requires self-confidence

No one can make you feel inferior without your consent.

~ *Eleanor Roosevelt*

When my younger son, Rafael, was three years old, I took him to a popular local violin teacher for lessons. I quietly observed over a period of several months, without saying anything about a number of methods I felt were not helping my child. Thankfully, I was spared the need to meet with the teacher to tell her my thoughts because before I could do that, she "fired" us from her studio.

Why did she let us go? For the simple reason that my tiny child barely had enough neck length to comfortably fit the violin under his chin, but I would not agree to the use of a shoulder rest, required by this teacher for all of her students. As an Alexander teacher, I knew that making the violin taller on his shoulder would cause my son to strain to hold the instrument, thus increasing tension and gripping in his neck, one of the worst things that could happen since excess tension in the neck always compromises the ease, freedom, and flexibility everywhere else.

Sadly, this teacher was not trained to see that different bodies require different instrumental setups, just as she was unable to see that different personalities require different teaching strategies. Thanks to her rigidity and despite her best intentions, she not only lost my son as a student, but I can easily imagine that many students who have passed through her studio have likely ended up quitting the violin due to lack of creative solutions and encouragement, and/or gone on to develop pain and other performance problems down the road.

Unfortunately, there are many, many music teachers out there who believe they know what's best, based on a standard formula that works for *them*, but who lack the imagination to experiment and adapt with new ways of doing things for the unique student who shows up in their studio TODAY.

The best teacher encourages the student to observe himself, listen to his body, get to know his own habits and personal idiosyncrasies, and work towards discovering whether something truly works for him or not, while also gently guiding the student on the path that, taking his uniqueness into consideration, makes the most sense to the teacher.

Ultimately, the best teacher teaches the student to gradually become his or her own best teacher, creating situations for the student to practice self-teaching through observation and experimentation from the very beginning. To do this, the teacher encourages the student to pay attention to the whole self with healthy detachment and practice the various suggestions proposed by the teacher with an inquisitive, playful, and open mind-body-self.

Even from a very young age, the student needs to learn how to become an excellent self-observer, more and more sensitive to what is beneficial to his whole self AND what will help him make progress with specific techniques; not just focus on improving those techniques directly.

Having an experimental attitude builds trust, as it honors the unique student's thoughts, emotions, and physical feelings, placing a higher priority on taking care of those than following prescribed advice or common practice.

The best teachers are attached to neither methods nor outcomes

A devoted and successful student brings joy to the teacher who cares!

Such a teacher presents her own best understanding of a concept with humility and with as much objectivity as possible. It's so important to remember that each and every person is entirely unique. No advice is right for every student; there is always an exception to every rule.

Things that work well for most people won't necessarily work for everyone. Here's why:

Some bodies can't or won't move and do things the way other bodies do.

Some people's minds can't or won't think and imagine the same way other minds do.

Some people don't feel or express emotions the same way others do.

A pervasive problem that even some of the best teachers tend to have is that much of their advice is unexamined, myopic, and based on habit, with its origins in one or more of the following:

1) tradition, or what is commonly accepted as true

2) what the teacher herself was taught

3) what the teacher has found works best for herself, personally

Good teaching takes all of these things into account. Great teaching becomes an art, however, when the teacher, letting go of what is commonly accepted if the student before her needs something different, willingly questions her own habits and beliefs. A great teacher is willing to step into the Unknown with the student, serving as a guide to exploring and discovering creative new solutions together that take the whole, unique student into account, along with all of his idiosyncrasies of mind, body, and character.

Unfortunately, since most teachers don't approach their students with this kind of flexibility and intent to learn together, they rarely open their advice up to question, contradiction, or alternative interpretation.

When a teacher presents her advice as the only "right way" to do something, discouraging a curious attitude willing to test things out and explore multiple ways of doing things, this can have a detrimental effect that mutes curiosity and slows down progress, especially in the case where the advice isn't, in fact, the best way forward for the student.

In the previous chapter, I suggested that you need to become more attuned to the quiet whisperings of your Inner Teacher, which offers you a built-in register of what is truly helpful to you and what is not. Even when you have—or have had—wonderful teachers, it is still essential to develop more and more trust in your own Inner Teacher: your Self.

My suggestion for you as you continue to absorb information from teachings outside of yourself is to first listen with an open mind, no matter where the advice is coming from. Be open to the possibility that it could be helpful, yet also be aware that it might not be right for you.

Give the advice a chance if its usefulness isn't clear to you at first. Try it out! Experiment with the idea for a few minutes or weeks. Find out what happens, and make sure you don't throw out the baby with the bathwater. You may just need more time with the idea, and even if it's truly a terrible idea for you, there's usually a kernel of useful truth hidden within even the worst advice. Get curious about finding that kernel; be grateful for all advice you receive, and you can't go wrong!

Lack of self-confidence is the biggest obstacle to your success

Many students question the advice of their teachers and experiment on their own only hesitantly. They may feel it's arrogant to do so, or too much curiosity may be actively discouraged by the teacher. Plus, the student's learned habits of people-pleasing and taking an authority's advice on blind faith may be deeply ingrained.

Of course, those in positions of authority (teachers, parents, school administrations, etc.) may actively encourage those habits because your lack of questioning makes it easier to guide you; it allows them to more easily uphold their power.

What you need to know as a musician is that people-pleasing and following advice blindly make it much harder to develop your ability to teach yourself once your teacher isn't there—and that's the most important skill you need every time you step into the practice room, alone with your instrument.

The best teachers teach you how to teach yourself, and that can't happen unless they are actively encouraging you to think, wonder, question, and experiment with what they give you. Without a teacher's nurturing guidance in how to work well on your own with the tools they give you, it's easy for you to become dependent on your teacher. Then when you try to perform and things maybe don't go as well as you'd hoped (and your teacher isn't there onstage with you), it's easy for your trust in yourself to be seriously undermined.

Lack of trust in your Inner Teacher (YOU) is the same as a lack of self-confidence, *and this deficit is the single biggest obstacle to your success on every level.* It is also the main ingredient in performance anxiety, and the common denominator to every single problem you face as a musician.

When you don't understand how to teach yourself, your progress will be seriously stunted and you simply cannot grow into your own as an artist. True artistry is a solitary, inner experience and a beautiful conversation between you and your higher Self.

An important lesson in self-confidence and self-respect

When I was a young teenager, I was incredibly fortunate to attend masterclasses given by several famous violinists in two European countries over the span of five summers. I hesitate to share the following story about one of them, but the life lessons I learned were so powerful I feel the need to include it here, without naming anyone.

In a gorgeous, stately old mansion in the outskirts of an old city, dozens of hand-picked performers and eager auditors assembled for the masterclass. I remember fondly (and with a twinge of anxiety) the giant wooden doors and the beautiful murals painted on the walls of the room; on one side, glass doors opened out into the rose gardens below.

Despite leaving my private audition as a twelve-year-old in tears because this master violinist, whom I will call Mr. Mann, repeatedly refused to allow me to play my beloved Bach, requiring me to perform everything else on the audition list except the one thing I knew and loved best (he said I was too young to understand Bach), somehow I was still accepted into his coveted teaching.

This was a very great honor, as the cream of the crop of professional violinists from all over the world flocked to this event every summer to play for and learn from the great master. Overjoyed, I felt incredibly grateful to be given this opportunity, and I learned so much as I listened to these incredible musicians playing repertoire I'd never heard before and getting feedback myself, directly from the master.

As a good student and adept people-pleaser, I quite easily listened to and followed Mr. Mann's teachings, absorbing his ideas (musical and otherwise), making them my own. I used to think of myself as a chameleon, in fact! Because of this natural adaptability, I could take his suggestions when I played in the class, imitate his playing, and easily produce what he wanted to hear. So, the master became very happy with me, as he did with anybody who possessed that kind of flexibility.

Over time, Mr. Mann and I developed a very positive relationship, and in our wonderful, long lessons he was very kind and playful with me. Eventually, he did allow me to play Bach, and even those lessons went well. One day, he played a surprise "Happy Birthday" for me, and yet again, on the last day of class, he handed over his Stradivarius for me to play on, when I didn't have my violin with me.

This positive rapport was not, however, what some attendees experienced. It could in fact be quite uncomfortable to watch how he at times related to some of the other violinists. Many played their hearts out at a technical level I could only dream of at that time, stunning the audience, while our teacher sat listening with his head down on a small table, resting it on his forearms.

Not infrequently he let a violinist play through an entire concerto without interruption. At the conclusion of the performance, the audience would go wild with appreciation, but our teacher would only look up slightly from his table with craned neck and mutter, "Do you have anything else?"

Whereupon the violinist would become disconcerted for a moment before conjuring up a new piece from memory and start playing it—with equally dazzling skill.

In some cases, Mr. Mann offered up a minimal critique, but all too often the poor student, trying in vain to imitate how the master had played a piece in demonstration, was unable to satisfy him. In that case, frustrated, the master would give up, in which case the lesson was over and the student dismissed, having received no praise or appreciation and very little instruction (if any at all) before being replaced by the next person on the list.

One day, all of that changed.

A young Asian woman from California was attending the masterclass that year, and it was her turn to play. Again, she astonished the audience as she played through an entire concerto (was it Brahms?).

When she finished, we heard the familiar "Do you have anything else?" from the master as he raised his head slightly from his arms, where it had been resting for the last half hour.

For a moment, there was silence. And then, I witnessed an event I will never forget.

Defiantly choosing not to be dismissed like too many before her, this woman, instead of scrambling to serve up another treasure from her repertoire, replied in a firm voice, "Why should I play anything else? You'll just tear it apart like you do everything else," whereupon she turned on her heels and left the room. Not looking back, she disappeared from the building and the masterclass, never to be seen there again.

A stunned silence cloaked the room. You could have heard a pin drop—even on the plush, carpeted floor. In shock, holding our breath . . . we all wondered what would happen next. How would the master react? We watched him with wide eyes, waiting . . .

"Break!!!"

"Break time!!!" roared the giant director of the masterclass as he rose up from the small round table where he always sat next to the master.

"Break!!!" Together, they quickly left the room to have their private coffee in the adjoining room, as usual.

The rest of us huddled together, almost afraid to mention what had just happened . . . we whispered, remarking on the weather, tea, and cookies, or we quickly stepped out into the rose garden for the relief of some fresh air.

When class resumed, our formidable teacher returned, quite changed after this unexpected rebuke by the student, his character and humanity having been exposed—like in *The Wizard of Oz*, seen from behind the curtain.

From that moment on, Mr. Mann's humility was on display. No longer did he listen to his students with his head down on his arms. No longer did he wear a bored expression of hopelessness on his face. Exhibiting instead a softer, kinder, gentler side of himself from then on, he listened and offered suggestions, doing the best he could.

Over the decades since, I've often thought about this experience: how this brave student dared to stand her ground and speak her uncomfortable truth fearlessly to a world-famous, revered authority. That woman became a powerful, anonymous role model for me.

Despite the wonderfully perceptive lessons I and many others were so fortunate to receive directly from this world-famous violinist, equally important was the one we received from this woman who was not willing to accept treatment she did not deserve.

I saw on full display why nobody, no matter how famous, admirable, or skilled, has the right to treat others poorly. I learned that it's possible to say no to an authority on a pedestal and accept the consequences with head held high. And I learned that showing healthy self-respect while prioritizing self-care is far more important than succumbing to the whims of any teacher whatsoever.

Since witnessing this event, I have called directly upon these life lessons and been so grateful to the Asian woman who taught me by example, willing to live with the consequences of being true to herself.

Maybe she will read this book one day and recognize herself . . . If that is you, dear reader, I thank you for being yourself, teaching all of us about listening to the wisdom of our Inner Teacher, and sharing your wonderful music that day!

Getting support

Rather than trying to build up your self-confidence directly by putting yourself in difficult situations like the one above, the programs teaching The Art of Freedom Method offer structured support coming from three directions, each of which contributes to building up a more positive sense of who you are.

My students enjoy a) one-on-one private coaching with me, b) self-study online courses and daily practice on their own, and c) powerful group learning experiences—because we all need feedback, encouragement, and loving support from outside of ourselves!

The private and group experiences my students get reinforce what they already know, deep down, to be true since our outer experience merely reflects what's going on inside of us. Through hearing frequent reminders of what's important, what to pay attention to, and how to learn effectively, students accept more and more responsibility for their own personal and musical transformation. And the more they apply the ideas coming from outside of themselves, the more they realize they can trust what's already inside.

By accepting more of the responsibility for learning through self-teaching, and by putting The Art of Freedom Method into daily practice, along with Primal Alexander Awareness Etudes (see Part 3 for practical explanations of these) my students gradually grow in trust and self-confidence, as they see themselves getting better and better at carrying out their intentions successfully, with ease.

Here's what my student Martie had to say along these lines:

"I did a small but somewhat stressful project over the last couple days that in the past would have been painful emotionally and physically. In the past, while I would have 'gotten through,' I might have felt miserable and paralyzed at moments.

"Because of the consistent practice that I have been cultivating with Jennifer as my coach over these past few months, instead I was able to really enjoy and appreciate the process, was pain-free, and I played not only with confidence, but also with a deep connection with the music, my colleagues, and my violin.

"I was really proud of myself (which is not something that is always easy for me to say). I can also say that the very best of myself came through in my playing (I created much of what I wanted to paint with a piece as an artist), which is so satisfying to be able to feel. It was empowering to know that I had choices, and to make healthy choices for myself.

"I love that I was not letting my protectionism (the toxic kind) be an enemy of so much that is valuable, beautiful, and incredibly worthy and relevant. I feel brave and strong. This work is changing my life."

~ Martie, Baroque Violin and Viola, Viola d'amore

As demonstrated by Martie, as we gain more experience, our trust in ourselves grows. Through our practice, we learn to support and take care of ourselves better (physically, mentally, emotionally, and spiritually), and we also begin to realize that the world is supporting us, in turn.

We start to embody the reality that we are all interconnected and interdependent, and the more we trust this essential Unity, the more our trust becomes justified.

Here are some varieties of trust to cultivate:

- Trust in All-Possibility, including the possibility that there is much more to who you are as an individual and what the world is than what you are currently able to comprehend. Trust that this "more" may be fundamentally good, positive, expansive, full of joy
- Trust in the human organism's natural capacity to organize our experience, self-regulate and self-coordinate, based on what it deems most advantageous to our survival and our personal desire to thrive
- Trust in the human capacity to self-witness with relative objectivity and to transcend our personal experience by harnessing the power of our imagination
- Trust in each person's ability to take full responsibility for her own well-being, by—given her past experience and personal make-up—making the best possible choices in any given moment
- Trust in your good intentions, regardless of how well or poorly you are able to carry them out; trust in the essentially good nature of all human beings, no matter what it looks like and feels like sometimes
- Trust in the experimental process of learning with curiosity and nonjudgment, and in your ability to change and adapt naturally to new circumstances in healthy ways

Building up your internal reservoir of trust is an essential ingredient for learning and personal transformation.

And yet, I don't recommend making decisions and leading our lives through blind faith; I think a humble, healthy skepticism that is willing to question thoughts and beliefs, and test things out through generous experimentation is necessary to keep us aiming in the direction of our goals.

When I teach my students, I'm aware that they are generally inspired to trust me, but I want to make sure they don't fall into the trap of blind faith (after all, what if a particular suggestion I make is wrong?).

Instead, I keep throwing the ball back in their court, saying, "I'm giving you ideas and suggestions for what you can practice in order to improve, but please don't take my word for it—what if I'm wrong!? Now it's up to you to go home, practice, and find out the truth of what you're actually doing and what actually works for you."

I can say this with a confident smile because from Day 1 of their working with me, I present my students with logical explanations to satisfy their minds; fresh experiences in their bodies that they know they've *created themselves* by thinking in a certain way; and I give them a simple, practical framework for home experimentation. This practice allows their creative spirit to feel inspired and sense that something subtle, joyful, and mysterious is yet to come!

Developing effortless ease with your instrument

As a musician, you know that in order to see improvement over time, you need to practice skills frequently. My mother used to tell me and her cello students that daily musical practice should become as natural and indispensable as brushing our teeth.

Primal Alexander introduces the concept that you need to practice the skill of improving the "use of your Self" (what I call Primary Practice—see Chapter 22) as much as possible throughout the day—whenever you remember—because the quality of your Primary Practice is what ultimately determines the quality of your musical practice, and the results magnify exponentially.

To make Primary Practice easier, Mio Morales introduced his Awareness Etudes, which, as explained earlier, are short, simple movement studies that help us pay attention to what's happening to ourselves as we engage in any activity with ConstructiveThinking, a Primal Alexander skill I defined in Chapter 12. (See Chapter 19 for more specifics about Primal Alexander Awareness Etudes and access the video training to learn your first Etudes here: https://www.artoffreedom.me/book/training.)

What we all want as musicians is a way to play our instruments with natural flow, ease, and effortlessness. We want to be able to achieve this because we've seen how magical it is when a musician plays with such ease that it seems utterly impossible and completely natural at the same time. Such art transports us from the mundane, and we want to tap into that for ourselves! I'll be sharing tips on how to play with effortless ease in Part 3 of this book.

Part 3

How To Make Music With Your Whole Self

In Part 3, I share my thoughts on the process of Inspiration and offer practical suggestions to help you find a better way to practice and perform with your whole self with effortless ease, by systematically applying the fundamentals of The Art of Freedom® Method and Primal Alexander™. I also share some of the common myths about practicing that can sabotage your success.

Dare to Question Your Habits and Experiment!

Let go so the right thing can do itself

We can throw away the habit of a lifetime in a few minutes if we use our brains.

~ *F. M. Alexander*

It's not unusual to watch a great musician play with such ease and grace that you cannot keep yourself from thinking: *Wow! She makes that look so effortless! I wonder how she does that!* The whole audience has that thought.

As musicians, we all want that effortless ease when we're "in the zone" or accessing a "flow state," in which there is a fluid, flexible quality that also transmits a sense of buoyant weightlessness and transparency.

When you play with effortless ease, there is a special, surprising quality that arises from being fully conscious and wholly present within your experience, yet at the same time you're in a sense separate and unidentified with that experience. You are able to overcome any difficulties or extraneous thoughts and rise above what you're doing by directing your mind and physical body to be free of attachment to feelings, desires, or results.

Effortless music-making is natural, free, and conscious. In those moments your creative spirit is allowed to move freely through your whole self, without anything extra (fear, negative thinking, overthinking, muscular tension, anxiety, etc.) getting in the way.

Playing with effortless ease gives you a vivid experience of transcending your earthly heaviness and solidity, in favor of an otherworldly oneness that is paradoxically also completely here and now.

When you are fully present, aware, inspired, and NOT doing the habitual things that are unnecessary and come along with extra tension, you create the space for effortless ease to shine forth.

The best art—full musical expression made with the greatest ease and depth of meaning—delivers this effortless experience. You might think that only the most highly skilled artists can attain this, and that it would take many years to taste it. You might also think it happens by chance, when all conditions are right and you get lucky. This is not the case.

I will never forget the day Teresa, who had come to me frustrated by her slow progress, stepped up to play the cello in my in-person class. Teresa is an avid music lover and was then a devoted beginner amateur cellist. Fascinated by the ideas I shared, she had been diligently practicing at home what I taught.

Quite a few weeks had passed before she brought her cello to class. To this day, I usually leave the actual application of my methods to music-making until after a student has absorbed the fundamental ideas and has been practicing their Awareness Etudes for at least some weeks.

The day Teresa brought her cello to class, I worked with her a bit before she began to play, giving her suggestions for how to quiet her overly critical mind and get her intrusive thoughts out of the way.

Now with a clear mind and relaxed body, Teresa played one long note, and we were all stunned by what we heard. She delivered the note with such absolute perfection that I stopped her right away and exclaimed, "Oh my goodness—that was so beautiful! If I'd had my eyes closed, I might have thought I was listening to Jacqueline du Pré!" (One of the most well-known and exquisite cellists of all time, who tragically died a young death at age forty-two.) Teresa's sound was magnificent: round, full, vibrant, pure—touching each of our hearts deeply.

This experience proved to me that if you are able to get out of the way and direct the mind-body-self well, with ConstructiveThinking, anybody, even a beginner, can play with effortless ease and masterful artistry. I have seen my students play like this many, many times since.

Is there a formula to access effortless ease?

I was once asked if there's a formula to make effortlessness happen, as if on demand, when playing your instrument. Is it possible to consistently access effortless ease?

Well, on the one hand, no, you can't actually make it happen directly, just as you can't command Grace; on the other hand, you CAN create the space and the optimum conditions for it to occur. In fact, under the surface, both ease and Grace are always here, revealed as soon as we get out of the way and open up to All-Possibility.

With the right conditions present, effortless ease is the natural result. And YES, you can access this consistently whenever you want, regardless of your musical skill level, once you understand how.

There IS a way to get there—a formula, a step-by-step system—that, when followed, achieves this. I teach it to all my students. The process, based on The Art of Freedom Method and Primal Alexander, involves learning how to:

- gain a better perspective on how the different aspects of your life influence your music-making, and vice versa, and apply tools to balance those aspects on a daily basis

- get better at self-observation, watching how you fluctuate constantly between states of relatively more overall tension and relatively less

- discern what you are doing that blocks creative flow and impedes natural, effortless movement, free of judgment, as the way we create tension can be extremely subtle, and we need to become more aware of this delicate interference through our intention and practice of this very specific skill

- get to know how you, in particular, in an endless variety of situations, interfere with your ease; then gradually reduce or eliminate the interference with ConstructiveThinking. As described earlier, the Primal Alexander Awareness Etudes are very simple thought-movement studies that offer an excellent framework for practicing this

- practice doing your ConstructiveThinking whenever you remember throughout the day, so that you can bring a more effortless Primary Instrument (YOU) to your musical instrument later

Once you understand how to access effortless ease without the instrument (and learning this is NOT hard—it just requires some knowledge and practice), you can start applying this process to more and more complex activities WITH the instrument. In my coaching programs online, I teach very specific ways to do this, including how you approach, lift, place, and play your instrument, which I call the Instrumental Compass (taught in my Level 2 "Skills Accelerator" course).

We are creatures of habit

To learn faster, you need to do less of what doesn't work and more of what does. That may seem obvious, but do you really know what's working, and what isn't? How do you know what to do more or less of when you practice?

The key to making rapid progress is learning to see your habits with more and more objectivity.

By design, most of our everyday thoughts and actions are habitual, based on neural patterns that we've learned and repeated (practiced) enough times that they have become automated. A 2006 study revealed that for the most part, a full 47 percent of our reported actions are running on autopilot while we're thinking about something else![16]

Clearly, such repetitiveness can lead to a lackluster life limited in scope and creativity, yet, on the other hand, thank goodness for habits! Without them, we wouldn't be able to do much of anything because we'd constantly have to reinvent how we do the most basic activities. Our habits allow us to talk, walk, and relate to the world, and our habits allow us to learn new skills with ever-increasing complexity.

Habits are simply an arrangement of neurons that have fired and wired together into a neural pattern enough times to become strong enough to be automated, running on its own, below the level of our conscious awareness.

Once an activity is a habit, the neural pattern can be triggered by a simple thought or feeling even without our awareness, much like computer programs initiated by other programs. In this way, most of our lives take place on autopilot, moving mindlessly from one thought or activity to the next. In fact, even though this is a human attribute, it is not specifically human since this is how other animals function, as well.

Living this kind of automated human-animal existence might not be a problem . . . if only our specifically human capacity to THINK didn't get in the way, causing the creation of tension-filled automated programs!

Unfortunately, many of our habits of thought and movement were not learned while in a tension-free state of effortless ease, which is why nearly all human beings carry around more tension in our minds and bodies than necessary. Even though it isn't our natural state and we

16 Wendy Wood, Jeffrey M. Quinn, and Deborah A. Kashy, "Habits in Everyday Life," Journal of Personality and Social Psychology 83, no. 6 (2002): 1281–97, https://dornsife.usc.edu/assets/sites/545/docs/Wendy_Wood_Research_Articles/Habits/Wood.Quinn.Kashy.2002_Habits_in_everyday_life.pdf.

don't have to live this way, many of us have learned how to think and move with *more* effort than ease, coming to believe that life is hard—that hard work is required to get ahead and be successful, and pain, effort, and tension are inevitable—sometimes, even desirable!

The good news is . . . even though all of that is true, it's only true when you look at it from a certain perspective. Because what you focus on, you get more of.

The REALLY good news is . . . *"We can throw away the habit of a lifetime in a few minutes if we use our brains."* (F. M. Alexander).[17]

However, learning how to do that consistently requires discipline, and most people don't exactly get excited about self-discipline!

But, what if self-discipline could be easier than what you're used to? What if the only discipline required to effectively change your habits and experience more ease was simply to be curious and shift your attention away from tension—what isn't working. And towards ease—what is.

Can you entertain the possibility that perhaps much of what you've come to believe isn't necessarily the only or best way to look at things, and maybe isn't even true?

I believe this open-minded shift in attention is the key to making good use of Alexander's statement and changing our habits rapidly, with ease.

What if we could literally open up our mind-body-selves to All-Possibility, step into new territory, and allow ourselves to have a completely new experience that is utterly removed from habit, and potentially much better for us in every way?

What if we could learn to think differently, change our priorities and shift our focus, and thereby create a new experience of life for ourselves?

What if we could do this on a large scale—bringing more balance to our life and our world as a whole—and simultaneously bring about changes that improve the most subtle and smallest details of our musical performance?

The Alexander Technique is the practical, problem-solving technique that allows us to step off the beaten path of the familiar and into the wide, promising expanse of the Unknown, with maximum ease.

---

17 F. M. Alexander, Articles and Lectures: Articles, Published Letters and Lectures on the F. M. Alexander Technique, Jean M. O. Fischer (ed.), (London: Mouritz, 1995): 197.

Since you can't know what lies ahead before you get there, this departure from the tried and true can be terrifying. But stepping into the Unknown is necessary if you want to find new, creative ways of doing things that work better for you than what you've been doing up until now.

What's more, the best music always contains an element of mystery and surprise. So . . . can you flip any anxiety you feel into excitement, and get curious about what's possible?

Three big keys to bravely stepping into Unknown territory are curiosity and experimentation, plus a willingness to be wrong.

Alexander said, "Don't come to me until you've first made up your mind to smile when I tell you that you're wrong!" He also wrote, "You all want to know if you're right. When you get further on you will be right, but you won't know it, and you won't want to know if you're right."

Perhaps jazz artists know this best. When, in improvising, they play an unintentional "wrong" note that doesn't fit in with what came before, the best of them can just keep going, picking up the "wrong" note and weaving it into what comes next, transforming what was "wrong" into something "right." Maybe there's no such thing as a mistake when you know how to learn from the past and turn lemons into lemonade!

In order to solve a problem, start by wondering and questioning

I have a very simple practice I teach to my students to help wake up their curiosity and start them looking at things from different perspectives. All you need do in this practice is let your mind ask questions. Begin with "I wonder . . .." or "What if . . . ," and see what your mind comes up with.

But . . . don't answer the questions! We are so conditioned to answering questions when asked, it can be hard to turn off that mental function. I encourage you to do what I call "open asking" instead. Just ask without expecting an answer. Make it a game!

Developing a playful, childlike sense of curiosity is so important as we begin to question the things we've been taught. Which is something that must be done in order to deepen your understanding or go beyond it, no matter how uncomfortable that might be at first!

In order to make a teaching your own, you first need to question it, experiment with it, taste it, and find out whether it works for you or not. And if it doesn't . . . be open to discovering or creating something new and uniquely yours!

Typically, so much practice time is spent doing what we've heard or been told is "right," without taking the initiative to find out if it actually works for us. But not every idea works for everybody! Not only that, but someone else's ideas can actually interfere with your progress if they aren't appropriate for your unique, individual makeup.

In the old days, before video recording and easy travel, people mainly relied on whatever advice they got from their local music teacher, and they had few other examples to inform them of different options. So, if their teacher's advice was good for them, they could progress if they followed the instructions; if the teaching wasn't appropriate, they would eventually either give up or keep trying hard, but without getting great results.

These days, with access to endless teachers, methods, performances, and video tutorials, it's easy for anyone who wants to learn to see that there are many different approaches to playing an instrument, with experts often offering conflicting advice. All it takes is a few minutes down the online rabbit hole, watching a few videos of master musicians play, to see that there are many different ways to approach an instrument and make great music, and there isn't just one "right" way at all.

For example, which is the right way to hold a violin bow? The Galamian style or Russian? Should you use a shoulder rest or not? Chinrest on the side or in the middle, high or low?

You can find many examples of excellent musicians playing with very different techniques, which is proof that there isn't just one right way. For example, just today, a perplexed new student of mine sent me this comment: "I recently had two masterclasses with world-renowned violinist/teachers . . . one told me to have full contact with the violin for security, and that it doesn't matter if the violin looks 'low,' so long as I feel secure and grounded. The other told me that the violin was 'too low,' and I needed to bring everything up." What's a musician to do?

It can be very confusing to receive conflicting advice, especially if an approach isn't actually right for *you*. And if you blindly follow someone else's advice, whether it's a respected teacher or a famous musician sharing tips online, you may end up wasting a lot of time.

Then if you don't get the results you were expecting, you can end up feeling like there's something wrong with you because you can't do what you believe is right, and/or you may end up blaming the teacher. Blame will get you nowhere, however, as it will just increase negative thoughts and energy and prevent you from moving forward with a positive attitude.

Instead, if you start by questioning the common assumption that there is one "right" way to play your instrument, and you open up to the possibility that there might be a better way for you than what other people are telling you or what you've been doing up until now, you will naturally find yourself asking this helpful question: "So, I wonder . . . what's a better way for ME right now?"

You may realize very quickly that you don't actually know the answer—and suddenly there you are, face to face with the Unknown, groping forward into the dark.

I call this space "The Land of I-Don't-Know," or "The Land of All-Possibility" (aka the LAP). This is definitely a very interesting place to be. After all, in the LAP of Mystery, anything is possible!

As this quote from an unknown source discovered by author Stephen R. Covey (often erroneously ascribed to Viktor Frankl) puts so well, "Between stimulus and response there is a space. In that space is our power to choose our response. In our response lies our growth and our freedom." (See Chapter 16 for a definition of Alexandrian inhibition, which further describes how we can make use of this space and power to choose our response.)

How you respond to finding yourself in the LAP will be pivotal, making all the difference to the speed of your progress and the fluency of your learning. You can't go wrong when you're in learning mode. As the star baseball player and manager Yogi Berra put it, "When you get to a fork in the road, take it!"

But how CAN you tell what's right for you?

Ideally, a built-in sensor would let you know instantly if an approach works for your system or not. Is your instrumental setup ergonomically appropriate? Is a particular technique suggested by someone else actually causing harm to your system and blocking your natural sound, or is it improving it?

Guess what? You DO have that internal GPS!

But you probably aren't aware of it; if you are, you probably override your intuitions in favor of a trusted authority, assuming that your GPS is wrong and the expert must be right. We have been taught, after all, to listen to our elders and our teachers, and to please those who would like us to comply.

We have NOT been taught that we have a wise, internal Self-Coordinator that we need to pay attention to, one that is constantly doing whatever it takes to keep us safe.

And because we're not used to listening to this inner GPS, its voice is too often drowned out; then we are less and less sensitive to the little warning signs it gives us all the time when we're going off-course.

What we need is a way to restore—and increase—our sensitivity, so that we can begin to trust it again. In order to do this, we need to be willing to take a good look at ourselves as we are, free of judgment, and find out how we typically do things already. What habits do we have, and what results are we getting?

We need to become our own science experiment, willing to find out what's working and what isn't.

Basically, you have two choices for how to meet the Unknown:

1) react from a place of fear, need, constriction, rejection, judgment, or doubt. This choice causes you to retreat back into the familiar Land of Habits, where you were before you peeked through the doorway into the Unknown;

2) respond from a place of love, openness, curiosity, willingness to learn, acceptance and confidence. Making this choice allows you to embrace new possibilities and have new experiences, from which you can learn and grow.

Daring to question your habitual beliefs, assumptions, and ways of thinking and moving can feel truly terrifying; it means becoming vulnerable, risking making mistakes—possibly even being seen making those mistakes. It means accepting that you are a "perfectly imperfect" human being with your own personal limitations to transcend.

It means, stop pretending you know everything or anything about how things work; let go of the need to understand and to know it all.

After all, do you have to know how your breathing apparatus works in order to breathe? Do you need to know which muscles and cells in your body are moving in order to lift an arm? Do you need to know which parts of your brain are activated in order to think?

When you walk down the street, exactly which muscles and cells and systems are involved to make that happen?

Of course, you don't know! Nobody does!

In the same way, you do not need to know which muscles are involved in singing, conducting, or playing a trill on your instrument. The "how" of any activity is, in fact, a great mystery, involving far more than meets the eye or the intellect.

The good news is, it's not our job to know how; that's the job of our Inner Wisdom, or Inner Coordinator. That mysterious and subtle energetic "life-stuff" within us, which organizes everything within us, enabling us to form an idea and watch ourselves take it into action with only the most minimal understanding of how we're doing it.

Of course, you need to have a basic understanding of how your musical instrument works and how to relate it to your body. But if you have an open attitude of healthy curiosity and you're willing to experiment as you learn, you will be able to discover what works well for you in any given context, even if you barely understand how or why.

How can this be possible, you ask?

Because it simply isn't the job of your thinking mind (your prefrontal cortex) to control your body or to know how your body carries out your intentions.

The job of your thinking mind is to create clear intentions (general and/or specific), and then get out of the way. Trust that the rest of your brain-body-self will coordinate everything in the best possible way in any given moment, to bring you closer to your goal.

Let your Inner Coordinator do it for you!

When confronted with a difficult choice, you can choose to respond differently—NOT habitually. You can let go of the interference and allow your system to go back to its natural effortless way of being/moving. ConstructiveThinking is a positive, ever-fresh way to respond that specifically uses the mind to get the unhelpful thinking mind and concordant overall tension out of the way.

When you are the master of your mind, knowing what to use it for, and then use ConstructiveThinking to get it out of the way, your Inner Coordinator is free to give you what you want, created with ease and grace. Let It work for you!

Here's an example: if you want to improve your tone quality, first, begin with a general idea of what that means for you. Listening to recordings of musicians who create a beautiful tone is just one way to jump-start your imagination, giving you an ideal to aspire to.

If you're a string player, you might know intellectually to hold your bow a certain distance from the bridge and pull it with a certain amount of speed and pressure to create the tone you want. But while you play, you don't want to have to think about those specifics.

Instead, you want your mind to be as quiet as possible or occupied with ConstructiveThinking, so that you are continuously available for fresh, new ideas to come and go as they please. When you are an empty, receptive vessel for Inspiration, your whole mind-body-self is ripe and ready to be spontaneously ignited by music's mysterious creative spark.

Rather than using your mind to micromanage what you're doing while playing (which will kill that mercurial spark, even if you're able to put on a dazzling show of technical wizardry), it's far more useful to direct your attention to incorporating any helpful information about how to play well *before* you play; then, once your intentions are clear, delegate those ideas to the systems beyond your conscious awareness, and trust that your Inner Wisdom or Inner Coordinator truly does know best how to carry them out.

By letting go of your belief that you know what needs to happen and your desire to be in control of the outcome, you give your system a chance to work out an even better way, which involves much less effort and far more freedom. When you get out of the way and allow it, this inspired creative process will surprise you every time.

THIS is what great art is all about. When YOU are surprised by what comes through you, and your audience hangs on your every note, wondering what's going to happen next; and then what happens is as surprising as it is natural—just like the surprising yet natural way snowflakes fall and autumn leaves scatter on the pavement. Like Nature, the best art is seemingly random and unpredictable, yet displays such perfect order that it could be no other way. Experiencing it is profoundly satisfying to the soul and fills the heart with expansive joy.

It is your wise Inner Creator that creates art through you, momentarily transmuting your human nature into a channel for inspired creation. This Inner Creator is fundamentally not other than YOU, and your personal ego needs to surrender the driver's seat for it to take charge and do its thing. This kind of artistic creation has a universal quality that is deeply intimate, yet entirely impersonal. Your job is to get the pride of knowing and the chaos of thinking out of the way to let your whole, integrated Self do what it's designed to do.

Letting go and letting yourself live in the LAP of Mystery—in the gap between stimulus and response—is your most powerful tool to access your innate creative freedom as an artist!

The willingness to take this leap of faith and learn from any mistakes that might happen along the way is what gives you the opportunity to explore new neural pathways that can lead to far more efficient ways of using your brain and body than the ways any other teacher could ever dictate to you.

Thankfully, even though it can seem easier to fall back into The Land of Habits and keep doing what FEELS safe, known, and right, simply because it's familiar (since you've been living there most of your life), you are never condemned to remain in that place of relative stagnation, accumulating rigidity and living a slow death by stress.

Even if you find yourself reacting to not-knowing in a way that causes you to shrink back towards the familiar and secure, based on information from outside (from a trusted teacher, parent, or famous artist who is convinced that their way is the best way, for example), in any given moment you can always make a fresh choice.

Asking, "What is right for me? What works best for me today?" with sincere curiosity, humility, patience, and faith, is an essential attitude that will carry you along a quicker, easier road to discovering your own unique way of making music with masterful artistry. In the next chapter, we'll look at some more ways you can set yourself up for success by ensuring a productive practice session every single time.

"So many look at music as endless 'have to's': Stand like this. Hold your instrument like that. Do you know all your scales and chords? Can you cite from volumes of music theory?

"I get all that. I really do. We all try to continue to master our instrument. And, yes, a lot of that depends on having some idea of what you're doing. But that's all a very slippery slope . . . and none of it is what I consider 'making music.'

"I could boil Jennifer's classes down to a single sentence: "That's interesting, but what if . . . ??" The possibilities are endless! Each moment of awareness opening the door to something new I might never have thought of.

"All of the 'have to's' might get one to the center stage spotlight . . . but it's being confident enough to risk the *what-ifs* that's going to make it *magical*. Isn't that why we all picked up an instrument to begin with? The magic . . . the joy of making use of that magic . . . and the freedom and confidence to explore those *what-ifs*.

"Music is much more about not being afraid to bare my soul . . . in the hopes that the listener understands something I might never be able to put into words . . . in the hopes that I touch them somehow . . . leave a part of myself they may never forget . . . and, in the process, feel the joy of knowing I made a difference. I got a LOT more out of Jennifer's program than I ever could have anticipated!"

~ Jim, Flute

Get Balanced and in Tune with Your Self!

How to have a successful practice session every time

Happiness is not a matter of intensity but of balance and order and rhythm and harmony.

~ *Thomas Merton*

Did you ever fall "out of tune" with yourself, becoming disconnected from the Source of your creativity, unaware of the subtle, quiet teachings of your wise Inner Teacher? This easily happens when you aren't caring for your whole self with daily dedication.

When we forget our heart's desire to connect and create from a sense of wholeness, it's hard to remember to focus on what matters most, and our lives will become misaligned and lack harmony. For example . . .

- Maybe your love life is great, but you're skipping practice sessions, neglecting preparation for your upcoming concert or audition, and the quality of your musical performance is slipping.

- Maybe you're learning new repertoire at breakneck speed, your technique keeps improving, and you're getting some really great gigs . . . at the expense of your partner or family life; or . . .

- Maybe you're managing to juggle all of your responsibilities—teaching, performing, exercise, nutrition, family, etc.—but you're left feeling stressed and secretly worried about pains in your body that just won't go away.

If you don't get "in tune" with your whole Self before you even pick up your violin or sit down at the piano, then it should be no wonder when things aren't as easy or consistent as they could be when you're with your instrument.

An obvious place to begin "tuning" yourself is to make sure you're taking care of your basic self-care needs. It's hard to think well if you're malnourished, dehydrated, or pushing yourself beyond fatigue! (On the Bonus Materials page you can pick up a Self-Care Checklist I created to help you with this: https://www.artoffreedom.me/book/bonusmaterials.)

Mark is a well-known pianist with a demanding year-round concertizing schedule; he holds faculty positions at several of the world's most prestigious music conservatories. When Mark came to me for private coaching, he was running on empty—with his days off typically spent flying back and forth between the schools where he taught—often learning music from a score on the plane. Or frantically squeezing in a little practice time with a piano, cramming for his next performance, sometimes with little more than a few hours to rehearse.

This air-tight schedule led to quite a lot of performances that were largely unsatisfying for him, despite the rave reviews and delighted audiences, because he knew privately that he wasn't fully tapping into his rich artistic potential.

Even though he always felt pushed, strapped for time, Mark still loved performing and teaching his students, and yet, the constant grind had been going on relentlessly for years, partly because, due to circumstances beyond his control, he felt a strong need for the paychecks.

Mark hadn't been able to bring full-bodied joy to his playing for a long time. He knew with his whole being that something needed to change. Not only that, but he was feeling more and more tension creep into his playing, experiencing pain more frequently, and frustrated daily by limitations in his technique that he believed were caused by poor posture that he felt incapable of correcting on his own.

One of the first things I do with a new coaching client is to ask about the other areas of their life, including rest, recreation, and basic self-care. In Mark's case, it was clear there was a need for change in several areas unrelated directly to music, but which—when addressed—could go a long way to bringing balance into his life. He was more than willing to look at his diet, spend time in Nature, and exercise more, and make some minor tweaks to his schedule to give him a little extra time in between appointments to slow down a bit.

Next, I introduced Mark to the five pillars of The Art of Freedom Method and gave him a taste of the Primal Alexander Awareness Etudes beyond TheCyCle, which he had previously learned from a video and had been practicing for about a year already.

Within just a couple of short weeks working together, Mark declared that he had just had *the most free and enjoyable performance of his life*.

Once Mark was able to find more balance in his daily life, we took a look at how he was thinking about each of his obligations and the specifics of his method of practicing his instrument. As we went along, we uncovered quite a few under-the-surface tension-creating habits, including some long-standing people-pleasing tendencies, erroneous beliefs about posture, and an overly careful approach to producing sound that caused him to hunch over his instrument, impeded his tone production, and limited his technical facility.

After a few more months of attending to his Self-Use and following the practical suggestions I gave him, Mark was astounded to recognize how much easier it was to play. His posture had improved noticeably without even trying and the quality of his performance was climbing to new heights, as reflected in his sound and musicianship. In fact, everything had gotten easier. More than ever, Mark was enjoying his life.

Balancing with the Five Pillars of The Art of Freedom® Method

So, how can YOU bring the different areas of your life into better balance and also develop your artistry with ease and joy?

As I did with Mark, I recommend that you begin by taking a broad look at your life as a whole, see where things are out of alignment, and make sure not to neglect basic self-care. Once you've begun addressing the basics, it will be easier to go deeper into balancing the more subtle aspects of your mind-body-self, aligning these with your daily activities and musical practice.

I've found that remembering the five Life-Pillars of The Art of Freedom Method on a regular basis, letting them inform your day and practice sessions, can be a smart place to start. As a reminder, the Life-Pillars are Purpose, Mind, Body, Spirit, and Artistry.

By consciously attending to your Purpose—your "Why"—and including in your awareness your basic bodily needs, your mental and emotional attitude, and your creative spirit, you can automatically feel more integrated and bring more balance into your day.

I often suggest to my students to spend a bit of time developing a "Life Mission Statement" (LMS): a general, guiding sense of purpose to serve as an anchor to your life. Having a general idea of what you want your life to be about doesn't need to be complicated, and your LMS doesn't have to be set in stone. If you don't have any idea what your LMS is, you can let it be as simple as a word that indicates something you value beyond a doubt. For example, the word "Love" is a perfectly valid LMS!

When you have an LMS, you can refer back to it whenever you're hesitant about making a decision. When faced with a difficult choice, ask yourself, "Is this in alignment with my LMS?"

Often, you'll find that more than one option will be in alignment with your LMS, in which case it doesn't matter so much which option you choose and you just need to pay more attention to how you're going about whatever it is you decide. Getting better and quicker at making decisions is a great way to make your life easier, and to instantly bring yourself into better balance.

Of course, finding balance is an ideal to aim towards, not something to achieve, grasp, or hold onto. Balance is not static; it is lively, ever-changing!

Balance is an equilibrium that includes all parts of a whole, which play and vibrate together as if dancing around a constantly reliable and always accessible center.

Actually, it may be more useful to speak about the process of "balancing," rather than aiming to arrive at a state of "balance." Here are a couple of examples of balancing in practice:

- Think of a clown balancing a plate at the tip of a long stick; the clown, stick, and plate all need to be in constant motion for the plate to keep spinning, balancing up there.
- Or think of ten Chinese acrobats, each balancing atop the shoulders of the acrobat beneath him, forming a tower. In order to continue balancing, they all need to be flexible, in constant movement. The first time I saw this act and noticed how much they were swaying, especially the man at the bottom, I feared they would all come toppling down, until I realized that their constant movement around a central vertical axis was what was holding them all up!

As Rumi so eloquently writes (in *The Essential Rumi*, translated by Coleman Barks):

> Your hand opens and closes, opens and closes. If it were always a fist or always stretched open, you would be paralysed. Your deepest presence is in every small contracting and expanding, the two as beautifully balanced and coordinated as birds' wings.

In The Art of Freedom, the play of balancing begins every time we reorganize ourselves by remembering the Five Pillars. These pillars serve as a unifying reminder of what's most important whenever we apply our primary instrument (the whole self) to the process of artistic mastery—with or without our secondary, musical instrument.

We step into this balancing process whenever we wake up our purpose with clear intention in the mind, coupled with desire in the heart, energized by our creative spirit, embraced and expressed through the body.

Making this balancing process part of your consciousness and bringing it into your everyday life as a new habit requires regular practice. In case you missed it towards the beginning of the book, you can download a Personal Life-Balance Assessment Tool from the Bonus Materials page: https://www.artoffreedom.me/book/bonusmaterials.

Creating new habits

As a musician, you know that repetition—practice—is essential for you to get better at anything.

This is because, as previously mentioned, the neurons in your brain fire and wire together in a particular way every time you think a certain thought or perform a certain action. Whenever you repeat a new arrangement of neurons firing and wiring together, you build on that connection and make it stronger. As the new pathway grows, it gradually becomes the preferred path for your brain to travel along the next time you want to perform that activity.

This is how we create, how we learn, and how habits are built.

The problem is, when we first attempt to think differently or do something new, our habit is drawn like a magnet down an older, proven pathway, which has successfully kept us alive and carried us towards the things we want, with at least some degree of satisfaction.

To change how we do things, we first need to stop our brain from traveling down the well-worn pathway of habit (in Alexander jargon, we call this *inhibition*)[18] and make a fresh, conscious decision to move along a new neural pathway (we call this *direction*), a path that is weak because it previously didn't exist.

Let's take a closer look at these two terms, which are used somewhat differently in Alexander parlance than in everyday language.

Two fundamental principles of the Alexander Technique

Inhibition

In the Alexander Technique, inhibition is more a physiological term than psychological (it's not the same thing as Freudian inhibition, which indicates a hesitation to act—something entirely different).

18 "INHIBITION": In the Alexander Technique, we use this term in the sense of physiology, not psychology (don't think of Freudian inhibitions in the sense of hesitation to act—that's something completely different).
To "inhibit," or "practice inhibition," is to actively stop the brain from firing neurons in a habitual sequence. That pause creates a space in which there is a split second of time to make a conscious decision that is new and unfamiliar.
We humans inhibit all the time, but we aren't aware of it. (That's why we don't immediately act on every random impulse we have.) The Alexander Technique teaches us to practice CONSCIOUS inhibition, on command.

To practice Alexandrian inhibition—to inhibit—is to actively stop the brain from taking an idea all the way from abstract idea into manifestation by preventing the firing of a neuron or neurons in a sequence. Inhibition allows us to "change our minds" or "change a habit" by redirecting the energy of a thought elsewhere, away from the habit. Inhibiting a thought/action introduces a momentary pause—a moment that opens up a bit more space in the brain to allow for a more conscious, new decision to arise.

We humans inhibit all the time, but we normally aren't aware of it. (That's why we don't immediately act on every random impulse we have.) The Alexander Technique teaches us to practice CONSCIOUS inhibition, on command. This is an essential skill for life, and also for music; it's what allows you to quiet your inner critic, fearful and negative thoughts, and it's what allows your finger to reach just a little bit higher than usual in order to finally play that note in tune!

Direction

The word "direction" in the Alexander Technique has several shades of meaning that overlap:

1) Sequential: You can give yourself a "direction" by thinking a specific thought that links to other thoughts, as in having a series of steps to follow. These thought-directions link together in a particular order to take you towards a particular goal, as when following a recipe or a map. You can give yourself a direction to move your arm or a direction to prevent your arm from moving, for instance.

2) Spatial: You can think about spatial "directions": up, down, left, right, forward, back, inward, outward, etc. The awareness you have of different directions in space influences the state of your body in relation to space as a whole. For instance, thinking only about the space in front of you (for example, when you are concentrating hard and overfocusing on the music in front of you) may cause your whole body to push towards it or pull back away from it. In both cases, the imbalanced spatial direction of your attention literally throws your physical body slightly off balance and increases overall tension as your reflexes kick in and your muscles work harder to keep you from falling over.

3) Energetic: You can "direct" your attention, and your whole mind-body-self as a result. There is an energetic component to this activity—a flow of energy that moves through you and through space in tandem with your awareness. As is commonly said in personal development and yoga circles, "Where your attention goes, energy flows." When you

practice the Primal Alexander Awareness Etudes, you become more sensitive to this energetic flow, or "easing," and more skilled at allowing the flow to go naturally where it needs to, in alignment with your purpose.

Two sides of the same coin

The combined application of inhibition and direction to our Primary Instrument (the Self) while making music is what allows us to access effortless ease and enjoy real artistic mastery.

In the Alexander Technique, inhibition and direction go hand in hand—you can't have one without the other. To keep things simple, I normally just use the word "inhibition" to indicate that both inhibition and direction are happening simultaneously.

Through the "non-doing" volitional act of inhibition, you let go of excess overall tension and a global, expansive easing up and out (aka direction) happens naturally. You can't "DO" direction—you ALLOW it. You could even say that direction "does itself."

To inhibit consciously, you need the intention—i.e., to give yourself the direction—to inhibit. In Primal Alexander, we do this by employing ConstructiveThinking, with or without words.

When you do your ConstructiveThinking, you watch in wonder as the ease begins to flow more freely, allowing the natural ebb and flow of healthy expansion-contraction to occur throughout your system. Sometimes it's a very subtle movement that you may not notice at all, but it always happens because we are designed this way. This is the natural flow that allows inspired artistry to happen through you.

Humans are designed to be upright

We are beautifully designed to be upright creatures, always balancing around a vertical reference!

When we consider the balanced design of the upright human body, we see that our weight is made to fall through our bones around a vertical axis. When we dare to let go of our habitual mind-body holding and egoic posturing, releasing habitual thoughts and their corresponding muscular tightenings, we can let ourselves free-fall straight down around that vertical axis, and the ground sends us right back up, restoring us to our rightful space and stature.

Our vertical axis aims simultaneously both down and up, our lives hanging in the balance, supported by both gravity and levity. Both are equally important; again, we can't have one without the other.

Not only are we designed to be physically upright, but in principle we are also spiritually upright. We need to let our egos fall humbly down, bowing to meet the earth, while at the same time our spirits soar up to the heavens above! Anything else results in a false pride or false humility. Too much "down" brings on heavy depression; too much "up" makes us haughty and "stuck up"!

When you let go of your habitual need to feel in control, things may feel confused or wrong at first. But with practice you come to trust that the body has a "righting" reflex that automatically—and quite literally—aids you in "standing your ground." This true groundedness (something much more subtle than what is commonly attempted by feeling your feet on the ground) affects your psychological well-being, too, as it becomes easier to stick to your convictions and speak your truth, as the woman did in the European masterclass I wrote about in Chapter 14.

Practicing conscious inhibition and direction gives us a natural path towards more fully embodying who we are as upright people—in mind, body, and spirit.

Gravity and levity work through every cell of our body

Have you ever seen a cat fall and land on its feet? I saw that happen with my own toddler once long ago, when he fell off the couch and landed upright. Amazing! Like other animals, we humans have a built-in "righting reflex" that helps us balance and brings us into right relationship with the ground from moment to moment—as long as we don't interfere with it.

This "righting reflex" knows how to organize our system around gravity; in a very real sense, our whole system knows where down is and where up is. In the same way, every bit of us has a sense of inward and outward directions, just as we can sense the difference between lightness and darkness. Everything around us and within us oscillates between opposites, falling into place and vibrating in harmony with all other things—as long as the natural design is respected.

When we get out of the way and let our "righting reflex" do its thing, we have a healthy, balanced sense of space and it's easier to know where we belong. When we feel at ease where we are, the music we make can then vibrate freely through our bones and energize our souls with a resonance that uplifts us and the world.

Inhibition-direction is natural. All we need to do is remember and respect our natural design and take up our rightful place, here between heaven and earth.

Moving from the Known to the Unknown

To better understand the skill of inhibition-direction and how it's the key skill that allows us to successfully change a habit, imagine you're trying to get from one end of a tropical jungle to another. It's oppressively hot, and you're highly motivated to take a cool, peaceful swim in the lake on the other side. You've been there many times, and you don't even think about how you'll get there . . . you just walk along the same path every day without a care in the world. A few hours of pleasant hiking later, daydreaming and fending off mosquitos, you're there. That's how an automated habit works.

One day, you bring along a friend. Your friend is surprised by how much the path curves and winds around to reach the lake. He suggests that you create a new, straighter path through the jungle to save yourself a huge amount of time and energy.

That makes sense to you, and you decide that you're willing to put in the time and experience a bit of hardship now so that you can enjoy using the easier path later.

The next day, you take your machete into the jungle, and start hacking away at the tangled vines and thick bamboo. As you do this, you gradually become aware of the poisonous undergrowth, snakes, and other harmful creatures you'd never noticed before. It's scary. It feels wrong, and you don't have the stamina to work on it for very long. Pretty soon, you put down the machete and go back to the well-worn path, ready for the cool reward of your swim in the lake.

The next day, you remember your long-term project, and get back to work on the new path. Again, you give up after a while and go back to the old path. It's so much EASIER to do it the old way—besides, it feels familiar, safer.

If you don't have a strong, compelling reason to get to the lake faster, you'll quit the project before long. If you do have a strong motivator, you'll be persistent and keep working on it so that, over time, you'll have a path that is obviously much better than the old one. All the time and effort will be worth it.

Once you've cleared the new path, you'll only use the old path occasionally, when you're distracted and suddenly realize that your feet have mindlessly taken you down the former path. But the more you consciously choose to travel the new path, the less that happens, and the more jungle plants grow and overtake the old path, which will soon cease to exist from lack of use.

This is how we change our major everyday life-habits as well as the stubborn little habits of our instrumental technique.

Establishing new routines

The hardest thing about adding something new into your life is remembering to do it! The second-hardest thing is to keep the new thing simple, interesting, and easy enough for you to feel successful when you do it, so that you're more likely to want to repeat it.

As James Clear writes in his # 1 *New York Times* bestseller, *Atomic Habits*, "The truth is, a habit must be established before it can be improved. If you can't learn the basic skill of showing up, then you have little hope of mastering the finer details. Instead of trying to engineer a perfect habit from the start, do the easy thing on a more consistent basis."[19]

An easy way to help you remember is to tack healthy new routines onto your already-established routines and use outer reminders to jog your memory. Here are a few ways to use external reminders:

- Choose a daily activity you already do automatically that you can use as an anchor, so you can link the new habit to it (for example, turning on your bedside light, brushing your teeth, opening the refrigerator, getting a coffee mug from the cupboard).
- Put a sign or sticky note in an obvious place associated with the established habit (on the lamp, the bathroom mirror, refrigerator door, coffee mug) to remind yourself of the new habit you want to create.
- Use phone reminders to jog your memory at the same time every day.
- Write your intention on a piece of paper and put it on your pillow so that you can program your brain at night to remember what you want when you wake up.
- Ask a friend or loved one, or a group of like-spirited people, to help keep you accountable. My group membership program offers a very powerful, supportive environment for my students to help one another with this, for example.

Now that you have some ideas for how to begin establishing a new habit, let's look at a powerful little routine that can help you with balancing and self-integration, by bringing the 5 Life-Pillars into your daily awareness at the beginning of your day and before you practice your instrument.

---

19 James Clear, Atomic Habits: An Easy & Proven Way to Build Good Habits & Break Bad Ones (Random House), 2018: 163–164.

The "Golden Period"

My first Alexander Technique teacher, Erik Bendix, didn't talk much in our lessons, but when he did, his words often made me stop, think, and wonder. Sometimes, it sounded like he was uttering a Zen koan (a koan is a paradoxical phrase or riddle, used in Zen Buddhism to demonstrate the inadequacy of logical reasoning and to provoke enlightenment).

At one point, Erik told me, "It will be easier to stop once you've started, if you stop before you start." Huh?!??

It took me a long time to unravel that idea, which has become a cornerstone of my own teaching. In fact, what he was saying was that it's easier to be conscious and aware of what you're doing while you're engaged in an activity (like playing the violin) if you take a moment to become conscious and aware *before you begin.*

In Alexander jargon, you could say, "It will be easier to inhibit (stop firing neurons in a habitual sequence that creates excess tension, for example), once you've already started moving, if you inhibit before you start."

I've come to really appreciate the time before the beginning of an activity as the magical time when, tapping into the vast power of the mind, we can create what we want to experience next.

I call this before-time the "Golden Period."

There are infinite Golden Periods within every twenty-four-hour day; in fact, every moment we become conscious is a Golden Period. Depending on how we divide time, a Golden Period can be an infinitesimal flash of a semi-second before placing a finger on a string; or it can be the weeks or months leading up to a performance.

Mostly, when I speak about the Golden Period to my students, I'm referring to the minutes we have with our instrument before actually producing sound. But right now, I'd like to talk about the Golden Period we can have in the morning, right after we wake up and before we spring into the activities of our day.

When uninterrupted (by an alarm clock, for example) this special gap between sleep and action is truly special—a time when your brain is still in a slower brainwave state, one that's optimal for learning and creating. This is a great time to be balancing yourself, by reminding yourself how you want to be, act, and feel throughout the day that's about to begin.

I've created a little routine to bring the 5 Pillars of The Art of Freedom into conscious awareness at this time (or any time), which I call the "5 Pre-Pearls" of The Art of Freedom.

The "5 Pre-Pearls"

You can use these Pre-Pearls before getting up, before starting work, before going outside, before practicing, before performing . . . or whenever else you'd like to bring more balance and self-integration to an activity.

There are so many ways you can use these! You can touch on each of the Pre-Pearls for just a few seconds at a time, or you can turn this into a longer, more substantive journaling practice. Feel free to experiment and find what works best for you, what speaks to your soul, and what is practically useful, depending on the context you're applying them to.

The 5 Pre-Pearls:

1. Purpose
2. Wonder
3. Shadow
4. Light
5. Self-Integration

Let's look at each of these in a bit more detail and see how they relate to the 5 Pillars of The Art of Freedom Method (Purpose, Mind, Body, Spirit, and Artistry):

1. Purpose / Desires / Goals

Ask yourself, "What is my Primary Concern?" (see Chapter 13) "Why am I doing this?" "What do I really want?" "What is my goal right now?"*

F. M. Alexander said, "You need to start with the mental attitude." This is the reason for these Pre-Pearls, and why we begin with the Primary Concern, which reminds us to wonder, *"What is happening to me right now, as I ______?"*

It's so important to give yourself a moment to get in touch with your experience in the moment, and to notice how your experience is connected to your heart's desires.

Remembering your purpose is a powerful motivator, and making sure your actions align with your purpose is the key to feeling good about whatever it is you're setting out to do—whether the results are ultimately successful or not.

When you ask yourself, “Why?” or “What do I want?” your answer could be a big, overarching life-mission statement, or a miniscule goal for your practice session . . . or any number of different kinds of goals.

If your answer is “I don’t know,” that’s perfectly fine, too. There isn’t a right way to do this. The important thing is to be open to All-Possibility.

Examples:

- My purpose today is to explore being my authentic Self when I practice.
- My purpose is to enjoy my day with loving-kindness, without rushing around.
- My goals today are to practice for one hour, buy shoes, call my parents, take a walk.
- My practice goals are to work on scales and that passage on the third page of the Bach.
- I don’t know what my purpose is. But I’m open to discovering what’s possible.

2. Wonder / Healthy Curiosity / Childlike “Open-Asking”

Ask yourself: “I wonder . . .” and wake up your curiosity.

The best thing about each of the 5 Pre-Pearls is that you get to ask questions and wonder about things, without needing to know the answers.

Can you step into “The Land of I-Don’t-Know”—the LAP (Land of All-Possibility, as introduced in Chapter 15) and enjoy the empty spaciousness, freedom, and unlimited potential that comes from unknowing?

Tommy Thompson, a wonderful Alexander Technique teacher, healer, and friend, calls it “withholding definition.” Can you inhibit the age-old habit of defining things with past definitions because you think and assume you know them already?

Can you appreciate a question, an object, or a person, and see them as if for the first time? What kinds of hidden surprises might you discover within if you approach them with wonder and fresh, childlike eyes?

What if you could approach an instrumental exercise, a scale, or a piece you’ve played a thousand times as if you were a beginner and you didn’t know what it was “supposed to” sound like?

Can you ask a question and let it go, letting it float up and away from you into the sky?

The most important thing is to give yourself the time and space for unexpected answers to show up in their own good time, without pushing or forcing, without trying to get an answer or figure things out.

An answer might show up instantly while you're practicing the 5 Pre-Pearls, or it might take days or years to show up . . . or never. Let go of the need to define your experience and know.

Our job is simply to ask and wonder, tapping into the natural awe we all experienced as little children. I sometimes call this Pre-Pearl the "I wonder" practice, or "Stepping into The Land of I-Don't-Know."

Examples:

- I wonder why I have such difficulty relating to Sarah when she's upset.
- I wonder why I still can't play that octave section in my concerto.
- I wonder why people go to war and kill each other.
- I wonder why I keep forgetting to take out the trash on Wednesdays.
- I wonder why people and animals have to sleep at night.

3. Shadow / Fear / Doubts

Ask yourself: "What am I afraid of?" "What am I worried about?" "What doesn't feel good right now?"

It's normal and natural to experience fear, doubt, and unpleasant or "negative" emotions from time to time. In fact, if you never experience any of these, that could be a strong indicator that you're not allowing yourself to feel the full range of human emotion.

If that's the case, you're also not allowing yourself to express the full range of *musical* emotion. If you want to excel as an artist, you need to be able to tap into any and every emotion that a composition may demand of you.

This Pre-Pearl is a way to gently expose the darker aspects of the human soul to the light of your conscious awareness; and in so doing, let those negative emotions breathe a little and dissipate over time.

I like to playfully call these thoughts "the Doubt Monsters," and I often help my students meet and dismiss them with ease. You don't need to understand why you have these Doubt Monsters, where they came from, what they mean, or what they're doing inside of you. You also don't need to know how to get rid of them.

For now, simply be aware that they're there, bring them up to the surface, and give them a little nod so that those parts of you know they are included, too. This is actually a profound way to practice Unconditional Love of yourself because those Doubt Monsters are actually part of you: they are neurons firing into thoughts in your brain, causing feeling-effects in your body.

However, these thought-feelings aren't particularly helpful. So, even though they need to be acknowledged, don't spend too much time on this. If you know how to do ConstructiveThinking, you can simply notice your reactions, do some CT, and move on.

Just as we do with the "I wonder" practice, notice the emotion and let it go. Literally give it UP: imagine that you're letting the Doubt Monster float up and out of you, and then move on to the next Pre-Pearl.

If the emotion is heavy and doesn't want to leave, that's perfectly fine. No problem. Don't judge it or try to fix or change it; don't identify with it. Just remove your attention from it and move on. If you can't do that, that's OK. Just move on.

If you have a lot of doubts and fears come up in response to this Pre-Pearl, don't worry. Don't be afraid of your shadow! Rather than running away and skipping this step, just spend a few moments naming your fears and noting their presence. Even a few seconds is plenty unless you want to inquire a little deeper.

If you want to spend more time on this step, you might like to set a timer and do some limited stream-of-consciousness journaling. Just write down whatever comes up for a few minutes. Then, no matter where you are in the process, move on.

Avoiding this step, fighting this step, or dwelling on it is usually not helpful because you just end up feeding the negativity, keeping it stuck under the surface. Since stuck emotions always translate into tension, which blocks healing energy, freedom, and creative flow, this step is an important part of the process of self-mastery and artistic mastery.

Experiment with this step and find what works best for you. There isn't a right way to do it.

Examples:

- I'm afraid of pain.
- I hate conflict!
- I really don't like when he does that. I feel bad, frustrated, and sad about it.
- I hate that I can't play those chords in tune yet, even after three months of practicing!
- I'm worried about my upcoming performance.
- What if I don't get that job? What if I can't pay my bills? What if I have to move?
- I'll never be good enough!

4. Light / Easy Affirmations

Ask yourself: "What's the opposite side of this Doubt Monster?" "What do I want to believe, instead?" "What are my Angels of Ease today?"

The Greek philosopher Heraclitus "asserted that the world exists as a coherent system in which a change in one direction is ultimately balanced by a corresponding change in another" ("Heraclitus," Encyclopedia Britannica).

Just as one coin has two opposing sides, whenever you experience a negative emotion ("Doubt Monster"), there is at least one corresponding positive affirmation on the flip side to balance it (I like to playfully call these "Angels of Ease").

Can you think of three Angels of Ease that you'd like to remember as you embark on your day or the activity you'll be engaging in after your Golden Period? These can simply be positive words to guide you, or direct opposites of what came up when you touched on your shadow.

You might like to write your Angels of Ease on a notecard to carry with you, or a sticky note to attach to your music stand, so as you practice you'll be constantly reminded of the positive ideas you want to embrace.

As with the shadow practice, you can keep this short and sweet. Unlike the shadow practice, though, you can dwell on these ideas as long as you like. These thoughts are like purifying medicine for the soul, whereas the Doubt Monsters are more like insidious poison.

Examples:

- The "3 Magic Phrases": I am free; I don't have to do anything; I have time and space (see the next chapter for more on the "3 Magic Phrases").
- I love life!
- Pain is my friend; my response to pain makes me stronger (see Chapter 5 on pain).
- I'm so grateful I can feel!
- I can handle conflict, rise above it, and find peace within myself.
- I am free to be who I am; he is free to be who he is.
- My chords are slowly improving; the more I practice, the more I learn.
- I'm excited about my upcoming performance!
- What if I get that job? I love that I might get that job!
- Great and unexpectedly wonderful things are possible for me!
- I love myself and I'm good enough for me right now.

The constructive use of positive affirmations is endless. I recommend to my coaching clients that they make the time to identify their personal "Doubt Monsters" and corresponding "Angels of Ease," and keep a running list of them to refer to frequently.

You can also record yourself speaking these affirmations and listen to them at important times, such as before you go to sleep, upon waking, and before a performance, to strengthen the neural pathways that will help you think this way. I share a very specific way to do this using ConstructiveThinking with my private coaching clients to get the most benefit from the practice.

Thinking positively has been shown to relieve stress and anxiety, as well as improve overall health and increase happiness. You have nothing to lose by making time for this step, and everything to gain!

5. Self-Integration

Even if you skip every other Pre-Pearl in your Golden Period, THIS Pre-Pearl is the absolutely indispensable step to include before you play your instrument—every time.

This Pre-Pearl reminds you to actively practice self-integration, bringing conscious awareness to your mind, body, emotions, and creative spirit—all at once. This is the time to practice embodied contemplation/meditation/prayer and/or do some ConstructiveThinking, along with TheCyCle or a series of Primal Alexander Awareness Etudes. I'll be sharing more about how to practice ConstructiveThinking and TheCyCle in Chapter 20.

Like every other Pre-Pearl, you can practice Self-Integration for just a few seconds or much longer. When my students begin studying with me, they are required to practice just a couple Awareness Etudes for less than five minutes, twice a day. These Etudes are so powerful that by doing them consistently every day, my students are guaranteed to improve: they start to let go of tension, their stress is relieved, their pain reduces, their anxiety softens, their musical technique gets easier, and their creativity flows.

When you make the most of your Golden Period by bringing the 5 Pre-Pearls into your everyday life and especially by doing your ConstructiveThinking before you play your instrument, everything you do afterwards is easier. Guaranteed.

This is because the Golden Period sets the stage for creative Inspiration to flow through you to make music with effortless ease.

To help you remember to make the most of your pre-practice Golden Period and the 5 Pre-Pearls, I've created a "Keys to Successful Practice" cheat sheet that you can download and print out to keep in your practice studio or instrument case. Access your Bonus Materials here: https://artoffreedom.me/book/bonusmaterials.

In the next chapter, I'll share my vision on the mechanics of Inspiration and how to consistently tap into this flow for ease of expression, technical facility with your instrument, and a full-bodied feeling of joy and success.

> "When I first went to Jennifer for lessons, it was mainly due to the pain I had in my back when I would practice my violin for long periods of time. I feel like I came with one problem I knew I had, but in the process of our lessons I fixed problems I didn't even know I had, and now everything feels better. I feel better physically when I play but also emotionally and spiritually. I have a greater sense of freedom and confidence, and I've also learned some awesome practice techniques.
>
> My work with Jennifer has gone so far beyond a musical standpoint, it has influenced every part of my life in a positive way. I've learned how to relax when I play, but it has carried over to every activity I do, and now everything feels better. What I love most is that every session with Jennifer is different and inspiring. I feel like I always leave on a cliff hanger—and can't wait to come back!"
>
> ~ Rachel, Violinist and Educator

You are Made for Creative Expression and Success

Stop interfering with your natural design and enjoy inspired flow

One who sees inaction in action, and action in inaction, is intelligent among men.

~ *Bhagavad Gita*

People have long believed that the creative process happens when a person is inspired by a higher power moving through the artist from beyond. That higher power could be a God or Goddess, an angel, or some kind of supernatural "Muse" or "'Genius" spirit who would either transmit lofty ideas to the artist or completely possess the artist by entering the artist's body, taking over their mind and emotions during the process of creation.

This concept is not unique to ancient times; versions of these ideas are still accepted as truth in many cultures around the world, including our modern-day Western world. In fact, you don't even have to believe in a higher power to be influenced by it.

A comparable modern-day version of this concept is common in the world of classical music, when classical musicians imagine they are channeling a composer's wishes and intentions, even when the composer has long since passed away. There is a kind of reverence for the composer, almost as if his disembodied and timeless spirit were watching from above, ready to react and judge the performance according to how faithful it is to the composer's desires. There can even be an indignant sense of betrayal or fear when a composer's instructions and apparent wishes, or the common style of the day, are ignored or flagrantly contradicted.

Whether you believe in the process of artistic creation as an inspired, supernatural process involving a higher power or not doesn't really matter. Because if you have the right understanding and attitude to be able to tap into the way the mind, body, and emotions are naturally designed to function when manifesting an idea into sound, you can learn how to make great art with spirited and effortless ease, regardless of what you believe is the source of that creation.

Personally, I like to think of great music-making as being inspired by the creative spirit or life-force within us, which I consider indistinct from the creative life-force that exists outside of us and within everything everywhere all around us. (As mentioned in the introduction, feel free to substitute whatever word you prefer to use for the source of creation if the word "spirit" doesn't resonate with you.)

The process of creative musical Inspiration

When you think of making music as a creative process comprising a sequence of events, it may look something like this:

1) A subtle idea exists somewhere within and/or around you.

2) There's a moment in which your being becomes aware of this idea—as if you were a radio receiver picking up wave signals from the air—and it becomes a part of your psychophysical, material reality. In the moment that the idea enters your mind, it becomes a thought, or a series of physical neurons arranged in a unique pattern, firing and wiring together within your brain.

3) If you have the intention to manifest that thought into sound, turning it into an audible idea, you allow that thought to continue traveling through your nervous system without interrupting it. Your nervous system carries messages from your brain to stimulate the appropriate cells and organic systems within your body that will allow your muscles to contract and release in an organized, coordinated way that moves the appropriate bones and body parts to play your musical instrument.

4) Your ideas are turned into sound by your musical instrument—or your own voice if you're a singer, or your arms and hands if you're a conductor.

All of this happens in a flash, and your musical idea is manifested into sound with effortless ease—as long as you don't interfere with your natural design, which is made to carry out this inspired creative process seamlessly.

If we didn't have an ego that believes itself to be separate from the world around us, this creative process could happen beautifully and easily every single time. The problem is, our limited thinking minds are conditioned to function in a mode that typically carries habitual excess tension along with it.

Our minds are not clear receivers of inspired ideas.

Our habitual fears, anxieties, worries, and ways of thinking clutter the beautiful spaciousness from which creative ideas emerge, blocking the free passage of those ideas through the mind-body-self.

Our bodies are not relaxed and open, ready to receive the brain's messages and instantly jump into coordinated action to carry them out; instead, they are stiff, stuck—confused by unconscious, old protective armoring.

Our hearts are not full of love and free-flowing positive emotions, ready to faithfully reflect, carry, and express the music's feelings; instead, our hearts are hardened as we cling fearfully to the past and worry about the future.

At the root of it all is our ignorance of our true being, our consciousness, our integrated reality, our oneness with all things within and without. We forget our true nature. We forget about our creative, unifying spirit, freedom, and love that flows everywhere without distinction.

Happily, it just takes a split second to wake up, remember, get re-inspired, and once more surrender to the natural flow of the creative process. Ease is always here, happening, waiting for us to merge into the musical, rhythmic river of life!

Here's what Ayn has to say:

"Working with Jennifer has changed my life. Before I started her classes, I felt like one of those sci-fi characters from another planet that had lost their superpowers and had to live on earth as a mere human. It had always been natural for me to have awareness of the "other planes of existence"—I could kind of soak in the surrounding environment. For example, I would never remember people's names, but I remembered their 'aura,' or energy. I would look at a plant and know it was not happy and what it needed would just pop into my head.

"But all that became totally blocked, and I remember thinking how horrible it was that this was the way other people live all the time. Not having this extra-sensitive awareness is like being blind. These days, I still have blockages, but I think I'm about 50+ % back.

"I'm now coming to the realization that I have an issue with self-expression with words and that is one reason I want to play the violin—but even that causes some tension whenever I play. What's so wonderful is that Jennifer always says something just at the right time that moves me along to rediscovery. OH! And I just remembered I used to have pain before working with Jennifer. I totally forgot I had pain when I started! :)"

When I teach people how to engage in this inspired creative process in a practical way, I like to use what I call "The Starbucks Analogy."

The Starbucks Analogy

In the USA, we have drive-through coffee shops (like Starbucks®) that allow us to quickly and conveniently get a drink without having to leave our car. We drive our car along the side of the building and pull up to a speaker where we can communicate with the employees in the shop, putting in an order for what we'd like to drink.

After ordering, we drive over to the pickup window to wait until it's ready. Then the employee hands it through the window, we receive it, and we pay.

This simple process is actually very much like how we human beings naturally and easily manifest our desires into reality.

Let's say you want to play your instrument. Here's how it goes:

1) <u>Set up</u>. You get your instrument and everything you need set up and ready to go (pull your car up to the speaker).

2) <u>Intend</u>. Clarify what you want. Decide what music you're going to play (put in your order to request your drink).

3) <u>Inhibit (and Direct)</u>. *Get out of the way* by clearing your mind and body of unhelpful thoughts and tension (move your car to make room for new orders), *delegating* the task to the appropriate systems in charge of carrying out your intentions for you (let those in the shop do the work for you), *trusting* that your brain-body-self knows how to coordinate itself to create the sound you want (trust that the employees back in the shop know how to make your drink), and *allowing* your music to be produced while

you watch and wait patiently for the result to be delivered (wait for your drink to be handed to you).

4) Receive. Your ears receive sound a split second after it is produced (receive the drink handed to you after it has been made).

5) Repeat and refine, as desired. Now that you have the result, is it actually what you wanted? Do you want something modified? Do you need to be more specific? Do new skills need to be learned before you can get the sound (or drink) you want? If so, go back to step #1 and repeat—now you are practicing!

As simple as it is, it's easy to get this creative process wrong by skipping steps, doing them in the incorrect sequence, or forcing the process through impatience. When we don't follow the natural and necessary "means-whereby" (Alexander's term—see below), chaos ensues, and we miss out on what we want. Here are just a few examples of what can go wrong.

1. Set up.

External setup: If your violin setup doesn't fit your body, your violin is missing a string, the strings are out of tune, or your bow doesn't have any rosin, then you can do everything else right, but you still won't get the best results.

Internal setup: Even more importantly, are you fully ready to make good music? If your mind is full of chatter, your body is tight and constricted, and your emotions are pulling you down, your musical ideas won't be able to travel easily from idea into sound; they'll become distorted along the way. You also need to have at least a minimal understanding of how to use the tools you have—for example, how to hold a violin and bow.

If you and your instrument aren't well set up, it's like entering a shoe store and asking for coffee, or speaking in the wrong language or a nasty tone of voice at the wrong window at the coffee shop. You can try and force the employees to make you a chai latte, but it will take an incredible stroke of luck or a lot of extra effort to get a happy result.

2. Intend.

Once your overall setup is adequate, you need sufficiently clear intentions. In Primal Alexander, we always make sure to make what's called the Primary Concern our primary intention, which is to find out what's happening to the whole self as we engage in an activity (see Chapter 20 for more on this). After you've established the Primary Concern, you can add on what I call "secondary goals."

What piece do you want to play? How do you want to play it? Are you working on a specific passage or technical skill? Do you want to play it in tune? With or without vibrato? What kind of mood do you want to evoke?

Clarifying intentions takes place in the prefrontal cortex, the conscious part of your brain behind your forehead. This is the thinking "command" center of your brain, where you have thoughts and ideas and decide what you want to have happen next.

The more clarity you bring to your intentions, the more likely you'll get the result you really want. Of course, the intention needs to be aligned with your setup. If you decide you want to play a Beethoven piano concerto, no amount of wishing will make that work if you're set up and ready to play the violin!

If you're a beginner violinist and want to play Paganini Caprices right away, that won't work, either, because your mind-body-self (your internal setup) hasn't learned how to refine and organize this request and carry it out yet. Too many components to that activity first need to be learned separately, and too many ideas are jumbled together that your system doesn't yet know how to coordinate. (An important method I recommend to solve this kind of problem, by the way, lies in my "Stained-Glass Practicing" technique, described in Chapter 21.)

At the coffee shop, if you tell the employee you want a drink but don't indicate what kind, you might end up with tea when you wanted a latte, or an iced drink when you wanted hot coffee. If you ask for an obscure specialty coffee that isn't on the menu, the employees in the shop won't be able to prepare that for you. Needless to say, if you order an airline ticket to Holland, you won't get much more than a quizzical look!

3. <u>Inhibit</u>.

This is the step most often likely to trip you up, and it has nothing to do with your level of expertise. Even the most accomplished, successful musicians can interfere at this point by—ignorant of how the mind-body-self is designed to function—trying to control and micromanage the process. By doing that, we actually interfere with it and reduce the quality of the result. (Alexandrian inhibition was more fully explained in the last chapter.)

Once you know clearly what you want, put that desire into the background (delegate it to the control of your subconscious brain and wise Inner Coordinator), and bring your Primary Concern and ConstructiveThinking to the foreground, using your conscious awareness and your prefrontal cortex.

This requires that you trust your natural ability to carry out your mind's intentions with minimal bodily effort and maximum ease and efficiency; and that you allow it to take the time it requires. Also, you need to understand that the thinking mind does NOT know how to coordinate the events that need to take place within the body to carry out an activity—that's not its job!

Instead of meddling with the Starbucks employees—going inside the coffee shop to show them how to make your drink—you normally trust that they know how to do it, right? Sometimes, it may take longer than you'd like, but there's not much you can do about that. Yelling at them won't make it go faster, and it may sour the flavor of your drink.

Your job isn't to speed up the process. Your job is to be clear, trust, be patient, and be happy while you wait! Paradoxically, standing back and letting the right thing "do itself" is the best way to speed up your learning.

4. Receive.

This may seem like the easiest step, but surprisingly, we can mess this step up, too. If we're so intent on controlling our outcomes, meddling by interfering with a job that isn't ours, we're no longer in the best state to receive what we're given.

If our minds are stressed and our bodies full of tension, we literally can't hear the more subtle nuances of intonation and inflection, and sometimes we'll even miss it when we're playing wrong notes.

The amount of time necessary for anyone to carry out this creative process will vary, and depends on many factors, including the quality of your setup, the clarity of your intentions, and your skill. It can take anywhere from two to twenty minutes to pick up a drink at the coffee shop; it can take just a fraction of a second, a number of minutes, or even weeks to notice improvement when you're working with yourself. Timing is not always predictable, but the need for patience is!

F. M. Alexander spoke about a comparable set of orders as happening "one at a time, all together." The ability to coordinate your thinking with your movements, using the steps outlined above, is a very valuable skill, worth developing, and it requires lots of practice! This makes deliberate, step-by-step practicing over time essential. We start with one intention and gradually layer on more intentions, once we learn the first ones.

Balancing ambition with gratitude

In spiritual terms, one thing missing in the schema above is having an embodied sense of gratitude. Can you be grateful for being able to produce a sound at all? What a miracle that we can have an intention, make a request, and the body moves to get any result whatsoever! If we are open to receive, we are also free to marvel at our input, and we are more inclined to wonder with childlike curiosity about our next step. How can we refine our request to be more in alignment with what we want next time?

When we're full of judgment, criticism, and resentment, it makes it much harder to learn and improve because our bodies always reflect our mental/emotional state and normally deliver exactly what we've ordered—as long as the system is free, open, and in good, healthy working condition.

As I described in Chapter 8, having needs and desires is perfectly normal and human, and it's actually healthy. In fact, denying our needs and desires and pretending we don't have any is unhealthy, since we're denying our human design and experience.

Of course, there are all kinds of goals—big and small, lofty and mundane.

You may have dreams of winning a competition or landing your dream job, performing challenging repertoire you adore, or performing to a sold-out crowd at Carnegie Hall.

Maybe you enter the practice room each day with the goal of mastering a specific technique, memorizing just one more measure of a complicated piece, or simply enjoying the sound of your instrument in one special moment, when somehow it all magically comes together.

Having goals becomes problematic only when we become too attached to them and start believing we need to acquire or achieve those things outside of us in order to feel a greater sense of wholeness, abundance, or joy. The truth is, the source of happiness lies within us, but we're too used to looking for and finding temporary happiness on the outside to believe that.

What we believe actually creates our experience of the world around us, and what we focus on we get more of.

The brain has a reticular activating system, specifically designed to pay more attention to what we tell the brain—what we believe in any given moment is most important.[20] When thoughts of lack and separation occupy a lot of space in the neural network of our brains, the mind starts to lean towards interpreting our experiences in ways that deliver that experience, thus, "proving" to us that our belief is justified. Paradoxically, when we think and make choices from a sense of lack, we actually create more of that feeling-experience of lack, deficiency, and incompleteness in our lives. A most-unwanted result.

---

20 Alia J. Crum and Ellen J. Langer, "Mind-set Matters: Exercise and the Placebo Effect," Psychological Science 18, no. 2 (Feb. 2007): 165–71, doi: 10.1111/j.1467-9280.2007.01867.x.

Thinking we need to get what we don't have pushes us out of our awareness of the fullness of the present moment. It's important that we don't let our desires become stronger than our internal sense of abundance, interconnectedness, and gratitude for who we are and what we already possess within and without.

No matter what your goal may be, your experience of the process of achieving it—and your fundamental experience of success—depend entirely on your attitude and what you're doing with your whole mind-body-self as you work towards your goal.

Two ways of achieving success

Ultimately, there are two ways you can go about achieving your goals, and your choice determines the nature of your experience and the relative quality of the outcome. Your two options are:

(A) Goal-oriented approach:

Make achieving your goal more important than attending to the moment-by-moment process required to get there. This is what Alexander termed "end-gaining": when your attempt to "gain" an "end" occupies more space in your mind than attending to what he called the "means-whereby" required to gain the end. To me, "impatience" is a good synonym for "end-gaining."

End-gaining—goal-oriented thinking and living—is always accompanied by an increase in overall tension, beyond what is actually necessary. That unnecessary tension not only makes the creative process more difficult, but it compromises the quality of the result.

This may not always be obvious, as mainstream society is essentially an end-gaining, goal-oriented culture, and, even when it's taking us in the wrong direction, end-gaining so often FEELS right. In fact, most of the world actually promotes this practice of achieving results quickly without any regard for harmful side effects to ourselves and others. Witness the sorry current state of the environment, mainly caused by human greed and short-sightedness, aka end-gaining.

Since end-gaining is the norm on a gross scale everywhere we look, it's no wonder that we usually don't notice when we and others are doing it on a microscopic scale. We aren't aware that we're bringing too much psychophysical tension to everything we do, and we don't make the connection between our end-gaining attitude and our physical pain, mental confusion, undue intensity, and the imbalance in different areas of our lives.

As Alexander put it, "This end-gaining business has got to such a point—it's worse than a drug."

Or . . .

(B) <u>Process-oriented approach</u>:

Make awareness of your moment-to-moment experience and the step-by-step process (what Alexander called the "means-whereby") required to achieve your goal more important than whether you actually achieve your goal ("gain your end") or not. In Primal Alexander, Mio Morales calls this witnessing of our present experience attending to the "Primary Concern."

Instead of approaching our desires with a high degree of tension-filled intensity, demanding the fruits of our actions to arrive faster, forcing answers, and trying to control outcomes, we can soften our gaze and shift our attention with childlike curiosity and healthy detachment to the present moment, wondering "What's happening to me right now, as I ________?"

When we make this our Primary Concern, we immediately shift out of the mindless and imbalanced way of being of the goal-oriented approach into a more objective state of observing our subjective experience. We discover that the only thing we truly have control over is where we place our attention; and this choice directly influences the quality of our experience in the next moment.

Paradoxically, as soon as we give up and let go of our habitual idea that our personality—our conscious, thinking mind—needs to DO something to be in control of ourselves, our actions, and even the world around us, we can finally stop fighting, striving, pushing, and forcing things to happen the way we believe they should.

When we let go of the illusion that our small mind is in control, we can finally relax and rest into the reality that an aspect of us is much deeper, grander, and wiser than our thinking mind, and *IT actually has control over our whole self and our experience of the world.*

Waking up to this allows us to remember the primacy of our BEING over our doing, and we can begin to accept what comes to us with equanimity—in calmness of mind and body. When we stop end-gaining by getting our overthinking ego-personality out of the way, we stop interfering with the natural order of things so our creativity can flow. This is when Inspiration can travel easily and effortlessly through the clean, empty space of our empty mind-body-self, transmitting ideas from the infinite space and pulsating energy of the universal Mind, or quantum field, into a form that we can perceive through our senses. This is how the creative process turns a musical idea into sound, with relative tension or relative ease, depending on the degree of intensity of our thought-interference.

What is true success?

The excess tension produced by end-gaining doesn't always prevent us from achieving our goals, but it does make it harder to achieve them; and it *always* compromises the quality of our results, not to mention our overall balance and well-being.

Identifying end-gaining as the root cause of our discomfort becomes particularly challenging when we are successfully accomplishing our objectives, despite the tendency to prioritize the end result. In fact, when we're used to success, it can even seem like a goal-oriented approach is *required* to get results!

People often get ahead professionally by concentrating hard, practicing long hours, prioritizing their goals over everything else, and pushing themselves beyond what's comfortable. They conquer fiendishly difficult repertoire, win competitions, get great jobs, and even become famous. The music they create, with the technical wizardry and even their passion, can be truly amazing.

But at what cost do they achieve this success? Are they healthy, happy, calm, at peace, and enjoying fulfilling personal and professional relationships?

True success is internal and subjective; it can't be determined by the outside. Those famous people may seem to have a perfect life and make perfect music, but I guarantee that if they've achieved a ten out of ten from the outside, if they are habitual end-gainers their success in life doesn't feel like a ten to them. Yet, if they knew how to make their music without all that end-gaining, they'd be able to play at a ten out of ten for themselves, and a *twenty* out of ten as seen from the outside!

We can look successful from the outside but feel like a failure on the inside. Contrarily, even when looking unsuccessful from the outside, we can feel successful and know with our whole beings that we've been truly successful on the inside.

Real success cannot be quantified; it can't be measured by the world's superficial standards. Great artistry depends on prioritizing inward over outward success, the Primary Concern and the present moment over end-gaining.

The wonderful thing is, when we are successful within ourselves, those who are able to see through superficial exteriors will perceive and deeply appreciate our real success. Great artistry shines far beyond quantitative concepts of speed, dynamics, and number of notes played. Great art communicates an ineffable quality that is subtle, perfectly responsive, and supremely flexible.

It possesses an ever-changing quality that cannot be reproduced; and at the same time, there is an inevitability that feels like it cannot be other than it is. There is no pretension, no artifice, no masking. It is innocent, pure, honest, and generous.

It pierces through the clutter and confusion of our minds like an arrow and uplifts it like the wind. It melts the heart like fire; carries and floods the soul like a river; and soothes and heals the body, just as we are supported by Mother Earth.

As you work towards a musical goal . . . ask yourself:

- How am I feeling? Do I feel strong, healthy, relaxed, and energized? Is my body calm, open, responsive, and flexible?
- What is my mental state? Are my thoughts clear, organized, and focused? Am I able to be aware of what's happening within me as well as what's happening around me? Am I able to easily shift my attention when something unexpected happens, or am I hooked into a rigid or judgmental way of thinking?
- What is my emotional state? Do I feel successful? Am I filled with joy, love, and gratitude? Am I enjoying the activities I'm engaged in right now? Am I in touch with my feelings, responding to the world and those around me with patience, love, and acceptance, even when things don't go the way I want?
- Is my life in balance? Am I giving sufficient attention to all the different areas of my life, adjusting as necessary, bringing more or less of my energy to whatever needs more or less of my attention in the moment and over time?
- How is my spiritual life? Do I feel inspired, creative, motivated, purposeful? Am I growing, evolving, and choosing actions that are aligned with my True Self and life purpose? Does my heart feel connected with the world and serving others around me in a way that is positive, deeply nourishing and mutually supportive?
- How does my artistry reflect all of the above? Have I been considering success on a more superficial level, or is there a freedom and spontaneity in my music arising from a quality of Inspiration and ease in my whole being?

Everything is connected

There's a certain attitude that goes along with end-gaining. End-gaining and its concomitant imbalance and suffering arise when we forget that we are intimately connected with the world around us and there is fundamentally no real separation at all.

The tension created by end-gaining is caused by fighting against this true reality that we are failing to see or unwilling to accept. In the instant that we bring our attention fully back to our experience of the present moment, conflict ends within us and tension drops away.

No longer trying to run from a potentially unpleasant future or painful past, and no longer pushing forwards towards a potential future reward or trying to go back to the illusory dream of a beautiful past, the mind can finally rest into silence and the body is free to relax.

The assertions that only the present moment exists and everything is "one" aren't just nice ideas or idealistic dreams. Neither are they simplistic or esoteric religious, spiritual, or "woo-woo" beliefs. These ideas are just as relevant to modern-day science as they were to the ancient sages from foreign lands and sacred traditions.

Let's pause for a moment and consider just a few things that the most up-to-date, cutting-edge science is discovering about the nature of the world, particularly in the fields of quantum physics and paranormal phenomena[21]:

- what we perceive and believe to be the physical world is actually made up entirely of vibrating energy
- energy is made up of waves and particles that change between those two states, and can even exist in both states at the same time
- waves and particles change their behavior when observed
- each atom, including every atom of your human body, is made up of more than 99.99 percent space
- space is made up of the interweaving of wave functions, particles, and invisible quantum fields
- it is possible to perceive the vibrations of energy in ways that go beyond our habitual concepts of time and space, and beyond our ordinary five senses of hearing, sight, smell, taste, and touch
- your beliefs about reality are based upon how you perceive and interpret the information received by your brain
- your perception shapes your experience of reality, and even influences that reality itself

21 Lynn McTaggart, The Intention Experiment (New York: Atria Paperback), 2013.

For an extensive and detailed bibliography on these topics, see *The Intention Experiment* by Lynne McTaggart.

What if you could open up your mind-body-self to the possibility that this energetic way of conceiving of reality may be far more true, accurate, and helpful than your habitual beliefs? What if you could let go of the idea that we live in a reality mostly made up of separate physical objects that can be perceived only by your five senses, within a sequence of separate events happening in linear time?

Consider Einstein's quote: "The distinction between past, present and future is only a stubbornly persistent illusion."[22] What if this perspective actually represents an aspect of "the truth that sets you free" because your recognition of the reality of our interconnectedness means you no longer need fear things, people, or events that seem separate from you and bound by time and limited by space?

Everything changes when you begin to draw the logical, practical consequences of these ideas, which run counter to pretty much everything we've ever been taught and conditioned to believe about how the world works.

When we forget about essential unity, we necessarily feel like something's missing, and we yearn to remember and experience this interconnected wholeness, unaware that we already have what we long for within us, as well as the ability to create new experiences that will help us remember the wholeness—or perfection—that we already are.

In the next chapter, we'll take a closer look at how to let go of habitual thoughts and beliefs that get in the way of your best music-making, and I'll share some powerful thoughts you can think instead.

RESOURCE:

You can download a printable "Practice Success Worksheet" with reminders of the process of creative musical Inspiration from the Bonus Materials page here: https://www.artoffreedom.me/book/bonusmaterials

22 Einstein: 1955—letter to the family of Michele Besso.

Choose Powerful Thoughts to Free Yourself and Your Music

Let go of limiting beliefs that block your musical expression

Whether you think you can or you think you can't, you're right.

~ *Henry Ford*

Now that you know how to wake up awareness of your Primary Concern, how to practice balancing your life with the 5 Pre-Pearls, and how to tap into creative musical Inspiration, let's explore some more ways to use the power of your thoughts and tune your mental attitude to experience more freedom and success in your life.

The truth is, our experience of the world and everything we create begins in the mind. I first realized this in a life-changing way that shocked my entire system to the core when I had my "kitchen epiphany" (see Chapter 9).

That's when I realized I was going about teaching all wrong: instead of giving my student total freedom to be herself, I was trying to fix her because I felt that there was something wrong with her sadness and downward energy.

Thankfully, the wise voice from inside of me stopped me in my tracks, saying, *"No! Not like that! She is free!"* That experience woke up a deeper respect and understanding in me of unconditional Love and what it means to have free will.

With this shift in perspective that allowed me to realize the ultimate freedom of my student, I consequently recognized the same freedom in myself and everyone else.

As I contemplated this powerful experience over the next days, weeks, and months, I began to realize a change in my own thinking that was influencing not only my teaching, but how I was relating to everyone and everything in life.

The thought planted within me—*"She is free!"*—led to the first of my "3 Magic Phrases" and, later, the development of what came to be known as "Freedom Directions," an outgrowth of that first "Magic Phrase." Just to be clear, I use the word "magic" loosely and in fun here.

These are my "3 Magic Phrases":

1) I am free.

2) I don't have to do anything.

3) I have time . . . and space.

Having shared these simple phrases with hundreds of musicians over the years, I've found that these thoughts can help us become free of some of the most important, old, limiting beliefs that keep us small and stuck. They allow us to stop hiding behind old protective armoring that no longer fits who we want to be, preventing us from realizing and fully experiencing the immense beauty and perfection of who we are.

When we approach these phrases with a childlike attitude of curiosity, they can evoke an instantaneous shift in perception that allows our minds and bodies to open up to a fresh, new, wonderful, awe-inspiring, and almost miraculous new way of perceiving the self and the world. To me, this IS truly magical!

Even though these thoughts have enormous potential, not everyone likes them right away, since the habits of the ego-mind may protest. After all, how many times a day do you think to yourself or tell others, "I have to do that"; "I don't have enough time!"; "I'll be free after ____ is over."

I once had a student (who later went on to become an Alexander Technique teacher herself) who—because they were so far from her personal experience—initially hated every one of the Magic Phrases.

"I'm free? Of course, I'm not! I have SO much I have to do before I graduate . . . so many pieces to learn . . . so many papers to write! And NO, I do NOT have enough time—or space in my life to be myself . . . I have a to-do list a mile long. I always feel behind. These phrases aren't true, and they just make me feel worse!"

And more recently, a student in his eighties wrote to me about the Magic Phrases:

> "Thinking about them opens a can of worms for me. There are many ways that I am not free. I am not free to ignore the law of gravity, it keeps me grounded to the earth. I can't fly off in space, no matter how much I'd like to do that. I am not free to stop breathing and hold my breath indefinitely. My body rebels."
>
> "Yes, I'm free to be me, but there are many physical limitations. My body may be free to experience an infection, or pain, which may stop me from playing the violin. My mind/body is free to experience dementia."

Maybe you can relate to some of these comments! I know it's easy for my mind to agree, too, until I pause and look a little more deeply within myself, with a real desire to learn the truth. That's when I remember that allowing something to be "free" is more about giving myself permission to fully and unconditionally accept its existence as it is right now, and less about wanting things to be different from how they are.

If it's hard for you to wrap your head around the idea that you are free, that you don't have to do anything, and that you have time and space, I often suggest adding the words "right now" or "to be myself . . . right now" to make them more accessible, as in "I am free to be myself right now."

When I do this, I always realize that—even if I don't FEEL free right now, I know that I truly AM free, in the sense of being able to choose my next thought, my next action. In a very real sense, I am free to have the experience of being myself that I'm having right now.

Nobody can think for me, make my choices for me, or take actions through my body, which is why I believe I am free. And I truly don't *have to do* anything right now. Even under the most extreme torture (God forbid), I would be the one having my own next thought and making my own next decision. Remember the extraordinary story of Viktor Frankl, who was able to maintain his dignity and claim his internal freedom even while trapped and enduring the horrors of living in a Nazi concentration camp (see Chapter 3).

Of course, there are research studies out there that seem to contradict the belief in free will, and there are all sorts of theories that we might not actually be making conscious choices at all—at least, not with our thinking minds. Are we puppets being controlled by some higher power or, like in a science fiction movie, machines directed by an alien being?[23]

23 W. P. Banks and S. Pockett (2007), "Benjamin Libet's Work on the Neuroscience of Free Will," in The Blackwell Companion to Consciousness (Blackwell Publishing, 2017), 657–70. Also see The Blackwell Companion to Consciousness | Wiley Online Books.

I don't think we're puppets or machines, but, considering that we can't actually know how anything works with 100 percent certainty (and science is always uncovering new information that contradicts what was discovered earlier), it seems to me that we can only operate on our own best guess, based on our own personal experience. Which is why I prefer to think practically, in a way that gives me the best results, as determined by self-observation and experimentation.

Experimenting to discover what is useful in this moment

Let's get curious and explore what is practically useful in this very moment.

Ask yourself: What actually makes a difference for me right now? Is it more useful for me to believe I am conscious and possess the free will to choose my own thoughts and actions? Or is it healthier for me to believe I'm a mindless puppet with no real control over myself?

Which belief produces a helpful result for me when I think it? Which thoughts help me feel more at ease, free, and happy? Which ones cause me to feel more restricted, uneasy, uncomfortable?

Try this experiment for yourself and see what happens:

Pause for a moment. First try thinking: *I have no control over my thoughts, and no free will. I am not free.* If you don't instantly feel a negative shift, wait for a moment and think it again a few times. Pay attention to what happens within you. What do you notice?

How does your body respond? What about your mood?

Now try out this one: "I am free to choose my own thoughts. I am free to be myself right now. I am free." Take your time; think it through.

What happens? How does your body respond? Did your mood shift at all?

Go back and forth between the two thoughts slowly a few times to get a better sense of the difference between: "I'm not free. I'm not free to be myself"; and "I'm free. I am free to be myself right now."

Try this experiment with each of the 3 Magic Phrases and find out how your whole system responds. Where does your mind go? How does your body feel? What emotions come up?

For example, put this book down for a moment and slowly think this phrase to yourself: "I don't have to do anything . . . right now . . . to be myself." Think it again. Three times.

What happens to you to your body? What thoughts come up? Is there a new mood or emotion?

If you find yourself breathing a little easier, relaxing a wee bit, or you smile in relief, that's an indicator this "Magic Phrase" is a helpful and constructive thought for you. It would be wise for you to think it often, and catch yourself when you try to convince yourself that you aren't free by telling yourself how much you *have to do*!

When I do the above experiment and consider how my system responds to each of these ideas, it's clear that I feel better when I believe in my own self-agency. Then, when I take action on this belief by choosing the thoughts that help me feel better and take me in a direction of more ease and happiness, the result "makes the meat it feeds on" (in Alexander's own words).

This odd expression means to say: if I think a certain way and get a positive result, that experience motivates me to think that way more often, which again gives me a positive result, which again motivates me to think more positive thoughts.

This experiment reinforces my belief in free will and the power to choose my own thoughts and create my own experience: I feel good, assuming this responsibility for myself, knowing that I have the power to improve my life by exercising my belief in free will!

This is why "I am free to be myself right now" is a practically useful thought for me to believe in.

Thought-experiments

When I share these 3 Magic Phrases with my students, I always suggest approaching them as little thought-experiments, with an element of childlike curiosity, free of judgment or expectation. We also discuss the different, and sometimes opposing, layers of meaning within them.

The surface meanings are often based on our instinctive habit and immediate feeling-response to the thought, while the deeper meaning reaches into something more rational and intuitive, in alignment with our whole being.

The truth is, you do NOT have to do anything right now—even if you feel compelled to. You always have a choice to not act, and there will always be consequences to every action or non-action. So, it may feel like you have no choice about doing what you "have" to do—because other people expect things of you, you have responsibilities, deadlines, or goals you want to achieve—but it is ALWAYS inside the framework of your choice. And whether you do them or not is ultimately a decision made by weighing the possible positive or negative, pleasurable or painful, consequences.

The problem is, if you don't acknowledge that you are free to choose your next thought and action/non-action, you are giving up your biggest asset as a human being—your power to choose. Instead, living by default, you put yourself mindlessly at the mercy of your habits and ever-changing feelings.

A challenging fact: If you're doing something, it's because you actually want to do it more than you don't. There's always a compelling reason behind what you're choosing to do, even if it's sheer laziness and refusal to buck the familiar. Even our habits are based on choices we initially made to engage in a new behavior, and you chose that behavior for good reasons, often based on getting what you needed to thrive and survive as a very small child.

That's why there's no need to criticize the choices we make. Something deep inside of you is making a smart choice, but if left unexamined, it's often based on an old reality that no longer exists, and therefore may no longer be useful or helpful. Acting on an old habit can even be harmful as it keeps you stuck and controlled by the past, keeping you trapped like a wild animal that slowly languishes and dies an earlier death from being held captive.

The most immediate problem is that we are living with conflicting desires going on within us most of the time: a part of us wants to do one thing while the other part doesn't; part of us wants to realize our freedom, while the other part has adapted to the comfort of the cage.

Example: How do you feel about practicing?

Let's take conflicting desires about practicing as an example.

When you decide to practice, is it because you want the positive results of practicing? Of course! We all know that if you do good practicing, you sound better; if you don't, you sound worse.

And yet, do you ever practice even though you'd rather be doing something else? Do you ever choose to do something else and then feel guilty about not practicing? Whether you're a student or a professional, the answer is probably yes!

When I was a child, I would often practice instead of playing outside with my friends or reading a book because I was supposed to be practicing, and because I cared a lot about becoming a better violinist. I also feared the possible consequences of not practicing! So, there would be times when I quietly resigned myself to doing "the right thing," choosing to practice while at the same time resentfully wishing I were doing something else.

The problem with doing one thing when you ALSO want to be doing something else is that you become "a house divided," split off from yourself. You are not bringing your whole self to what you're doing.

Part of you is practicing, while another part of you is inwardly elsewhere. Your mind is distracted, wandering off to other things and places. Your body innocently follows your wayward mind, which is trying to pull your body away from where you're sitting or standing to join your thoughts, wherever they are. Your emotions may reflect that tug-of-war with a mixture of resentment, frustration, sadness, or boredom.

All of this internal conflict is a jumbled mess that shows up in your mind as a lack of mental clarity, producing excess tension, stiffness, and compression in your body. The resulting lack of mind-body coordination gets in the way of your instrumental technique, making it harder to get messages from your brain to your fingers, and making it harder for your fingers to move because excess tension prevents free movement of your joints and muscles.

Clearly, internal conflict compromises the quality of your music, which is why it's helpful to have a practice like the 5 Pre-Pearls and 3 Magic Phrases, to help you sort things out and make a more conscious choice based on what you really want most. When you commit to your actions with your whole self, you'll feel more empowered, in charge of your experience.

This inner strength gives you a heightened feeling of safety and security, which allows you to bring a more relaxed mind and body, and a more enthusiastic spirit to your music.

Not only will your musical practice session flow with more overall ease, but you'll also have more fun! And when you're feeling good and enjoying yourself, it's easier to tap into a more open, experimental attitude for effective learning, and absorb and rearrange information in your brain for quicker progress.

"I had a really good audition yesterday. I did Awareness Etudes and Constructive Rest* very consistently leading up to it, which really paid off because it was the first time I could actually feel myself easing while auditioning, and I wasn't gripping the instrument or hunching as I used to.

"It was also the first time I got through that particular set of pieces in an audition without a memory slip because I did the thing you suggested of imagining how I want it to sound rather than listening to myself.

"Walking around the building the day before and taking everything in, I had plenty of thoughts like *I am so not prepared to do this*, but I was able to just say no to that and choose something else. Saying it was a fun audition would be a bit of a stretch, but it was a satisfying ending to the work I put into it and decently representative of who I am as a player.

"I've been thinking about this audition for three years and had every worst-case scenario go through my head, so I'm very happy for how it ultimately turned out, and no matter what the results are, I am excited by what I learned about myself! Thank you again!"

~ Lucy, Violinist and Educator

** Constructive Rest is a method for lying down in a semi-supine position that originated in the dance world. I mainly recommend it for students experiencing pain, to be used in conjunction with ConstructiveThinking and/or contemplation of the 3 Magic Phrases. While lying down in this position can be therapeutic in itself, the practice of Constructive Rest is not taught in Primal Alexander and is not essential to The Art of Freedom Method.*

Freedom Directions

There are so many ways to use the 3 Magic Phrases! The first Magic Phrase ("I am free") is particularly versatile and works best if applied in certain ways. I like to call these variations Freedom Directions because using these phrases allows us to consciously direct our thoughts, energy, and actions in ways that free up the whole mind-body-self.

There are a number of helpful corollaries to the phrase "I am free."

Believing that other people and even inanimate objects are also free to be who and what they are in any given moment can help you develop a healthy detachment and independence from them. This helps you let go and unhook yourself from people, things, and events that trigger you, becoming less reactive.

Freedom Directions give you permission to be exactly who you already are, having the experience of being yourself-right now. You are free to think whatever you're thinking, feel whatever you're feeling, and do whatever you're doing. To me, this is the very definition of personal freedom.

We are always free to be and experience ourselves exactly as we are, in mind, body, soul, and Spirit:

The MIND is free . . . to think or not think . . . whatever it is thinking or not thinking, right now.

The BODY is free . . . to feel or not feel . . . to move or not move . . . exactly as it is, right now.

The EMOTIONS, SOUL, and SPIRIT . . . are free . . . to show up and be experienced—or not—just the way they are right now.

The catch is, in using Freedom Directions you realize that giving yourself the freedom to be yourself requires that you grant the corresponding freedom to everyone and everything else, too! Freedom Directions are both personal and impersonal: they are applicable to ME, YOU, and the whole WORLD—even Nature and inanimate objects:

> I am free . . . to be exactly as I am right now.
>
> You are free . . . to be exactly as you are right now.
>
> The world is free . . . to be exactly as it is right now.

The Freedom Directions are a wonderfully practical way to practice acceptance of the things we cannot immediately change, by granting all things permission—or freedom—to be as they are. Remember the Serenity Prayer?

> God, grant me the serenity
>
> to accept the things I cannot change,
>
> the courage to change the things I can,
>
> and the wisdom to know the difference.

Freedom Directions are liberating. By remembering their truths, you are totally accepting the reality of the present moment—positive or negative—with discernment, yet free of judgment. This open acceptance is a necessary precursor to experiencing your own innate freedom to choose.

Once we can accept our current experience of reality, we can choose our next thought/action with conscious awareness, a choice that will immediately take us in the direction of either greater openness, spaciousness, and ease, or less overall ease, or dis-ease.

With freedom comes responsibility and liberation from mindlessness

It's important to point out that Freedom Directions are not an excuse to justify, judge, or moralize. Freedom Directions have nothing to do with declaring something "right" or "wrong."

No matter what you decide to do with your freedom, every personal choice—thought or action—produces a consequence. Every action has a corresponding effect or multiple effects, even if those effects are hidden and not immediately obvious to you, or appear to be different from what you intended. "As you sow, so shall you reap."

Without acceptance (which also occurs when you practice ConstructiveThinking or inhibition), your mind-body-self is resisting the reality of the present moment, trying to change and control it, pushing your mind around and pulling your body off-center.

When you are fully accepting of the present moment, you aren't rushing forward or running away from the future, and you aren't nostalgic for the past or regretting what is over and gone. Your mind and body are poised, experiencing the fullness of this moment: here and now—ready and equipped for the unexpected freshness of the next moment to spontaneously arise.

When you realize the truth of your innate freedom, you also realize that this awareness comes with a greater sense of responsibility. Nobody else is responsible for your thoughts and actions, and therefore, nobody else is responsible for your results.

When your mind is unconsciously generating habitual thoughts, making mindless decisions and acting on automatic pilot, almost as if you were sleepwalking through life, it's easier to forgive yourself later, once you realize your mistakes and understand what caused you to make them; it's also easier to forgive others when you realize most people are acting on old programming that way too. As Jesus said, "Forgive them, Father, for they know not what they do."

However, in the moment that you wake up to the higher reality of your conscious awareness and realize that you have the awesome freedom to choose your next thought and action, you become responsible for the creation of your next experience.

As you become a "co-creator" of your experience with your Higher Self, it starts to dawn on you that freedom is both liberating and an awe-inspiring responsibility. When you assume full responsibility for your own well-being, your thoughts, feelings, and reactions, your life takes on an incredible new depth and breadth of meaning.

Our innate freedom is immense, timeless . . . fathomless. It is a Great Mystery, impossible to grasp with the limited understanding of our thinking mind. And yet, we can experience it wholly in the instant of this very present moment when we decide to realize our freedom to fully be who we are. Freedom Directions give us a glimpse of what's possible if we journey further in this direction.

All of this might sound abstract and purely theoretical, but it's actually a very practical way to bring more consciousness into your everyday experience, as well as how you choose to make music.

After all, don't you want your music to flow with freedom, ease, and spacious abandon? Don't you want to feel unfettered in your body, mind, and emotions?

Freedom in your music isn't something you can fake; it flows spontaneously from fully embracing yourself as a free creative spirit. Creating music that flows freely isn't possible without first accessing that kind of freedom within your whole self.

How to Use Freedom Directions

Freedom Directions are a great way to bring your awareness back to the present moment and entertain the idea that anything is possible. To use Freedom Directions, simply apply the following sentences to anything you are noticing, within you or without, and observe how thinking this way makes you feel in your body:

"I am free to ______________________."

Examples:

"I am free to think about lunch while I'm playing scales."

"I am free to feel nervous about tomorrow's performance."

"I am free to move stiffly or with ease."

"____________________ is free to ____________________."

Examples:

"My friend is free to think poorly and make bad decisions."

"My friend is free to feel upset."

"My friend is free to blame others or to take responsibility for her actions."

Here are some examples of scenarios when using the Freedom Directions can be helpful to both your own well-being and that of those around you:

- Scenario 1: The weather has been exceptionally good, and you feel guilty for having skipped your practice sessions the last few days.

  You can think: *I am free to feel guilty. I am free to feel bad about myself, and my body is free to feel heavy. I am free to take advantage of good weather and not practice if I don't want to. I am free to sound bad when I don't practice. I am also free to start practicing again now. I am free to think differently, so that I can feel better and improve my mood. I am free to let go of guilt and notice a deeper joy within me. I am free to practice and feel good about myself and be happy. When I feel happy, I am free to share that positive energy with others.*

- Scenario 2: Your stand partner keeps complaining about the conductor and keeps forgetting to turn the page on time.

  You can think: *I am free to feel irritated by my stand partner because he's making it harder for me to enjoy the music. I am free to feel angry and impatient. I'm free to feel tight in my body. I'm free to wish he'd shut up and turn the page on time!*

  Hmmm . . . I don't like how I feel right now . . . I am free to think differently . . . My stand partner is free to be who he is. He is free to complain. He is free to be annoying. I am free not to like him. I am free to enjoy the music, even when he turns the page late. I am free to remember my reason for being here. I love music. I love people. I am free to feel grateful. I am free to feel good, even when my stand partner doesn't. I am free to ignore my stand partner.

I am also free to take action. For example, I can communicate openly with him, letting him know what I think and feel about his attitude and actions, and I am free to ask him to make a change.

- Scenario 3: You arrive at the venue to play a gig a few minutes before it starts. As you walk onstage, you realize it's freezing, there aren't any stand lights, and you can't do anything about either problem. You're shivering and you can barely see the music. Your hands are stiff.

  You can think: *I am free to shiver and feel cold. I am free to squint and lean forward to see the music. I am free to feel angry about these conditions. I am free to feel very uncomfortable, shaky, and tight. I am free to feel bad, and sound bad as a result. I am free to blame others for how I sound.*

  And yet, the hall is free to be cold and the stage is free to be dark. People are free to be thoughtless and inconsiderate. I am free to sound bad, and others are free not to like my playing. I am free to play the best I can and let go of what's impossible to change. I am free to find what feels good within me and focus on that. I am free to think differently so that I can feel differently and have a different experience. I am free to let go of expecting things to be different from what they are. I am letting go, giving up, and enjoying what I can. I am free to find things to be grateful for and let this way of thinking give me joy.

  I am also free to take action. For example, I can refuse to play and quit, I can complain, or I can speak to someone afterwards in the hope that I will never have to play in these conditions again. I can also choose to transcend my discomfort and focus on the beauty of the music, and give the best gift I possibly can to my audience, despite the inhospitable circumstances.

You can see from the above examples that the way you interpret the facts in each scenario—how you decide to think, how you choose to respond determines your experience: how you feel and what happens next.

In all of the above scenarios, it would be very wise to apply The Art of Freedom Life-Pillar #1 and remind yourself of your ultimate Purpose. What is most important to me? What do I want deep down, more than anything? Which choices of thoughts and actions will best align with my Purpose?

When you use your free will to make choices that align with your Purpose, and add ConstructiveThinking to the process, you are stepping through the doorway to ease, and everything will flow into place much more naturally.

The Magic Phrases and Freedom Directions are a wonderful way to let go of the limitations and constrictions of your ego, more consciously preparing the ground of your being for the creation of inspired music. Reflecting on them gives us a deeper understanding of what's possible, and they're a great antidote to the negative thoughts that keep us chained to our old habitual ways of thinking and acting in the world.

In the next chapter, we'll look at how the way you think and your manner of concentration can influence the quality of your practicing, and therefore your performance.

RESOURCE:

I've created a handy PDF reference guide for you to keep the fundamentals of The Art of Freedom Method at your fingertips. You can access it here: https://www.artoffreedom.me/book/BonusMaterials

Boost Your Confidence with True Concentration

To get the results you want, be aware of what you're actually practicing

> A universal characteristic of insanity is inflexibly doing the same thing over and over while hoping for different results. Flexibility in the face of changing circumstances, by contrast, is a hallmark of mental health.
>
> ~ *H. Stephen Glenn and Jane Nelsen*

In order to risk courageously baring our souls in front of an audience, we performers need to develop a healthy sense of self-worth and self-confidence. For some, this strong sense of self comes about naturally and is nurtured and protected by a healthy environment and good teachers. But most of us need to learn how to do this for ourselves anyway, regardless of our circumstances.

Cultivating the confidence and poise needed for excellent performance requires three things:

A) Self-knowledge: a growing understanding of yourself and the habits that get in your way;

B) Dedication: the willingness to learn how to overcome those habits, and humble dedication to that process;

C) Practice: excellent practice skills, made up of general musical knowledge, specific techniques, and effective learning methods.

All three components need to be present at the same time for the development of true artistic mastery, yet I've found over the years that most musicians overemphasize the third component (the one that requires the most direct study of a musical instrument) while minimizing—or completely ignoring—the significance of the first two (which stress the need for Primary Practice: self-observation, introspection, and personal growth).

When you have a strong desire to grow and succeed as an artist, your self-confidence will naturally grow along with your understanding of the essential interdependence of these three elements, as Alexander affirmed with this odd turn of phrase, "It makes the meat it feeds on."

What he meant was that the positive results of good practice habits will produce the self-confidence and motivation required to keep practicing; that will in turn continue to produce good results. Your steady improvement is guaranteed through this virtuous cycle of cause and effect.

A virtuous cycle

Jason is a professional cellist who started my introductory course soon after the end of the pandemic, with only a few weeks to spare before his solo performance of the Dvořák cello concerto with orchestra. Like most musicians at the time, having recently emerged from two years of minimal live performances, Jason felt completely beside himself with nerves. Doubting his ability to get through the high-profile concert without falling apart onstage, he contacted me for help.

After just three weeks of following my guidance and diligently practicing the basic Primal Alexander Awareness Etudes I gave him, Jason noticed that he was feeling much calmer. I taught him about the Golden Period and how to focus on his Primary Concern whenever he could, before and during the performance.

I also told him that he was "diving in the deep end," and not to expect himself to be able to incorporate much of what he was learning into his actual performance so soon, since combining good "use of self" with playing a musical instrument is a very complex activity, considered an advanced skill in my programs. Most of my students don't learn this until they've worked with me without playing the instrument for at least a couple months; we keep it simple and easy by introducing the instrument slowly over time. I told him to celebrate if he had enough presence of mind to remember to do his ConstructiveThinking even ONCE while onstage!

But Jason had this performance scheduled, and he was determined to make the most of what I was teaching him as quickly as possible so that after such a long time away he could enjoy a successful return to the concert stage.

To his wonder and delight, the more he practiced the Etudes I gave him, the more awareness he was developing, along with more conscious control over his reactions. He began to connect his thoughts with his physical experience, realizing he could choose different thoughts to get a different result. When he thought about not having enough time to practice or having "wasted" precious practice time going to the gym every day before the concert, he soon realized that this way of thinking was harmful and counterproductive, as it contributed to his stress.

Every time he started thinking in a self-critical way with increased worry and self-doubt, the tension in his body would increase, he realized, making it harder to play well. As he rapidly got better at identifying these self-sabotaging thoughts in the moment, he was able to nip them in the bud and start thinking more constructively sooner, since he was practicing the exact skills he needed for that by doing the Awareness Etudes.

More and more throughout the day, as he practiced his ConstructiveThinking—with and without his instrument—Jason started to feel better and play better, which motivated him to pay even more attention and do more of this Primary Practice. Allowing himself to reap the benefits of this virtuous cycle inspired him to keep up his Primary Practice all the way up to and through his successful performance of the Dvořák.

In our group class afterwards, Jason shared that this was one of the most unusual performance experiences he had ever had, in that he was more aware than ever, and even though he had a few small memory slips, it didn't matter at all because he was able to recover quickly and the audience didn't even notice. He said people came and talked to him for nearly an hour afterwards, telling him how moving the concert was and how much they appreciated how he shared his soul with them through the music.

Within days, Jason signed up for my more advanced course to keep developing his knowledge and practice of The Art of Freedom Method, which has helped him profoundly in other areas of his life, as well. Here's what he wrote just a few months later:

"The Art of Freedom has been invaluable to me. First, as I prepared for a huge performance and then two weeks later when I got my second cancer diagnosis in five years. As I recovered from surgery I didn't go to Jennifer's classes or even post much in the Facebook group.

"But I did the three basic Primal Alexander etudes daily (known as the "Tripod"), which made it possible for me to be calm enough to conceive an outcome I wanted rather than collapsing in panic and fear. Not only that, I was able to bring the healing I wanted to fruition: my most recent biopsy has shown no evidence of any malignancy or dysplasia.

"I have performed several times since my recovery in high profile situations and have had zero performance anxiety, and I've felt at one with myself, the audience and my spirit."

~ Jason, Cellist and Educator

Being open to All-Possibility is essential to making this process work. My students who simply follow the process with an open mind ready to discover new, easier ways of thinking and moving make steady, consistent, and noticeable progress.

Even professional musicians need better practice skills!

Over the years that I've been sharing The Art of Freedom Method and touch-free Alexander Technique, helping hundreds of musicians overcome all kinds of psychophysical barriers to making great music, I've come to realize that even highly skilled professionals often hit a plateau in their musical skills and suffer from the realization that they aren't fulfilling their potential. This keeps them from fully enjoying their best performance and often prevents them from working with better colleagues or getting the better jobs they long for.

Some of these musicians had a poor musical education early on, and therefore never learned the best ways to practice. But even those that *did* have good teachers and were taught sound practice and performance techniques, may still suspect underneath it all that something is missing. They sense that their musical technique is stuck, never getting past a certain level, and that something is intruding upon their ability to fully and freely express their most heartfelt musical feelings with their audiences.

I know from experience that nearly all musicians—even those at the top of their game—can benefit greatly from learning the uncommonly effective, holistic practice skills I teach.

Sadly, however, most musicians who have put in the hard work and long hours of diligent practice over many years are typically unaware that their problems are nearly always related to wrong assumptions about how to concentrate. In addition, they unwittingly apply flawed practice methods, which often slow down their progress—or even backfire and make them sound worse. (See Chapter 22 for four common myths that can sabotage even the best performers without their being the wiser.)

If you aren't sure whether your practice methods are adequate, it's really hard to feel confident about your playing because you can never really trust your skills to come through for you when you're onstage, facing the moment of truth!

When you've put in lots of hard work but still lack confidence—or even feel like an imposter—it's easy to feel like there's something inherently wrong with you, and maybe to make up for that, you steel yourself to practice more and even harder.

The problem is, if you don't understand how to practice your music with superior use of your whole self, you can practice all day long for the rest of your life, yet you still won't be able to express yourself with the kind of freedom, ease, and technical facility you desire.

In addition, you'll much more likely be plagued with physical problems such as increased tension or pain when you play, as well as mental or emotional difficulties like mind-wandering, performance anxiety, uncontrollable moods. All of the above go hand in hand with a fundamental lack of self-confidence stemming from practicing without conscious, constructive awareness of your whole self.

Central to the quality of your practice is how you concentrate

The way you pay attention and focus your mind on whatever you're doing (whether that's a technical passage in your music or how you type an email at the computer) matters enormously! The quality of your attention makes ALL the difference between a solid performance, with consistent technique and beautifully expressive flow, and a strained performance easily thrown off by anxiety, unexpected mistakes, and unhelpful thoughts.

Way back in Chapter 3, I introduced the concept that there are essentially two ways to concentrate. Let's revisit this idea and see how the way you concentrate affects the quality of your practicing.

Like most people, when you were a student, you probably learned that concentration involves narrowing your attention and you likely experienced a corresponding increase in overall tension, even if you weren't aware of it (young children often resist concentrating for this very reason). Over time, "hard" concentration starts to feel normal; never do you guess there might be any other way.

In fact, many people feel like their work has no real value unless it's "hard" work—they need to feel a certain level of tension while engaged. This fits the twisted idea that if things feel too easy, they can't be right. Brought on by the "no pain no gain" philosophy and the puritanical idea that struggle and suffering are good, we conclude that if what we do feels too easy or we're having too much fun, then we're being lazy or doing something wrong. We should buckle down and put in more effort!

Unfortunately, when you work on your music in a way that subtly raises the tension levels in your whole mind-body system, practicing can actually slow down your progress and sabotage your performance, even when you've worked really hard and prepared in a conscientious, systematic way.

It's pretty obvious if you think about it: if you concentrate hard when practicing and your tension levels are higher than when you're calm and centered (like when you're meditating or relaxing at the beach), then your muscles will be contracting more than they need to.

That makes it slightly more difficult to breathe, move your fingers, shift your arms, make smooth bow changes rapidly, play with exactness and precise intonation—or, respond instantly to the whims of your conductor, who suddenly decides to take an entirely different tempo in performance than what you'd rehearsed!

Concentrating "hard" also makes it harder to think creatively on the spot. The fact is, in a performance or at an audition you need to be ready for anything—totally resilient, adaptable, and responsive to whatever comes your way, both physically and mentally.

When you're used to concentrating "hard," you might *feel* like you're ready for anything, alert and ready to pounce, but in reality you are more "fixed" than "free" in both mind and body as your mind and body are geared up with excess tension and *set* for things to go a certain way. This makes it much harder for you to spontaneously shift direction and bounce back from whatever throws you off: the sudden wrong note you just played, the string that slips out of tune in the middle of your audition, the reed that isn't doing what you'd expected it to, the shoe that pinches your toes, the sudden dryness and freezing temperature in the concert hall.

What you need to know and can learn through systematic training and abundant practice (which is what I teach my coaching students in great detail) is that *true* concentration does *not* involve narrowing your focus and making things hard or intense.

On the contrary, it involves *softening* your focus and letting go of expectations, while developing a light, carefree quality of heightened attention, bright like quicksilver. F. M. Alexander called it "quickening the conscious mind." In this context, the word "quickening" carries the dual meaning of awakening and increasing speed.

Developing this kind of true concentration places YOU and your well-being at the center of your awareness. Everything else (bow, reed, sheet music, conductor, audience, etc.) is secondary, and is organized in a broad, spacious sphere of attention relative to your experience of yourself.

This way of concentrating allows your body to automatically reflect that spacious mental freedom by releasing excess tension and becoming more fluid and mobile.

When you concentrate on your music while placing a higher priority on what is actually happening within YOU, making this your Primary Concern instead of prioritizing the effect you're getting with your instrument or how other people may be reacting to what you're doing, the result is a much greater sense of calm and confident self-control. That ease allows the music to be expressed naturally through your body and your instrument, without your technique and expression being blocked by excess neuromuscular tension.

If you've ever meditated or practiced mindful contemplation by quietening your mind-body-self with single-minded focus (with a focus on prayer, art, or Nature, for example), then you've probably had a taste of such true concentration.

Even though focused contemplation is natural, it is not typically our habit, and you may have noticed that getting better control over your mind can seem like a Herculean task! If it seems hard to bring your mind to stillness when you aren't doing much of anything else, just imagine how challenging this can be if you try to do it while performing the Tchaikovsky violin concerto in front of an audience of a thousand people!

This is why we start out very simply and slowly in my coaching programs, first learning true concentration skills away from the instrument with Primary Practice, then bringing our Primary Practice into our musical practice sessions. In that way, we come to realize that it doesn't matter so much what activity we're engaged in—whether it's meditating on a cushion, doing the dishes, practicing the violin, or performing at Lincoln Center.

Our Primary Concern, wherever we are, no matter what we're doing, is always the same. When we ask ourselves, "What's happening to me as I __________?" we are instantly brought back to the present moment with full awareness. We wake up, we come back to who we truly are, and the relative quality of what we produce becomes less and less important. As we care less about results, we become more content, able to let go of excess tension. Paradoxically, this is the exact moment that the fundamental quality of our actions improves, without even trying.

What you practice is what you get better at

Just as what you focus on you get more of, you also get better at what you're practicing. With repetition come stronger neural networks and easier recall. So, it makes a lot of sense to be vigilantly aware of what you're actually practicing—far beyond the notes on the page! *How and what are you practicing?*

Are you getting better at playing that piece you're performing next month *with ease and joy because you're focusing on ease and enjoying yourself* as you practice?

Or are you getting better at *worrying about the hard parts and getting distracted* by the noises down the hall as you play through your piece?

Do you systematically practice letting go of worries and paying attention to the note you're actually playing right now, so that the music is free to flow naturally without a forced sound, and without rushing?

People tend to forget that they are not just practicing music when they practice; they are necessarily also repeating habits of mind and movement. When you repeat things with a certain attitude, that attitude becomes habitual and over time you develop an automatic response to similar problems.

For example, if your automatic reaction to seeing your instrument in its case is guilt, thinking, *I really should be practicing*, then the corresponding physical tension produced by that guilty thought is what you'll bring to your instrument when you finally take it out of the case. You will have an automatic neural network association of "instrument—guilt—tension," which will then, once you start playing, be more likely to trigger new unhelpful thoughts.

Because the excess tension you bring to the instrument when you finally pick it up will make it harder to play with technical facility and free-flowing emotions, you'll be more likely to be judgmental about yourself. You might think: *Oh, that sounds bad. I should practice more. I'm too tight. I need to relax!*

So, if you're bringing these kinds of self-critical thoughts to your practicing, along with their corresponding physical tension, clearly you are practicing "how-to-play-my-instrument-with-less-satisfaction-and-more-tension." You will get better at *that* the more you practice.

And you know what? What you practice is what you bring to the stage.

You won't suddenly feel better about yourself and perform with effortless ease, freedom, and joy onstage, tossing aside the guilt and tension you've been practicing with up until that moment. If you want to perform with self-satisfaction, effortless ease, freedom, and joy . . . well, then it follows that you need to bring those very qualities to your practice.

This whole book is about recognizing that the way you think and move habitually through your day is the same manifestation of "you" that you bring to the practice room. Your habitual unhelpful thoughts and excess tension bleed into what you do with your instrument and suck the life out of your music when you're not looking.

You are practicing YOU all day long. Then, in the practice room, you simply reinforce YOU + Musical Instrument. Why would you be any different with your instrument in the practice room when the door to your studio closes? Why would you be any different onstage from the YOU who practiced at home?

Of course, you might *feel* different from day to day, and you might feel more nervous or excited in performance, but underneath, you're exactly the same person with exactly the same tendencies that you bring to endlessly changing circumstances.

The Art of Freedom Method and Primal Alexander shine the light of awareness onto the YOU of the present moment. By shifting your attention to yourself as a whole, you can begin to notice your habits of thought and movement whenever you remember. And you can make a conscious choice at any time to step out of the vicious habit of mindlessness and constriction to create a new, conscious habit of making your Primary Concern primary, bringing your full presence into the practice room.

Looked at this way, there isn't really any difference between practice and performance; in both situations, you're just being YOU.

Once you recognize that your fundamental Purpose and your overall well-being—your Self-Use—are far more important than anything else, including the speed of improvement at your instrument, then you can more readily play the long game of musical mastery.

That means you can become more patient with yourself when things in your playing don't change as rapidly as you'd like them to because you know you're going in the right direction. And you can be confident about that direction when, as much as you can, you're doing your ConstructiveThinking and prioritizing your Primary Concern when you practice.

This is the key to fundamental improvement that lasts and transfers to ALL skills you engage in—making it easier to do whatever it is you're doing.

In the next chapter, I'll explain how the Primal Alexander Awareness Etudes offer you a very practical, step-by-step progression to make bringing your True Self to your musical practice sessions easier and easier over time.

Apply this Problem-Solving Technique to Your Practice

Focus on what's already working instead of obsessing over what's not

The only way to do great work is to love what you do.

~ *Steve Jobs*

Do you know why you practice?

When asked why they practice, most musicians will respond with the simple answer: "to improve my playing." Of course, if you think about it, what we're doing when we practice is *continuously solving the problem of how to create what we intend* so we can get what we want.

In Chapter 2, I wrote about the importance of having a deeper sense of life purpose in mind when you practice, which will serve as a whole-person anchor to keep coming back to when you lose your way or things get difficult.

And in Chapter 16, I described how you can set up your practice sessions for guaranteed success by making good use of your Golden Period and clarifying your intentions, using the 5 Pre-Pearls of The Art of Freedom Method. From the Primal Alexander perspective, our most important goal is always the Primary Concern—namely, to be present and find out what's happening to us from moment to moment, as we engage in any activity.

Once you've reminded yourself of your purpose and your Primary Concern, you can then attend to what I call "secondary goals," which are more specific to your personal goals as a musician. You are likely to have multiple secondary goals, such as improving your intonation, speeding up your vibrato, memorizing a piece, projecting with a full tone, or increasing your rhythmic accuracy.

When you bring any number of intentions to your consciousness, it becomes clear that a big reason for practicing is to solve the specific problems of how to achieve your goals in the most effective, efficient way possible.

But watch out! Whenever achieving goals is involved, it's easy to let habitual end-gaining (attachment to results) slip into the picture, so that you miss enjoying the process of getting there and subtly reduce the quality of your results.

Primal Alexander teaches you how to problem-solve without end-gaining by repeatedly reminding you to make your Primary Concern more important than your secondary goals.

Do you spend more energy on finding problems than actually solving them?

There are always endless things that we can improve!

In order to know what needs more work, it's essential to be as discerning and objective as possible when we reflect on our playing. Making comparisons to an ideal sound in our mind is important so that we have a clear idea of the music we're aspiring to create, and it's helpful to have positive role models to learn from as we refine our musical concepts.

However, we need to be very careful in making comparisons. When we fall short of our expectations, we need to be on the lookout for subtle end-gaining. End-gaining (caring more about getting results than engaging in the process) can trigger negative reactions that make us feel bad about ourselves and destroy the enthusiasm we bring to our practice. A hypercritical attitude can really work against us and tear us down if we let judgmental thinking creep into the mix.

Overemphasizing the search for flaws and succumbing to the negativity bias can make you overlook and undervalue what already works. This can turn practice into a laborious task rather than an enjoyable experiment that leads to rapid learning. It's worth noting that many teachers indirectly and unconsciously encourage excessive and unhealthy fault-finding in their students.

There's a common misconception that teachers are mainly paid to identify and solve their students' problems. Consequently, instead of focusing on the overall experience, well-being, and ease of the students in the moment, teachers often dedicate most of their time to finding mistakes and highlighting tension, prioritizing the negative aspects over the positive ones.

How we approach and address the need for improvement is crucial. Does the teacher point out issues with ease, objectivity, and encouragement? Or is there an underlying dissatisfaction and an unspoken (or spoken) pressure to work harder?

When a disproportionate amount of time in a lesson is spent on identifying and fixing flaws, it's natural for the student to adopt the same mindset during individual practice sessions between lessons.

This approach shifts the focus of practice from enjoying the process and the music being created to obsessing over what isn't working.

Consider this: do you want more problems to solve? Or more solutions to problems?

Do you want to experience more tension . . . or more ease?

If you want more solutions and ease, you need to learn how to direct your attention more skillfully towards the easing within you, which will gradually reveal the most natural solutions to your problems.

Widening your field of attention with "Ima"

One of the very first things I teach my coaching students is how to expand their attention to include the ever-present ease within their being. The quickest way to learn this begins with being able to differentiate between relative tension and relative ease or flow in your body.

Because you get more of what you focus on, when you give more attention to tension, pain, anxiety, or mistakes, the overall tension level in your system will increase—even if you manage to feel a bit more relaxed in one *part* of your body when you do that, or you're able to fix a specific technical or musical problem on your instrument. Bringing tension to how you work on a problem is not the best way to solve it; bringing ease to the problem IS.

Once you've learned to sense easing in your system as opposed to tensing, the next skill you need to learn is how to further expand and unify your field of attention. That way, you will notice not just the specific "problem spots" that are loudly in the foreground of your experience *but also* the quiet places of calm and ease in your body—what's going well—that are more subtle and ever-present underneath.

If you pay too much attention to mistakes, you'll tense up as you do that and be more likely to repeat those mistakes or make new ones.

Of course, that doesn't mean at all that you should deny your pain or your mistakes! On the contrary, listen to them, include them in your experience . . . and then move on.

It's like learning how to care for a toddler throwing a temper tantrum (your pain sending you messages loud and clear). First, you listen, giving her your full attention for a moment with loving acceptance ("I'm here for you; I hear you; I see you; I love you"). And you stay with her without expecting her to calm down immediately.

After a little bit, you move away to pay some attention to another toddler (a different part of your body that feels a little less painful, or relatively silent, comfortable or easy), who is sitting across the room by herself, quietly coloring with a smile on her face.

In this way, you keep shifting your attention with mild curiosity from places of relative tension in your body to places of relative ease. There is no judgment in this process, just as there is no judgment of little children when they're hurting.

Mio Morales calls the specific practice of compassionately noticing and acknowledging what's showing up in the body as described above "Ima" (which means "now" in Japanese). I think of "Ima" as a "pre-Awareness Etude." With Ima, you learn to shift your attention from one area of your body to another with detached curiosity, acceptance, and self-compassion.

As a first response to extreme performance anxiety, or if you're in the midst of a strong fight-flight-freeze (startle) response, Ima is my most highly recommended tool. If you feel like you can't think straight and you're unable to calmly do your ConstructiveThinking under stress, Ima is your go-to solution to bring your mind back into the present moment within your body.

This very grounding, centering, and calming practice is sometimes more immediately accessible in situations like these than the kind of ConstructiveThinking we do in the Awareness Etudes—which are taught right after Ima.

Ima is very powerful in its simplicity, making us aware of natural abilities that we have but don't normally make use of consciously. With Ima, we learn how to:

- shift our awareness from outside the body to places within the body
- listen to our body with detached curiosity, acceptance, and compassion
- define and differentiate between places of relative tension and relative ease in the body
- find out what happens when we pay more attention to either tension or ease
- give ourselves time to be with what's uncomfortable and accept the reality of our present experience, free of judgment or expectation
- allow our experience, including the feelings in our body-mind-self, to change and flow according to the quality of our presence and what we choose to pay attention to

Once my students learn Ima (this typically happens right away on Day 1), I teach them ConstructiveThinking (as defined in Chapter 7). As mentioned, there are many ways to do ConstructiveThinking, but in Primal Alexander the most common form is a question because as we wonder about the answer, a healthy sense of curiosity and directed movement within us automatically awakens. Usually we begin practicing ConstructiveThinking by asking, "Where else do I seem to be easing a bit?" as described in detail in Chapter 12.

Alexander Technique is a problem-solving technique

Mio often calls the Alexander Technique a "problem-solving technique." The ONE real problem we ever have is right now, and it can be summarized by this one question, "What can I do NOW?" The ONE solution then presents itself just as simply: be present, here and now.

> But how do you do that? *Just be yourself*, my father told me.
>
> But how? *Wake up and redirect your attention to what already IS.*
>
> But how? *Make your Primary Concern primary*: "What's happening to me as I ______?"

Then . . . notice what's already working. Get curious about the easing within and around you. Do some ConstructiveThinking (CT) by asking yourself: "Where else do I seem to be easing a bit?"

And then . . . let your next decision arise and move you from that easier state. Making your decisions from a place of ease and integration is an invaluable skill. It improves the quality of your music! (More on smart practice skills in Chapter 21.)

In the beginning, we learn how to do CT using words. And the sentence "Where else do I seem to be easing a bit?" is our doorway into an easier, wordless way of being.

This shift in our attention, or the way we concentrate and focus, is initiated by CT just as a tiny pebble dropped into a still pond of water initiates a gentle ripple of vibrations that continue until something else disturbs the pond, when the activity of CT needs renewing and the mind is brought back to the present moment.

ConstructiveThinking is a serenely calm, yet active state of alert awareness. Thinking this way is natural, but not habitual, and we need to learn how to activate it through our will, remembrance, and ever-renewing conscious choice.

With practice, it becomes second nature to let go of our attachment to our habitual, learned, narrow way of thinking/living and watch ourselves moving with ease and grace much more often, without even trying.

This is what we aspire to as musicians, and what allows us to enter a flow state and experience "effortless" mastery more and more often.

The Primal Alexander "Awareness Etudes"

By doing ConstructiveThinking in the way I've described, a student quickly learns it's possible to concentrate in a way that highlights the effortless ease of BEING instead of the effortful work of DOING.

Of course, Alexander's "quickening the conscious mind" requires practice, which is why Mio Morales introduced the daily Primal Alexander Awareness Etudes into his method of teaching. The Awareness Etudes give students a very simple framework to improve the quality of their concentration (or change their experience of it) by getting curious and noticing the relative tension or ease they bring to their movements.

Once they can do these movements easily, they can then practice paying attention to the easing within themselves during each step of the Etudes, to become more sensitive to when they interfere with that flow. As soon as they catch themselves interfering, all they need do in that moment is renew their ConstructiveThinking, thereby instantly letting go of the excess tension and reorienting themselves back towards greater ease.

Mio likens this process of sensitive redirection of your awareness with ConstructiveThinking to what happens when you drive a car down the road. You can't just aim the car straight ahead, push the gas pedal, and expect the car to keep going straight by itself. If you don't constantly make small adjustments to the steering wheel as you're moving, the car will gradually veer off the road. The hands of a skilled driver make those adjustments automatically.

But you don't actually know what it feels like to make those micro-adjustments until you get behind the wheel for the first time. Novice drivers need to learn what it feels like when the car starts straying off to one side, and then how to consciously direct their hands to turn the wheel and aim the car straight ahead again. With practice, you start noticing smaller changes in direction sooner, and your adjustments become quicker and smaller.

In time, your brain makes those tiny adjustments immediately and automatically, so that you don't even have to think about it. In this way, you have the impression that the car is going straight even though there are constant tiny fluctuations of movement away from the center and back. The one thing necessary for this process to happen with effortless ease is your wakeful, conscious attention to aiming the car as a whole towards where you want it to go.

This is exactly how it works with your body-mind-self. First you need to know what you want and where you want to go, and you need to keep that in the back of your mind. If you lose sight of your purpose or fall asleep, or you keep focusing on what's wrong or not working, that's like taking your eyes off the road. And sooner or later, you'll find yourself in a ditch or end up in New York when you meant to go to California!

Once you're clear about what you want (effortless ease in playing your instrument, for example), through constant practice you develop a greater sensitivity to the subtle changes in overall tension within you. You start catching yourself more often when you're thinking in a way that increases that tension and interferes with your natural ease. Over time, your ability to respond and let go in the moment (inhibit and direct, to use Alexander's terms) happens faster and becomes more automatic. Just like when you drive a car, all that's required for your chosen activity to happen with effortless ease is your wakeful, conscious attention to aiming yourself as a whole towards where you want to go and surrendering to the natural movement—led by your Inner Coordinator—that enables you to go there.

Some say it this way: "Let go and let God," or "Let go . . . and go with the flow"!

Two basic Primal Alexander Awareness Etudes

This ever-renewing process of noticing and redirecting your attention away from what you don't want and towards what you do want with overall ease may sound abstract, but developing this skill allows you to solve any problem at all in life and in music with more ease and flow—and I'm not exaggerating. AND there's actually a very practical way to learn it.

In music, we might describe good practicing simply in terms of "stop—think—play." But once you recognize that *directing your Primary Instrument (YOU) well* must take precedence over what you're doing with your musical instrument, you can appreciate how the practice translates into "being present—ConstructiveThinking—moving" your whole self. As if it were an extension of your own body, your musical instrument moves as a result.

Because when you improve the way you use your mind-body-self and apply your whole self in a general way to your music, any specific problems with your instrument begin to work themselves out, just like the car that stays on the road without your needing to think about it, in a very real sense, the music begins to "play itself" when you're paying more attention to the quality of your Self-Use.

In my Level 1 self-study course, the first thing you learn is how to improve the quality of your awareness and move with more ease *without* your musical instrument. You learn to do this in a very systematic, step-by-step way by practicing a few short, very simple Primal Alexander Awareness Etudes twice a day for just a few minutes at a time.

Basic Awareness Etude #1: TheCyCle™

TheCyCle is the first Primal Alexander Awareness Etude I teach my students. A meditative etude, TheCyCle takes less than three minutes to complete and involves barely any movement. Primarily, its purpose is to develop the skill of ConstructiveThinking without the added distraction of engaging in activity. Although versions of TheCyCle can be done anytime, anywhere, under just about any circumstances, it's normally done seated with the eyes open.

To practice this Etude, you softly cradle each finger, one at a time, with the opposite hand and slowly count to four on each finger. After each number, silently ask the CT question "Where else do I seem to be easing a bit?" with a light, detached curiosity that doesn't require you to look for a feeling or expect an answer.

Don't try to (or expect to) feel a result in your body. No matter what happens (whether you feel something or not), simply move on to the next number and ask the question again, with the same kind of childlike wonder that has no idea what to expect but accepts whatever shows up.

As you cycle through your ten fingers, simply notice whatever comes up (in your thoughts, body, or mood) as your nervous system gradually begins to calm down, and your whole system has a chance to lighten up a bit.

Many of my students report tremendous benefits just from doing this one Etude for a while; for example, relief from pain, calming of the nerves before an audition or performance, relaxation during an MRI or while having dental work done, easing of relationship conflicts, better decision-making, and relief from insomnia.

TheCyCle is the best pre-practice warmup I know, and it can help anyone, not just musicians.

> "TheCyCle has been so healing for me it has literally changed my life! Noticing the ease in my body drastically reduced the amount of pain I was dealing with on a daily basis from chronic health issues, stemming from a severe car accident, scoliosis, and other traumatic events. Doing TheCyCle has allowed my body to feel better than it has in twenty-five years, when I was first diagnosed. Never did I think I could feel this good again! It has been healing for mind, body, and spirit in so many wonderful, unexpected ways. And continues to be healing.........I do TheCyCle and my Awareness Etudes several times a day, every day, no exceptions."
>
> ~ Angèle, Harp

In my group class online, I currently have an Art of Freedom student, Rosy, a young violin teacher and dancer of Armenian descent who lives in Syria. She has undergone unthinkable trials over many years, dodging a war in her hometown of Aleppo, witnessing violence, death, bombings, and unrelenting destruction around her.

Most recently this year, she endured the horrific and traumatic experience of the major earthquake and aftershocks that decimated villages and killed nearly sixty thousand people across Syria and Turkey.

I reached out to Rosy as soon as I heard about the earthquake, greatly concerned for her and her family's welfare. Thankfully, she could connect to the internet right away, posting in real time. I am still moved as I write this . . . thanks to ConstructiveThinking and our work together, Rosy was able to begin processing her trauma as soon as the first earthquake hit. She wrote to me, "My whole body is shaking! Doing lots and lots of Ima!" By helping herself like this, she managed to stay strong and help many of those around her in turn, by passing along what she had learned, coaching them to do Ima and TheCyCle.

A few weeks later, in class, Rosy asked me how she could help her violin students, who, being young children, were all especially traumatized by the earthquake. Thankfully, she had already been meeting with them and helping them get their minds off of current events by drawing pictures of their violins and sharing their love of music together. When she asked me what more she could do, I recommended that she turn Ima into a playful children's game, helping them identify the relative tension in their bodies and redirecting their attention to experiencing more ease and comfort within.

After that, I suggested that she could get creative and do mini versions of TheCyCle with them. She was overwhelmed with gratitude to have these simple, yet profoundly powerful tools at her disposal to help herself, these children, their families, and so many more to stay sane and healthy in the face of immense and overwhelming multiple disasters.

I will be forever humbled by the power of ConstructiveThinking, grateful for the Awareness Etudes Mio has invented that help make being human so much easier.

Basic Awareness Etude #2: MJ™

The next basic Primal Alexander Awareness Etude is called MJ (named after two celebrities with excellent movement coordination, Michael Jordan and Michael Jackson).

MJ is the first Etude to introduce very simple movements using the arms and hands, and it takes a total of about thirty seconds to complete. This little Etude teaches the vital skill of awareness in activity, comprised of how to (1) inhibit your habitual reaction to the intention to move by doing some ConstructiveThinking immediately before moving; (2) allow the movement to happen naturally by itself as it flows from the easing elicited by the ConstructiveThinking—just as a leaf begins to move with the stream as soon as it falls into the water; (3) with detached curiosity, watch the easing happening within yourself while your arms move, noticing when/if you interfere.

During the Awareness Etudes, you practice doing your CT and wondering: *What happens to the sense of easing as I move? Does it continue or go away? Do I notice an increase of tension at some point in the movement, or do I continue to flow with ease all the way through the movement and beyond?*

At first, you may not notice much other than your arms moving, but as you practice MJ (and the many other movement Etudes) over time, you learn to bring a unified field of attention to what you're doing, and you become highly attuned to subtle fluctuations in your awareness and the subsequent tensing or easing of your muscles.

With regular practice, you develop the subtle sensitivity required to guide your body, arms, and fingers in flow to play your musical instrument with expert skill and masterful artistry.

The systematic, daily practice of the basic Primal Alexander Awareness Etudes takes just five minutes or less to complete in total, so they're extremely easy for anyone to fit into even the busiest schedule.

After learning the basic Etudes, my students are introduced to a series of Awareness Etudes that include a wider variety of movements, gradually becoming more complex as they move through Levels 1–3 of my self-study courses. Some of the later Etudes are based on Jin Shin Jytsu (a Japanese self-healing art), Tai Chi, and I Chuan.

The effect of the Awareness Etudes can be unexpectedly beneficial for your overall well-being as you start moving and responding to events with more calm acceptance and less reactivity and tension—so much so that it warrants prescribing these Etudes in a way similar to how a doctor prescribes antibiotics: I tell my students to take two sessions per day and don't skip a dose if you want to get the best results! :)

We practice these Awareness Etudes in my live group classes, along with playful games we make up together based on the basic Etudes framework, which help us relate the process to unexpected real-life events and performance situations. In addition to the Etudes & Games sessions, we have involved discussions in which we address all kinds of physical and emotional obstacles that can get in the way of effortless and natural music-making. During our master-classes, I help students apply an easier way of being and paying attention to their instrumental technique, phrasing, habitual thought-patterns, and so much more. Classes are always stimulating, fun, and deeply insightful!

Applying ConstructiveThinking to your musical instrument

After learning how to move with more ease and conscious control without a musical instrument, you are then ready to begin applying ConstructiveThinking to how you move *with* your instrument.

As before, this is done with very simple things first, such as thinking about, approaching, lifting, and placing the instrument, then playing just a few long notes. I introduce these movements in a detailed Awareness Etude sequence I've developed called the Instrumental Compass.

For each musical instrument, there is a different Instrumental Compass, since for approaching and playing every instrument a different process is involved. The most complex Compass I've ever developed with a student is the Bassoon Compass, as it requires quite a lot of steps to take the instrument out of the case and put together the different parts. Even soaking a reed becomes part of the Compass!

The value of the Instrumental Compass lies in looking mindfully at each small activity that needs to happen before we can make music. Usually, those activities have become so habitual that we're not even aware we're doing them, and we tend to rush through them to get to the "important stuff" of making music.

We forget that EVERY activity we engage in is the "important stuff," and what we do with our whole mind-body-self as we get ready to play is just as important as the music. The Compass teaches us to make the most of our Golden Period (the time before; see Chapter 16), so we can do lots of ConstructiveThinking prior to actually making our first sound, and in this way optimize our chance of flowing into that first note with effortless grace.

When you mindlessly rush through the motions of getting ready to play, you bring all of the residual tension from your day—and every other time you've rushed through those movements in the past—to how you play *this* music.

If you take your instrument out of the case and rosin your bow with lots of excess tension, you're very likely to bring your bow to the string with the same tension, then transmit that tension into your vibrato, and it will be pulled out of the string for the world to hear.

Yes, we can hear your tension when you play—even if you're completely unaware of it. But don't worry—we can also hear your ease and joy! :)

So . . . which one do you want to experience, and which one do you want us to hear more of?

If you want your audience to relax and enjoy the resonant sounds you make and the technical passages you toss off with relative ease, then it's really worth prioritizing what you're doing with your attention and the quality of your "use" *before* you begin, just as much as while playing. The quality of your practice session and the music you make is absolutely guaranteed to be more successful all around when you pay attention to what you're doing with your whole self before you begin.

This is why I teach my students to practice some form of the Instrumental Compass as part of their regular warmup routine, along with TheCyCle and any other Primal Awareness Etudes in their repertoire.

Over time, my students are able to apply ConstructiveThinking to any aspect of their music, including their teaching. Here's how one of my students, a bass player, conductor, and school-teacher has brought the Awareness Etudes into his teaching, as well as his own music-making.

"When I began studying with Jennifer Roig-Francolí, I had a vague idea that the Alexander Technique could help me with the aches and pains of being an aging musician. I'd been playing double bass as a semi-professional for over forty years, and it felt like it was all catching up with me. I had no idea how radically working with Jennifer would change not just my playing, but my teaching practice and my life.

"I knew but never fully realized the connection between how we think and how we play or even how we are physically in the world. The daily Primal Alexander Awareness Etudes have made me feel more grounded and less rushed; they've given me a greater sense of ease, even under the fire of a difficult rehearsal, performance, or practice session . . .

"One indelible memory I have is of the first time I led nearly a hundred of my orchestra students (grades 8–12), prior to a concert, in some of the Etudes Jennifer taught. I was astounded not just by the level of focused energy in the warm-up room, but by the quality of our performance that evening. I've never wavered in my belief in the power of Primal Alexander since that evening.

"I know that the techniques I've learned from Jennifer and Mio help students . . . I've gone from a teacher who tended to micromanage every bit of setup in my students, to someone who helps their students find the 'easier' ways to do things. This doesn't mean I let things go, but I try to get their thinking and observational powers engaged so they notice the best positions and solutions. In online lessons it can be difficult to get your students to hold the bow or the instrument correctly, but by approaching these issues using Primal Alexander as modeled by Jennifer, I'm helping students discover for themselves how to do things more easily. How to play with better technique.

"Instead of detailed assignments when I've identified something they need to work on, I urge them to experiment and 'see what happens.' It's taken some of the drudgery out of online lessons and practicing. It's given us the freedom to explore and devise new games and solutions. Jennifer's Art of Freedom Method has definitely made music more fun (and yes, I did learn to play more easily and hurt less as a bass player, too)!"

~ Joseph, Conductor, Educator, Double Bass

With regular practice of the Awareness Etudes, my students dramatically improve the effectiveness of their practicing, acquiring more and more complexity, as they learn how to combine ConstructiveThinking with the most current practice strategies based on cutting-edge research. We'll be looking at some of those combined practice strategies in the next chapter.

RESOURCE:

Learn how to do Ima, ConstructiveThinking and TheCyCle from my companion video training here: https://www.artoffreedom.me/book/training

Adopt Smarter Practice Strategies for Stellar Performance

Improve on current practice techniques with ConstructiveThinking™

This is much too serious to get too serious about.

~ *Marjorie Barstow*

Everyone knows how important it is to practice regularly in order to improve a skill, and most people also recognize that paying attention to the *quality* of our practice is essential for mastery. To this end, there have been countless books and manuals written on musical pedagogy, and many research studies have been done to find the best ways to learn and improve skills.

What is much less recognized, however, is the fact that the relative effectiveness of any methodology, no matter how well researched or clearly proven it is to work, is entirely dependent on the quality of Self-Use (mind-body-self coordination) the musician brings to it. Somehow, this stunningly obvious fact has been almost entirely overlooked by researchers, teachers, and performers, and the concept of Primary Practice is completely ignored.

Even the most skilled and successful musicians are largely ignorant of the concept of Primary Practice and how essential it is to incorporate this awareness into their musical practice sessions for true artistic mastery. Lacking this understanding prevents them from fully enjoying the fruits of their hard work in performance, since they can always sense that something elusive is missing and whatever they produce never feels quite "good enough."

This deep lack of self-confidence keeps them stuck in a vicious cycle of hard work—subpar performance—disappointment and frustration—renewed hard work, etc. This sequence of events is a main contributor to physical discomfort, injury, performance anxiety, mental disturbances, and emotional suffering, all of which will only increase over time if left unaddressed. And the most effective, long-lasting solution to any of these is by remembering to prioritize your Primary Concern—how you use your mind-body-self from moment to moment—and to do your ConstructiveThinking as often as you can remember to.

In the previous chapter, I shared how students of The Art of Freedom Method first learn how to improve the use of their Primary Instrument (the whole self) through Primary Practice away from the music, and then how they begin to bring that improved use of self to their musical instrument.

The next step in their artistic development is to begin applying their improved Self-Use to the music itself. This is where it becomes essential to have a good working knowledge of the best learning methods and practice techniques based on cutting-edge research.

Knowing what to practice and how to practice it well is equivalent to having your own best teacher by your side 24/7. When you know how to apply your whole self to every aspect of musical practice in the most efficient and effective ways, it's impossible NOT to watch your skills improve!

> "When I joined Jennifer's program, something miraculous happened each week! My music-making became easier and more enjoyable because I was pain-free, and certain fears began to melt away. It was like a musical rebirth! My shoulders evened out without forcing them (I have scoliosis), a newfound freedom emerged, and I realized I could be the powerful musician I've dreamt of being since I was nine. Jennifer's knowledge and wisdom guides you to making incredible music— completely in ease. As a performer and educator, I believe every musician and teacher should take a course with her!"
>
> ~ Lacie, Vocalist, Violinist, Fiddler, Recording Artist, Educator

In this chapter, I'd like to share three practice concepts, central to The Art of Freedom Method, that bring my students consistently excellent results. The nuances are far too numerous and subtle to be expressed here verbally, so I'll just give you a broad overview of what's possible, in the hopes that you'll be inspired to reach out and learn more directly from me.

Let's begin by looking at the importance of what is known as "deliberate practice."

Deliberate practice

> *Fundamentally, the theory of deliberate practice posits that development of expertise requires incorporating a self-reflective feedback loop into the skill delivery or development (i.e., practice) process, rather than simply performing a task repetitively until mastered. To achieve maximal efficiency, time for self-reflection, and instantaneous feedback are vital for allowing the learner to self-adjust and make improvements before engaging in the next task. Mastery is thus achieved through repeated cycles of focused practice and self-editing, with each cycle emphasizing one or more aspects of a desired skill.* [24]

There's no question that to improve your music-making, deliberate practice is absolutely necessary. The study does add the caveat that "One important requirement for successful implementation of deliberate practice is a qualified teacher or preceptor to guide the process, shaping the student's reflections, and providing feedback." But what qualifies a teacher to give the kind of in-depth, holistic feedback required for true artistic mastery goes far beyond what is normally taught in a pedagogy class. Besides, even if a teacher IS uncommonly well qualified to teach deliberate practice, most students only see their teacher for an hour or less each week, being left to their own resources the rest of the time, which easily allows the end-gaining habit to seize the upper hand.

As it says in the description above, deliberate practice involves focus, time for self-reflection, instantaneous feedback, self-adjustments, or self-editing. Therefore, qualitative deliberate practice requires:

- the ability to focus with true concentration and an expanded field of attention as described throughout this book, especially Chapters 19 and 20
- the ability to make good use of your time by being alert and present in the moment, without pushing ahead or dragging behind
- the ability to observe yourself while performing a task and recall what happened with relative objectivity, so that you can accurately assess what worked and what didn't
- sufficient knowledge and creativity to come up with the best possible solutions to improve your performance, so you can decide what you need to do less of, and more of

24 Joyce M. Wang and Joseph A. Zorek, "Deliberate Practice as a Theoretical Framework for Interprofessional Experiential Education," Frontiers in Pharmacology 7: 188 (2016), published online July 7, 2016, https://doi.org/10.3389%2Ffphar.2016.00188.

- the ability to self-adjust through experimentation, with a curious and non-judgmental attitude, and without end-gaining or becoming overly attached to the results

Without these essential skills, the self-reflective feedback loop of deliberate practice will always be subject to the inaccuracies of what Alexander called "faulty sensory appreciation" (when you think you're doing something, but it turns out you're not, or when what you're feeling doesn't accurately reflect reality), and you'll end up wasting a lot of time repeating tasks with wrong ideas and excess tension. For example, you might think you've corrected your intonation, but when you listen back to a recording, you can hear that the passage is still out of tune; or thinking you're sitting straight and your shoulders are relaxed when you play the piano, when in fact, a video reveals you're hunching over the keys with your shoulders raised.

For this reason, even musicians who know about the concept of deliberate practice can spend a lot of time practicing and still end up sounding worse! It's not necessarily because they don't know how to practice well, it's because *they don't know how to use themselves well and pay attention to what really matters while they practice;* they are in the habit of prioritizing their Primary Practice neither in daily life nor with their instruments.

Combining deliberate practice with the improved Self-Use brought about by The Art of Freedom Method and Primal Alexander will ensure that the self-reflective feedback loop takes the whole person into account, thus, is based on more accurate feedback. This kind of practicing is more fully conscious and far more effective than deliberate practice alone.

With better Self-Use, you will be able to make better use of your time, the accuracy of your senses (including your sight, hearing, and touch) will improve, you'll be able to think more clearly and come up with better solutions to problems much more quickly, and you'll bring a more relaxed body to your practice, which will enable you to carry out your new ideas with greater mobility, responsiveness, ease, and joy.

Improving on mainstream practice methods by adding ConstructiveThinking

Deliberate practice is the necessary overarching umbrella that contains all other practice methodologies. Some of the most common practice methods I include in my teaching are:

* Imagery, visualization, or what is commonly known as "mental practice" (which I prefer to call MindFlow Practice—see below)

* Whole-Part-Whole learning model

* Chunking (what I prefer to call Patterning)

* Chaining
* Spaced, or Distributed, practice
* Interleaved practice
* Retrieval practice

Even if you overthink, overfocus, and overdo, bringing a high level of overall tension to your practice, it still may be possible to play just about anything better in a limited sense when you use any or all of the above-mentioned practice techniques. You may be able to memorize your piece, play all of your double-stops in tune, and get up to speed. You may even win that competition . . . But at what cost to the general quality and depth of your artistry and your well-being down the road? Every time you interfere with your natural design—the way the parts of your mind-body-self are meant to work together efficiently, in harmony with your Spirit—and every time you block the natural easing and flow of Inspiration within you, what you're doing is essentially self-destructive and will either subtly or grossly affect the quality of the music you're making.

Mindless practice makes it literally harder to play your instrument because of the excess overall tension in your system that results from not being present to your experience in the moment. The quality of your sound will suffer, along with the musical expression of your phrasing, the ease in your timing, and the facility of your technique.

Conversely, when you add CT into any of the above practice techniques, you will dramatically improve their effectiveness, and ensure that what you're doing is actually helping you improve in the long run, instead of potentially giving you quick short-term wins that feel like you're doing the right thing when you're actually taking an unhelpful detour in the wrong direction.

I'd like to dedicate the remainder of this chapter to presenting two important Art of Freedom Method concepts which involve combining standard practice techniques with ConstructiveThinking. I call these new practice methods "Stained-Glass Practicing" and "MindFlow Practicing." These concepts are new, yet they are natural to how the mind-body-self organizes itself for optimal learning.

When you absorb these two meta-concepts and apply them at every level of your practice, from the biggest vision of a whole piece down to the micro-details of the smallest note, you truly have it made!

The quality of your practice is guaranteed to improve dramatically, and your performances will happily follow suit. Not only that, but you'll feel more confident, in control of what you're doing, and the well-being of your mind-body-self will improve, too. With consistent practice and dedication, soon you'll be able to skyrocket your abilities towards becoming the best artist you've always dreamed you can be!

'Stained-Glass Practicing'

What I call "Stained-Glass Practicing" (SGP) combines the concept of deliberate practice with ConstructiveThinking, so that an overall sense of ease and effortlessness are infused into every step of the learning process. When you bring conscious awareness of ease into every aspect of your practice, easing automatically becomes an integral part of your performance.

The concept of SGP comes from my experience watching my mother make exquisite stained-glass windows and lamps in our basement, and drawing the analogy years later between creating a work of stained-glass art and perfecting a piece of music.

To successfully manifest any idea, you need to begin with the end in mind. So, whether it's a piece of music or a stained-glass window, you start by having a good idea of what the finished work of art will look or sound like before you begin.

When you first start working on a window, you'll have a detailed pencil sketch of the complete design to work from. If you're a musician, you'll either have the sheet music in front of you, a recording to learn from, or a general framework of ideas in your mind (if you're improvising or composing your own music). Taking in the big picture of a pre-composed piece may involve first sight-reading through a complete piece of music to get a better idea of what it's about, or listening to a complete recording of the piece.

In both art forms, once you have the big picture in front of you, you can start to take in the formal structure, recognize patterns, and see what smaller sections, tools, and skills you'll need in order to create the piece.

Once you understand what's involved and you have the appropriate tools at hand, and you've developed the necessary techniques to be able to make or play the piece, you can start working on it.

With both stained-glass art and musical practice, you'll need to work on each piece of glass or section of music separately before you can put it all together, but you'll also need to keep coming back to the big picture from time to time to make sure things are fitting well and the pieces of glass will fit harmoniously into the whole.

As an aside, the practice of going back and forth between big-picture practicing (playing through large sections or the entire piece of music) and highly detailed practicing is known as the "Whole-Part-Whole" method.[25] This is a very useful technique to help musicians keep their practicing balanced, since many of us tend towards either playing through long passages without paying enough attention to detail (which can lead to sloppy playing and learned mistakes), or having an overly myopic attention to detail that forgets how everything flows together musically as a whole (which can lead to technically accurate but musically dull performances).

Whether it's a piece of glass or a section of music, when you take the time to work mindfully on one small piece at a time, you can make good decisions about what you want that piece to look or sound like. You choose the shapes, color, texture, size…vibration, speed, dynamics, pitch, etc.… create balance among how the sections relate to each other… and smooth out the rough edges so the piece connects well with the adjoining pieces. In this way, everything will fit harmoniously into the overall pattern when you put it all together.

Once you're happy with the small pieces you've created (you have a beautiful, well-shaped piece of glass, or your musical technique and expression are flowing well), you'll need to have some sort of a substance to connect them.

In a window, the gaps between pieces of glass are filled with pieces of molten lead that hold the pieces together so the window can exist as a whole and be seen in its entirety. Without the lead connecting all the individual pieces, everything would fall apart and lose its meaning.

But what happens when the work of art is intangible and ephemeral, as in music? What holds the notes, the phrases, and the bigger sections of a piece of music together, so that the mind can make sense of the whole piece, even as each note disappears in the very instant it has been revealed?

No art form can exist without the artist, and the relative quality of a work of art is directly proportionate to the degree of conscious awareness brought to its creation. This becomes obvious in the case of the performing arts, where the artist is required to be present from the beginning to the end of a work's expression.

Since a piece of music merges back into silent nothingness as soon as the musician stops playing and the sound disappears, music requires a very high degree of consciousness to be infused into and between each and every note. This awareness is the subtle golden thread that connects every aspect of music-making, and it is the light of awareness that shines through, uplifts spirits, and makes the qualitative difference between a performance born of Stained-Glass Practicing and music-making that ignores the consciousness of the Self.

25 Richard A. Swanson and Bryan D. Law, "Whole-Part-Whole Learning Model," Performance Movement Quarterly (March 1993), https://doi.org/10.1111/j.1937-8327.1993.tb00572.x.

This requires self-effacement, inner silence, quieting of the ego-chatter in the mind, so that the whole mind-body-self becomes a conduit for the musical idea to be carried into sound with minimum interference in the moment.

As Thomas Merton wrote in his book *No Man Is an Island*, "Music is pleasing not only because of the sound but because of the silence that is in it: without the alternation of sound and silence there would be no rhythm."

I've written this whole book to emphasize how the entire self must be involved in the process of artistic creation. To be fully present and committed to your art with your whole self in the act of creation is a very lofty ideal, and yet ConstructiveThinking is the practical, simple, and instantaneous solution to the seemingly impossible and unachievable goal of artistic mastery.

Think of ConstructiveThinking as a skillful medium you can develop to access the life-stuff that holds the notes together and gives your music meaning. This skill is what allows the artist to tap into her creative essence, Being-Consciousness-Bliss, and potentially transcend her earth-bound humanity, her music to become a window offering both a glimpse of the Divine and a way to share that sacred vision with others.

In my coaching programs, I teach my students exactly how to practice with ConstructiveThinking, bringing more awareness and ease into a piece of music one step—one gorgeous piece of "stained glass"—at a time.

MindFlow practice instead of "mental" practice

One of my pet peeves is the term "mental practice." To me, this term just reinforces the wrong idea that the mind and body are separate entities, and that practicing without a musical instrument must be a mental or non-physical activity. In fact, *all* modes of practicing require the participation of the whole self—mind, body, emotions, and creative spirit.

I propose that we honor the unity of the self and our desire to make unifying music with effortless ease and flow by replacing the limiting term "mental practice" with the more inclusive, holistic term "MindFlow Practice." Using the term "MindFlow Practice" (MFP) reminds us that the human organism is an integrated energetic system constantly in flux; a hierarchical system in which the Inner Wisdom of the whole self directs the movements of the mind, which are then reflected by the body (see Chapter 19).

When people talk about so-called "mental" practice, they typically mean rehearsing music in the mind without using the musical instrument. The funny thing is, most teachers who recommend "mental" practicing intuitively recognize that awareness of the body needs to be included in this process. However, the way they recommend to do this is problematic and can easily backfire when they advise students to imagine and rehearse *how it feels in the body* to play the passage of music they're working on. Some teachers go even further by suggesting the student actually move their fingers along with their thoughts.

These suggestions can be more harmful than helpful if a student is unable to first imagine the music (hear or visualize it internally) *without reacting to it by subtly increasing tension* (which in those who have not been specifically trained in the subtleties we're discussing here usually goes unnoticed). This requires having the ability, as is described throughout this book, to consciously inhibit the movements of the body that would normally follow upon having the *idea* to move.

When I first began studying the Alexander Technique twenty years ago, I was shocked to discover that I was completely unable to *think* through my music *without feeling* a corresponding muscular activation in my arms, hands, and fingers. I had been doing "mental" practicing ever since I could remember: when bored in school, riding in a car, or falling asleep at night. This definitely helped me learn things faster, but it also solidified the tension that I was bringing to everything I was thinking about, subtly working against the facile execution of those passages.

Now that I've been teaching the Alexander Technique for nearly as many years, I realize that my initial experience of instant muscular activation when thinking of playing my violin is extremely common in musicians, and it can take a good amount of time to unravel this reactive habit.

Why is it so important to be able to think of music without reacting to the ideas physically? Because without this ability, any rehearsal ("mental" and/or "physical") will simply reinforce the unhelpful psychophysical tension habits that are already present and make them stronger.

This might not be a problem if it weren't for the fact that our psychophysical state is always changing from moment to moment and from day to day, depending on innumerable factors, many of which are unpredictable.

When things feel different from how you rehearsed when your psychophysical state was different, you're likely to become disconcerted and get thrown off your game if you're not used to rapidly adapting to and rising above the changing states of your body-mind-self.

Which means if you're depending on the memory of how you *think something should feel*, but then your body is in an altered state due to performance nerves or any other number of reasons (what you've eaten, how you slept the night before, how you related to others backstage, etc.), you'll find yourself in trouble. What you're doing with your body will end up, by definition, feeling quite different.

Your likely response will be to try to make your body feel "normal" again, the way it felt when you were relaxed at home. Basically, you're fighting against and not accepting your current reality, and your instinct will be to try to change how you feel. This reaction will likely cause you to shift your awareness down into your body, abandoning your prefrontal cortex "throne" (see Myth #4 in Chapter 21) and leaving yourself vulnerable to all kinds of unhelpful thoughts and tension taking over, throwing off your performance as a result. This is at the root of most performance anxiety.

What makes MindFlow Practice different?

MindFlow Practicing is a catch-all phrase that I use with my students to describe the conscious psychophysical work we do in relation to our music without making sound directly with our musical instrument.

What distinguishes MindFlow Practicing from ordinary "mental" practicing is the addition of ConstructiveThinking, which allows you to rehearse your thoughts and movements with ease in the body, as you consciously release overall tension whenever you notice it creeping into your experience.

By minimizing the unnecessary habitual movements normally involved in playing your instrument, you can more easily sense the subtle energetic changes and muscular tensing reactions that, when you're playing, are always there under the surface, but which are obscured by the sounds and internal "noise" produced by the physical movements.

So much of our playing is polluted by end-gaining thoughts and intentions, such as wanting to get the notes right, not wanting to mess up, caring too much about what other people think, listening to the quality of our sound in a judgmental way instead of discerning to learn, etc. But most people don't recognize that the tension produced is in reaction to their THOUGHTS, and is not a direct result of how they are moving with their bodies.

The cause of tension is not in the physical body; its source lies in the mind. This becomes glaringly obvious once you've been practicing Primal Alexander Awareness Etudes for a while, as you become more sensitive to the difference between what happens when you simply do your ConstructiveThinking and what happens when you imagine yourself playing your instrument or think about playing a difficult passage.

As you alternate between noticing overall easing in your system and thinking about playing, you'll very likely notice that your system gears up to get ready to play, or tenses up in response to what you might think of as difficult. It can be extremely instructive to suddenly experience an increase of tension, even when you're not moving at all and your instrument is completely out of the picture.

Once you start to accept that the deeper source of your tension lies in how you are thinking about playing your instrument *and not in how you actually play it*, you'll gradually come to realize that the bulk of the work you need to do *has to take place first in the mind*, but with full awareness of how your thoughts reverberate in the body.

You can't just focus on your thoughts alone; you need to know how those thoughts are affecting your neuromuscular and energetic systems by including your whole self in your awareness; then, based on what you discover, you can make changes in how you're thinking so as to allow for more easing in your body and flow in your music.

There are endless ways to do MindFlow Practicing (MFP)

The special power of MFP lies in the direct access it affords us to our creative imagination, since we're taking the actual physical movements of playing out of the equation. There aren't any rules when it comes to MindFlow Practicing, as long as you put it into the bigger context of The Art of Freedom Method, making your Primary Concern primary, and with a carefree attitude of experimentation and self-observation. And, of course, lots of ConstructiveThinking.

One of the biggest benefits of MindFlow Practicing is that it can be done anywhere, anytime, under just about any circumstances, with more structure or less. You can include MFP as an essential portion of your regular practice time, or you can do it freely when you're out walking the dog, babysitting your neighbor's child, planting a garden, or washing the dishes.

More formal practices of imagery/visualization/audiation are extremely valuable practices that fall under the general umbrella of MindFlow Practice, all of which I teach in great detail to my students. MFP is one of the most valuable resources I use to help students prepare for auditions and performances, or to overcome anxiety.

MFP doesn't always come naturally to musicians, and I've had more than one student tell me they find visualization to be difficult but definitely a skill very much worth developing. I remember one student in particular who found it nearly impossible at first to imagine herself performing her cello with ease. Every time Carla imagined herself playing in front of an audience—or even walking onstage in an empty concert hall—she felt her whole body tense up.

Over time, though, with just a few minutes of daily MindFlow Practice using the simple instructions I gave her, she improved to the point where she could imagine herself performing challenging music in front of an audience with joy and effortless ease.

Since the creation of our experience begins in the mind and is fed by our belief in ourselves, as Carla systematically practiced her Awareness Etudes and gradually improved in her ability to visualize, she noticed that her performances began improving greatly as a result.

This is very significant, because the truth is . . . *if you can't imagine doing something with ease, you won't be able to do it with ease.*

As the genius scientist Albert Einstein, also an accomplished amateur violinist, said, "Imagination is everything. It is the preview of life's coming attractions."

Now that you have a better idea of how dramatically your practice skills can be improved with The Art of Freedom Method, I'd like to help you avoid some pitfalls caused by several common myths about practicing that can slow down your progress and sabotage your performance if you buy into them.

Four Common Practice Myths that Sabotage Success

Avoid these pitfalls caused by wrong ideas about practicing

Primary Practice: the practice of noticing and prioritizing the quality of awareness you are bringing to your experience of your whole being as you engage in any given activity, at any given moment.

~ *JRF*

This chapter presents just a few of the massive but very common myths about practicing that I've seen many people follow unquestioningly. If you adopt them, these wrong ideas can really hinder your progress. My hope is that you'll be more likely to notice these when you come across them in the future, and that you'll then refer all ideas (yes, even mine!) back to your internal GPS—the intuition of your own, wise Inner Teacher—to discover what works best for you!

Five common practice myths to watch out for:

MYTH #1: 10,000 hours of practice are required to master a skill.

MYTH #2: You need to work directly on a specific problem in order to solve it.

MYTH #3: Scales are the answer to improving your technique.

MYTH #4: Building up your "muscle memory" is the key to playing with confidence and consistent accuracy.

BIG MYTH #1: You need 10,000 hours of practice to master a skill.

TRUTH: The speed of your progress is highly individual and is determined by a combination of both quality of practice and quantity. In all cases, HOW you practice is far more important than how MUCH.

Skillful mastery can certainly be acquired in less than ten thousand hours when there is an abundance of qualitative Primary Practice, both with and without your musical instrument.

Primary Practice is my term for the practice of noticing and prioritizing the quality of awareness you are bringing to your whole being as you engage in any activity, in any given moment.

When the quality of your holistic awareness is improved through Primary Practice, you can improve your musical skills much faster than most people believe, and as the time you spend attending to that is increased—with or without your musical instrument—the need for musical practice time can be substantially reduced.

I can't even begin to tell you how many musicians, including highly skilled professionals, have confessed to me that they are struggling with physical and/or emotional pain related to their music-making. Despite having "done everything right" in the pursuit of mastery by prioritizing study, dedicated practice, and hard work, these musicians still don't feel at all like they've mastered their instrument. Instead, they feel like they've definitively reached the limit of what's possible for them, always falling short of the elusive mastery they've pursued over a lifetime.

They feel like imposters. They feel inadequate, like there's something wrong with them, and they fear they'll never be good enough, even though they've spent far MORE than ten thousand hours diligently honing their skills the way they were taught, in the best way they know how.

The good news is that I've been able to help these musicians, and plenty of amateurs, too, to see through the common mistake of prioritizing quantity over quality, and I've helped them feel successful and hopeful that mastery is indeed possible for them.

If you're an adult who wants to master a skill, or if you're a young adult who feels intimidated by an amount of practicing that seems impossible for you, then I promise there's a goldmine of ease and success waiting for you, hidden within the skill of Primary Practice!

If you commit to learning the uncommon breakthrough techniques I'm sharing here and apply them to the skill you wish to master, then mastery is yours for the taking in far fewer hours than experts and common assumptions tell you. Indeed, if you follow the process diligently and consistently, your mastery will be inevitable and practically effortless.

Where did the 10,000 hours of practice myth come from, anyway?

Musicians take it for granted that they must spend a substantial quantity of time practicing a skill—indeed, multiple years. However, the specific number of ten thousand hours derives from the 2011 book *Outliers: The Story of Success*, by *New Yorker* staff writer Malcolm Gladwell.

Based on studies he looked at, such as one by a Swedish psychologist who interviewed violinists from a famous Berlin music academy, Gladwell argues in Chapter Two that to achieve mastery of a skill, you must practice ten thousand hours, distributing the hours in any way over time. However, many music teachers interpret this to mean a large number of hours on a daily basis in the belief that this cuts down the overall amount of time. I've had many students tell me their teachers required them to practice six or even eight hours every day.

The main problem with the Berlin music academy research study is that it focuses primarily on quantity of practice, ignoring the immensely important factor of quality. The research, based on feedback from subjects who displayed a certain degree of mastery in their area of expertise, did not take into account their practice methods. It is highly probable that the subjects in the study did not know how to use the power of conscious inhibition, or ConstructiveThinking, and therefore they did not have the very best practice methods at their disposal.

To me, this is a major flaw in the study because in my experience as a mind-body-movement expert and coach for musicians, I can see that most musicians who may be said to have achieved mastery still apply much more effort than necessary in playing their instruments. This tells me they needed much more time, by far, to achieve their degree of mastery than was actually necessary, had they known more efficient ways to think, move, and practice.

Not only this, but there were many people in the study who mastered their instrument in much LESS time (ten thousand hours was just the average time it took), indicating that those people may have had superior practice skills than others.

In my experience, students who have learned how to play with less tension and who are integrating ConstructiveThinking with the most up-to-date practice and learning methods (as presented in Chapter 21) learn much faster than those who do not have this skill. The "quickening of the mind" that takes place with this skill speeds up the learning process, increasing the effortlessness and overall quality of everything they do.

The myth of 10,000 hours of practice is based on three wrong assumptions:

1) People know how to practice well (not so!)

Most people actually don't have good practice skills; they aren't very good at coordinating themselves, managing their minds, or organizing their time. They waste a lot of time and energy in the practice room, unnecessarily repeating things they can already do, and sometimes even doing things that slow down progress. When you're practicing the wrong things and not paying attention to your Self-Use, as described throughout this book, practicing can even be worse for your playing at times than not practicing at all!

2) Practicing is defined by time spent with your instrument (not so!)

Even before the ten-thousand-hours research, a long-standing, prevalent belief assured us that it takes a large quantity of time practicing *with a musical instrument* to achieve mastery. There's also a universal belief that it's better to practice your instrument than to not practice it at all. Also, very little credit is given to the powerful skill of MindFlow Practice, in which time spent attending to the music without your instrument can be even more productive than time spent with it.

These beliefs have led most musicians to feel better about themselves whenever connected to their instrument for a certain amount of time—even if they're forcing themselves to practice, the quality of their attention is poor, and their end-gaining attitude is negatively impacting their overall well-being.

The ten-thousand-hours myth has also led to a lot of unnecessary and unhealthy guilt (resulting in unhelpful overall tension) when a person decides NOT to spend as much time with their instrument.

3) Practicing is defined by time spent focusing on the music (not so!)

When you recognize that the quality of your Primary Practice—how you use your whole self throughout the day—is the single most important factor in improving the quality of your musical practice, you begin to understand how important it is to pay attention to your Self-Use away from your instrument, even when you're occupied in doing something completely unrelated to your music.

In fact, the bulk of your practicing takes place away from your instrument, when you're not even thinking about it. Not only has new research shown us that the brain keeps learning during practice breaks, when you're resting or doing something else, but the Alexander Technique has demonstrated to us that it is the quality of your attention and how you use your whole self throughout the day that determines the quality and effectiveness of *all* of your actions, including your musical practice.[26]

Potential pitfalls of believing in Myth #1

An older adult student of mine recently told me: "I've occasionally given thought to working out a strategy for getting in ten thousand hours of practice and found it to be possible if I practiced six days/week, four hours/day *for eight years*. Perhaps if I had begun learning the violin as a child and gone to a conservatory, that would have happened."

The Ten Thousand Hours Rule may indeed lead you to mastery, *but only if your practicing is sufficiently qualitative*. Sadly, with many people who attempt to achieve mastery, even *one hundred thousand* hours of poor practicing won't be enough to be successful!

In addition, if you believe quantity is the most important component, you can easily become discouraged and give up, believing that mastery is impossible for you, once you realize how long ten thousand hours actually is!

This myth can easily lead adults to believe they've missed the boat and mastery is practically out of reach for them. After all, adults usually have jobs, families, and other obligations that would make it impossible for them to get in the "required" number of hours.

Why condemn yourself to the idea that mastery is impossible for you, simply because of a belief in a fallacy?

Alternatively, you could adopt this myth and deceive yourself into believing that you're on an inevitable path to mastery, when you aren't, since you're paying more attention to the number of hours practiced than the quality.

If you make practice choices based on this myth without taking into account the information offered in this book regarding qualitative practice, you are likely to end up, in the best-case scenario down the road, *accepting* defeat when you finally realize that your goal will be forever out of reach. Or, in the worst-case scenario, you may end up frustrated, feeling like a failure, full of pain and anxiety, or even injured—all because you believed you needed to push yourself to practice a certain number of hours.

26 Medical News Today, "Why Taking Breaks Is Important for Learning New Skills," How taking breaks helps your brain learn new skills (medicalnewstoday.com).

But isn't quantity of practice important?

Yes, of course quantity is important. But not in the way most people think!

I have worked with countless musicians who were told that to achieve success, they needed to practice a prescribed number of hours, sometimes as much as eight hours every day.

Many forced themselves to put in the required hours out of obligation, despite internal resistance and personal desire to practice less; unsurprisingly, they injured themselves as a result. (See Chapter 8 for more on conflicting desires.)

Others put in the required hours out of intense desire to succeed, but their zealousness led to rehearsing with far too much tension, something unsustainable over the long term.

Yet others had poor teachers who taught them unhelpful habits, which could never lead to excellent technique and musicianship because what they were getting was simply bad, ineffectual advice.

Even if you fill your practice time with the best techniques, gleaned from the best teachers, the only way to stay physically healthy and emotionally balanced in your life and while practicing your instrument is to have your priorities in order.

Having your priorities in order means you are giving due attention to the 5 Pillars of The Art of Freedom Method on a regular basis (see Chapter 16), constantly renewing your commitment to a higher Purpose, and being very present when you practice by paying attention to your Primary Concern and your essential Being as much as possible.

In this way, you are bringing the highest standard of quality to the practice of your musical instrument, and you can't help but be successful every step along the way. Consequently, you cannot fail to enjoy artistic mastery if that is what you want!

Ultimately, Self-Love, love of music, and devotion to a higher Purpose provide the magnetizing attraction that makes it EASY to commit to practicing because it's enjoyable and deeply meaningful to you.

The qualitative infusing of immediate, timeless Presence into your practice is very different from the forward drive and intense passion brought about by egoistic ambition. Pushing yourself to practice more through an iron will or through fear, instead of calm, confident Love, comes at a steep price. Even if a certain degree of instrumental mastery and professional success is achieved in this way over time, true artistic mastery will remain perpetually elusive and out of reach. The inevitable result will be a life out of balance—tainted by frustration.

In short, I believe it is quite possible for a person to achieve the same (or even a superior) level of mastery in far less time and with much less effort than is commonly thought.

How to go beyond Myth #1 by redefining practice

In this book, I have effectively redefined the idea of practice from a holistic perspective, to include taking responsibility for what you are doing with your whole self, independent of what the activity is that you're engaged in. As mentioned previously, I call this Primary Practice.

Once you start learning how to practice your Primary Instrument (YOU) with more conscious, constructive awareness throughout the day, you'll soon come to see that you can get much more done in much less time with your musical instrument than the Ten Thousand Hours study purports to be necessary—because you're shifting the focus away from the specifics of what you're doing with your instrument and towards how you are Being your whole self.

The Art of Freedom Method for conscious living and masterful artistry delivers a much simpler, faster, and more enjoyable way to achieve musical mastery—simply by living your life fully, with awareness and ease, and then bringing that ease of Being to your music!

BIG MYTH #2: You need to focus and work directly on a specific problem in order to solve it.

TRUTH: Once you have sufficient information, the best approach to solving a problem (for example, improving a specific technique) is *indirect and holistic*.

I will never forget when Sarah entered my studio one day, terribly distraught. Her senior recital for her bachelor's degree in music was scheduled for less than a week away, and she felt woefully unprepared to play the Sibelius violin concerto on the program.

Nearly in tears, she told me that her teacher had forbidden her to "make music" or practice anything other than intonation until her intonation was "perfect." But Sarah told me that the more she worked on her intonation, the worse it got.

I calmed her down, reassuring her that it probably wasn't that bad. However, when she played part of the piece for me, I had to admit—I won't say atrocious, but it was pretty terrible! Of course, I didn't tell her that.

From my perspective, Sarah's teacher was making a big mistake, but as a musician's coach (not my students' main "music teacher"), I would never criticize anything Sarah was telling me she was being taught by her music teacher. Instead, I opened up a dialogue, asking questions that might lead her to think about the problem differently.

I asked Sarah if she'd like to do an experiment. Desperate to try anything at that point, she nodded agreement.

First, I asked her to set aside her violin, and we spent a few minutes practicing some Primal Alexander Awareness Etudes together. As she did this, her attention slowly began to shift away from what wasn't working and what was upsetting to her, and she started to lighten up, becoming curious, aware of the easing that she could newly sense in her body.

After a little bit, we began to chat about the Sibelius. How did she feel about the piece? Did she know the story behind its composition? What was the emotional mood the composer was trying to evoke, and how did it make her feel? What did SHE want to bring to the piece, personally, and how might it move her audience?

We talked about anything BUT intonation.

I rarely play my violin for my students, but in this case I was eager to play a passage of the Sibelius myself (I've always loved the piece!). So, I played the first page for her, adding in plenty of spoken commentary, painting vivid images of the stark mood evoked by this concerto, which was written in Finland, soon after the death of the composer's daughter.

By the time I'd finished, Sarah was transported into a rich, meaningful world devoid of any thought of instrumental technique. When I then asked her to pick up her violin and play the music how *she* felt it, she had long forgotten about her troubles with intonation.

To the astonishment of us both, the music that emerged was heart-wrenchingly beautiful, and nearly perfectly in tune. Sarah's soul had been longing to be let loose to feel and express the meaningful emotions of this piece, but the prohibition her teacher had put on not allowing her to "make music" until she had fixed her intonation had effectively put her in a straitjacket.

Of course, she was suffering, and her intonation was suffering right along with her! When we suffer, our music suffers—unless we know how to process that suffering by letting ourselves feel the pain and offer it up, entering the flow of ease within us.

When I asked her what playing the piece was like that time, she immediately responded, effusive and glowing with enthusiasm. Mentioning the intonation didn't even cross her mind.

When I pointed out that her intonation had been greatly improved, she suddenly realized what had happened and was overcome with emotion.

"But I didn't even THINK about the intonation that time!!" she cried.

It's always our thinking that gets in the way, isn't it?

This is how, when our priorities and intentions are clear and in place and we give our technique some space, it naturally improves itself.

Unfortunately, Sarah's teacher had unwittingly (and with the best of intentions) caused her priorities to be skewed, which, when she followed his instructions, caused things to get progressively worse.

His injunction to focus ONLY on the specific problem, without letting her make music until the problem was fixed, not only caused Sarah to focus on something she was *doing wrong* instead of the rightness and lightness of her *Being*. This approach was also exaggerating the importance of intonation, which is such a small part of the whole musical package—making something less important bigger and bigger, outweighing and overshadowing what is TRULY important: transmitting the meaning of music as a deeply, fully embodied, soulful whole.

A similar thing happened recently, when an adult beginner violinist played in the masterclass portion of my weekly group class online. Kenya felt frustrated because she couldn't get through more than a couple measures of a phrase without tensing up. When I had her play the phrase the first time, her intonation was very off, but neither of us mentioned it since our focus for that lesson was something different.

In between repetitions of the phrase, I gave Kenya suggestions to help her do her ConstructiveThinking while playing, while simultaneously noticing the easing that arose in her as a result. Each time she played, things improved. By the third and fourth time she played the phrase, her intonation was nearly perfect.

When I asked about her experience, Kenya reported that she felt much more relaxed and she was aware of the improvement. When I specifically mentioned her intonation, she said she knew that it had also gotten better. But when I inquired as to whether she'd been *trying* to play more in tune, she was surprised and immediately said, "Oh! I wasn't even thinking about it."

When I asked Kenya how she'd made the improvement, a broad smile came over her face as she made gentle swaying gestures with her body and violin; then she said, "My mind kind of went blank for a minute . . . the music was in my head . . . and it worked."

The other nine musicians in the group who were watching the lesson said the transformation was stunning.

These are just two examples of how specific problems (in this case, intonation), can improve dramatically without our even thinking about them, as long as we are prioritizing the whole over the parts, the general over the specific, and our experience of the Self-Instrument (our Being) over everything else.

When we overthink, we inevitably overfocus on what is secondary instead of what is primary, we end-gain, and things get worse.

When we have a clear intention, let go of the desired outcome, and focus on the "means-whereby" to achieve the goal, things are allowed to flow naturally, and they start to work the way they are intended to.

I have seen this phenomenon repeated again and again, with a great variety of techniques on a variety of instruments, with all kinds of musicians.

Of course, this approach presupposes that we have the basic knowledge and sufficient sensitivity required to solve the problem at hand. For example, both Sarah and Kenya needed to understand what good intonation is before they could delegate fixing their faulty intonation to their Inner Coordinator. Had they been unable to hear the difference between a C# that is in tune and a C# that is out of tune, they would need to work on developing that sensitivity first (ideally using ConstructiveThinking for that, as well), before expecting themselves to be able to play in tune.

An important key to making this process work is to understand the natural process for goal manifestation, as described in Chapter 17.

BIG MYTH #3: Scales are the answer to improving your technique.

TRUTH: As useful as they are, practicing scales is NOT the answer to improving your technique; neither is the practice of any other technical exercise with your instrument. HOW you practice is far more important than WHAT you practice.

On the very day that I'm writing this, one of my students, an oboist named Félix, confessed in one of my group classes that he used to practice scales assiduously for two hours every single day, because he had been trained to believe this was necessary.

Thankfully, my students are open to trying new ways of doing things!

Félix told us that, after exploring different ways of practicing that I recommended—especially, integrating ConstructiveThinking into his practice—he discovered that his two hours of scales practice was actually counterproductive, as he would typically be tied up in knots and feeling discouraged about his abilities when he was finished.

On the other hand, he said in the next breath, he has hit upon a system in which he sets a timer for six minutes (the amount of time that works for him personally right now), and he now spends just six minutes daily on scales. After that, he works on any number of other technical exercises that he has on the practice agenda for the day, for just six minutes each.

I wasn't surprised in the least when he announced that his playing—including his scales—has improved much more quickly by practicing this way, in literally one twentieth of his previous time spent on scales!

Granted, scales (and many other basic technical exercises) are extremely useful to include in your practice routine, and I do recommend using scales as a foundational exercise to work on a huge array of specific techniques—anything from intonation to vibrato to strategic positioning of fingers.

But my students have come to understand through practical experience that no technical exercise can ever be what makes the difference between mediocre instrumental technique and masterful artistry.

After all, it is entirely conceivable that a musician could achieve a high degree of mastery of his instrument without ever using scales as a systematic part of his practice method, whereas, it is inconceivable that a musician could ever become a true master without having superior conscious control over his mind, body, emotions, and creative spirit, and knowing how to apply such self-mastery to his instrument.

Félix now understands, from experience, that his rapid improvement is due to a complex combination of factors, many of which I touch upon in this book, which can all be summarized by one thing: Félix is getting better at the use of his Primary Instrument—how he uses his mind-body-self as a whole—and therefore, he is bringing a better-coordinated self to his oboe practice daily.

The result? A rapid and marked improvement in his musical skill in much less time than it would have taken without the new knowledge he is now applying on a daily basis.

What Félix discovered through questioning his beliefs and experimenting with new ways of practicing was that the key to artistic mastery does not lie solely in the practice of scales or any other technical exercise on your instrument. Again, it is the quality of your Primary Practice (attention to how you use your whole self in any activity) that determines the degree of musical mastery you can achieve.

"When I first considered working with Jennifer I was skeptical because it's harder for me to trust an online program than 'real life' offers, and money was short since I was a student at the time. However, soon after getting started, Jennifer impressed me by noticing in great detail when and how I would tense up or find ease on the basis of what she saw on her screen during our video call, and taking the risk turned out to be worth it.

"I had had chronic pain in my chest for many months and had lost hope that it would ever go away. After our first session I felt the pain fade for the very first time and I teared up from joy. Over the course of the first few weeks my pain completely disappeared and it hasn't come back to this day.

"The fact that everything is online turned out to have an empowering side-effect: Every little success is a result of your thinking! No hands-on therapist required. I've had ups and downs as in every learning journey and my commitment to her practice has sometimes wavered, but I do always come back to it and not an hour passes by without me doing ConstructiveThinking.

"I've had extremely stressful orchestra auditions that I managed to overcome (and win!) in great part thanks to what I learned from Jennifer. Tension under pressure is still my biggest challenge and sometimes I feel like I am back to zero, but of course that is not true. The kind of musical situations I find myself in are increasingly demanding and we cannot expect to be robots that function with the same level of ease under any circumstances without fail."

~ Félix, Oboe

BIG MYTH #4: You need to build up your "muscle memory" and practice remembering how things *feel* on your instrument in order to improve your technique, memorize music better, and perform with confidence.

TRUTH: So-called "muscle memory" is an activity that takes place in the motor neurons of your brain, not your muscles. Relying on your memory of a physical sensation, trying to recreate it by focusing on how things feel in your body, is a major hidden contributor to performance anxiety, self-doubt, inconsistent technique, and failed skills under pressure.

Your muscle cells change as you use them, and with repetition your brain's motor neurons create habits which are stored as memory; this makes it easier for you to repeat learned movements, even after a certain time away. This is where the expression "It's like riding a bicycle" comes from.

This so-called "muscle memory" explains why people who play an instrument during childhood can generally lay it aside for decades, focus on an unrelated career, family life, etc., and still come back to that instrument as an older adult and not have to start over again from scratch. This is truly a wonderful thing! Thank goodness for motor neurons and unconscious habits!

However, the learning process happens most easily and gives us the most control when we apply deliberate practice with conscious awareness by (1) formulating a clear intention of what we want to do; and then (2) inhibiting, or letting go of, that desire while entrusting it to our "Inner Coordinator" (unconscious processes, including our brain and every muscle cell), which will produce our desired outcome for us.

When we mistrust and meddle with this natural learning process by trying to impress a physical sensation—the feeling of a movement—onto our memory by paying attention to how a body part *feels*, we actually slow down the learning process.

This is because, as we take our thinking "down" to the physical body part in question (for example, paying attention to what our fingers feel like while trying to play double stops in tune, or "mentally" rehearsing that feeling away from the instrument) our attention is no longer "up" in the prefrontal cortex. That's where our attention needs to be as much as possible, so we can do the ConstructiveThinking that allows us to be ready to receive and interpret the feedback sent up to the brain from the muscles via the nervous system. We need to be alert and present "up" there so we can immediately and creatively respond with the best next step.

Here's how the chain of command is designed to function best to carry out a desired action:

1) We become conscious of a clear intention in the prefrontal cortex (I want to play this double stop in tune).

2) This intention is quickly and automatically conveyed to other, unconscious parts of the brain that activate the motor neurons and other bodily processes needed to carry out the requested activity.

3) These unconscious aspects of the self (our "Inner Coordinator") wisely coordinate the entire organism to carry out the desired intention in the best way it knows how in that given moment, predicated on the information it has, the current conditions, and our previous experience.

4) Unless more information/learning is required or something else interferes with the transmission or reception of the message, the desired movement happens as intended (the double stops are played in tune).

As long as we don't interfere with it, this process works smoothly and seamlessly—even miraculously, since nobody actually understands exactly how every tiny detail works! Of course, most of the time we DO interfere, without even realizing it.

Putting aside the interference that can be caused by certain injuries or diseases, normal interference in flow happens within each of us many times a day, when we send a contradictory or incompatible request from the brain that compromises or cancels out the original message before we are able to carry it out.

This is why one of the most important reasons to regularly practice Primal Alexander Awareness Etudes is to increase your sensitivity to these subtle interferences; once you become aware of the interruption of easing within you, you can inhibit what is blocking the flow, thereby allowing your intentions to pass smoothly from idea in the brain to muscle and back up to the brain again with effortless ease.

We practice ConstructiveThinking to actively minimize the kind of interference that stems from conscious or unconscious thoughts that can send mixed or contradictory signals, sabotaging our best intentions.

Here's an example. If you think: *I want to play that double stop in tune*, and then you add, *but I'm really worried that it will be out of tune because it's so hard and I'll never be able to fix my intonation and I should probably just quit the violin once and for all because I'll never be good enough*, you're muddying the original request with lots of end-gaining and fear. Those thoughts trigger a fear-based reaction that increases muscular tension, which will then become part of the neural learning network—and therefore the memory—of how you play that double stop. Therefore, you're unlikely to get the result you actually wanted when you started to practice.

To put all of this simply: when you focus on how something *feels*, your attention goes down into the body and you're no longer up in the creative, conscious, command region of your brain. Consequently, you're unable to do the ConstructiveThinking you need to let go and let things flow. That means the ability of your system to effectively carry out your intentions will be seriously compromised, as it will be left largely up to chance, at the mercy of your distracted, undisciplined mind, which generates all kinds of additional tension. This effect is likely to magnify when you're under stress, like when you're about to take an audition or perform onstage, which is why it's best for you to begin developing the skills here well in advance of a stressful event.

In Chapter 15, I shared the "Starbucks Analogy" to illustrate how our intentions move from idea to manifestation. Here's another analogy to help you understand the interdependent, yet hierarchical roles of the mind and body, which are crucial to understand if you want to improve the quality of your practice and improve your skills faster.

The Monarchy Analogy

Imagine that your physical body is a vast expanse of land ruled by a monarch, and that monarch is your mind. Everything in the monarchy is beautifully designed to function well, and there is peace in the land—as long as the monarch and everyone else in the realm are doing their jobs well.

Your job as a monarch is to sit upon the throne (located in the prefrontal cortex, the conscious command center of your brain), creating laws and making requests for what you'd like to have happen. You make things happen out in the fields (the remote parts of your body like your fingers and toes) by informing the ministers of your castle (located in other, unconscious parts of your brain and your nervous system) of what you want.

Your ministers then carry those messages out to the fields (through the nervous system) and tell the peasant farmers who work there (muscles and other physical body parts) what needs to be done. When the farmers are healthy, happy, well-cared for, and they have the knowledge and equipment needed to work the fields to produce the desired crops, the farmers easily and agreeably carry out the desired actions as requested.

Once the monarch's messages have been sent and your intentions have been acted upon out in the kingdom (your body), the ministers instantly return to the castle (your brain) to inform those present of the results. If you haven't left the throne in the meantime, you'll be right there to receive the news, and you'll be able to more accurately interpret and assess what to do next. Which is when the cycle repeats itself, and the monarch issues the next request to the body through its ministers.

But what do you think would happen if the monarch didn't trust her ministers to do their jobs, and she decided to continuously leave her throne (prefrontal cortex) in the castle (head) to go down into the fields (body) and micromanage the farmers (fingers, or other body parts), telling them what to do without having a bigger picture of the state of the lands as a whole (the whole mind-body-self), and without the specific knowledge of how the peasants should carry out the task at hand?

Just imagine . . . disgruntled ministers, confused and offended farmers (what does the monarch know about planting crops?!) . . . and a throne left empty for usurpers hungrily waiting for their chance to launch a coup!

Imagine that a coup does take place; wild insurrectionists (random negative thoughts) take over the castle, but the crowd has no real leader. They end up pushing one another on and off the throne. Chaotic chatter fills the land, the ministers now incapable of coordinating ideas and making anything good happen in any consistent way. Fear and anxiety rule, and the people are desperate for competent, constructive leadership.

The good news is that once this monarch realizes what's happening, she can instantly teleport back onto the throne; thankfully, the people give her another chance to be present and rule the kingdom well.

However, if the land has been without a ruler and living in disorganized chaos for any length of time, it will take quite a lot of healthy discipline and persistence for her to bring trust and good coordination back to the country again!

Moral of the story: aim to return to your prefrontal cortex throne room and think clear, constructive thoughts as often as you can remember to; don't go down into your body to try to feel out what's going on, micromanaging your body parts and trying to make them do what you want; listen to your ministers and trust your wise Inner Coordinator that keeps everything in order, alive and flowing according to the design of the kingdom; be on alert to receive the information your bodily senses send you, so that you can make your next best decision based on information as accurate as possible.

Here's a common scenario, illustrating what can happen when you're used to relying on how things feel instead of trusting the natural process I've outlined above:

On Monday, you feel happy, calm, relaxed, carefree after a good night's sleep and a great weekend. Your fingers fly over the fingerboard without the least bit of difficulty, and your heart swells with joy. You're amazed by what you're able to accomplish, and you marvel that the passages that seemed difficult yesterday now feel easy. You're pleased that all the time and effort you've been steadily putting into your practicing seems to be paying off.

On Tuesday, you receive bad news about the state of your finances and the failing health of a loved one. You have indigestion that evening and don't sleep well, consumed with worry.

On Wednesday, it hits you that you have only ten days left to practice for your audition; you feel woefully unprepared. You scramble to find more time to practice, rushing through your daily activities to get to the practice room sooner, but when you pick up your instrument, nothing seems to work: your fingers feel clumsy, your rhythm is erratic, and your intonation is suffering. Gone is the amazing sound of a couple days ago; you're plagued by repetitive thinking about how your playing will never be good enough to win an audition.

On Friday morning, your friend invites you to a mock audition at her home that evening, and you say yes to the opportunity. All day you feel excited and find yourself mentally rehearsing your excerpts whenever you have a free moment, remembering how good everything felt on Monday; but the closer it comes to the time to play, the more anxious you feel.

When you get out your violin to tune, your heart is racing, your hands are freezing, your bow shakes. As you perform your excerpts, you feel terrible, making little mistakes all over the place that you've never incurred before. You feel horribly frustrated afterwards and just can't understand why everything felt and sounded so different from what you did alone in the practice room just a few days ago.

This kind of thing happens when we rely on our "muscle memory" and "mental practicing" of how something feels in the body instead of rising above that by making our Primary Concern primary and applying intentional ConstructiveThinking.

Basing our practice on how the body feels is like building a house on the shifting sands of a beach, since every aspect of the self is constantly changing, influenced by the environment. One day the tide is high; the next, it's low. The sands move with the tides, reflecting the phases of the moon, just as the body reflects our state of mind.

Relying on how something feels or our memory of how something felt under past and different conditions is a mistake, plain and simple, and it is the biggest cause of inconsistent technique, unreliable performance, and our corresponding feelings of frustration, disappointment, insecurity, inferiority, and helplessness.

RESOURCE:

To help you apply what you're learning here, make sure to download your "Keys to Successful Practice" cheat sheet from the Bonus Materials page here: https://www.artoffreedom.me/book/bonusmaterials

Conclusion

It's simple. Just let go! ☺

All spiritual traditions stress the importance of Self-knowledge and surrendering the egoistic tendencies of our personality to let something greater flow through us, a "Spirit" that is free to move and uplift us, guiding our actions with Inspiration and grace for positive results in the world and beyond.

Even those who aren't inclined towards exploring spirituality will acknowledge the importance of overcoming selfish and controlling tendencies, becoming more present and living more mindfully in the moment, pausing to consider before speaking and acting, and embracing better ways to deal with stress. In so doing, we open ourselves to experiencing greater peace, improved well-being, more fulfilling relationships, and true success in all of our endeavors, including our artistry.

Whether you choose to think in terms of allowing "Spirit" to move through you, or you prefer to simply "let go and go with the flow" so your whole self can function more freely and naturally; whether you believe the "ego" is something to be extinguished or you prefer to consider it as an integral part of you to be developed in a positive way; and whether you want to "improve" or you want to peel off the ego layers to reveal who you already are.... the fundamental question remains: *HOW do you do it?*

I hope reading this book and experimenting with the ideas is helping you answer that question, and I hope you're also slowly discovering that you don't need to fully understand how... because that's not actually the job of your thinking mind. Let go of your need to know, and you'll know what I mean!

Why is letting go so important for musicians?

I've given many examples throughout this book of what can happen when you end-gain, but here are a few more reminders, in case you're still wondering why letting go with your whole self is so important for you as a musician. These examples illustrate what can happen when you're hooked into your thoughts and feelings, without letting them flow through you and letting them go.

- End-gaining makes it harder to play complex, technically demanding passages with ease and accuracy.

  Moving your arms, hands, and fingers quickly requires swift, clear communication between your brain and your body. Excess muscular tension means muscles are being held in a contracted state more than necessary, which reduces flexibility and range of motion, and makes it harder for you to quickly press and release your fingers or change your embouchure to move from one note to the next.

  Clearly, you need to be able to let go in your body for necessary releases to happen easily; but you can't let go in your body if your mind is trying or thinking too hard, or if you're in an emotional state that shows up in your body as muscular tension.

- Feeling conflicting or negative feelings towards your stand partner, conductor, a friend, or your spouse?

  If you don't know how to let go and rise above turbulent emotional states by letting it all flow through, up and out of you, the hardening quality of emotions like anger will affect the way you communicate with others as well as your playing. Your sound reflects your state of being; if you are in a contracted emotional state, your sound will be smaller and tighter than when you're experiencing a neutral or expansive state. When you are open, free, and loving, your sound will also be more open and free, and it will project naturally. Without being forced, your sound can vibrate freely to pierce and melt the hearts of those who are open to listening.

- End-gaining increases mind-wandering. Are you in charge of your mind?

  First of all, mind-wandering is normal, human, and not "bad." But it does compromise the quality of whatever it is you're doing, since you're taking some of your attention away from the task at hand so you aren't fully present.

There are infinite ways the mind can get distracted, and all of them reflect an attachment to something limited and partial, which is not the whole.

We either get hooked into paying more attention to things happening outside of us and forget our inner world; or we pay too much attention to what's happening inside of us (our thoughts and feelings) and become disconnected from what's outside. When your attention is split and out of balance, your body reflects that imbalance. Again, tension increases, and your music suffers.

Letting go of end-gaining is healthy detachment

Letting go of end-gaining is a kind of internal decluttering—a minimalism of the whole self that allows us to stop doing whatever is unnecessary and gets in the way of natural flow of energy and well-coordinated movement. I find it helpful to think of this process as "healthy detachment."

Healthy detachment isn't just a mental or spiritual concept, of course, and it certainly isn't about separating yourself or dissociating from your experience. On the contrary, healthy detachment allows you to unify your experience with expanded awareness as you're detaching from a partial point of view. As with all natural human qualities or "virtues," while conscious letting go is a choice initially directed by the mind, it is a necessary activity which requires the inclusion and active participation of the whole self.

To consciously let go or practice healthy detachment requires an ever-increasing awareness of what is happening to our whole selves in the moment—our minds, bodies, and emotions. Without this consciousness, even if we think or feel that we are letting go, the result will be short-lived and largely ineffectual.

For example, you might be very much aware of having too much tension in your shoulder when you play. So every time you practice, you work on relaxing and letting go of your shoulder. When you relax your shoulder, it seems to release, so you believe you have "let go" of the tension, and you move on. However, a few minutes or days later, you notice that the tension has creeped back in, and you're back to where you started. Either that, or the tension "moves" to another body part, and now you have to work on letting go of your wrist or unlocking your knees instead.

You can go back and forth like this, feeling tension and working on letting go of various body parts for years, with only relative success. This is simply because you're working with parts instead of the whole.

Rarely do we realize that the whole self needs to be involved with the process of letting go. But as soon as we start looking at everything through the lens of the interconnectedness of the mind, body, emotions, and spirit—and our internal and external worlds—we can at last start to appreciate that letting go is not a partial process.

Once you understand that letting go is holistic—it doesn't happen in parts—you need an effective process for letting go. Thankfully, that part is extremely easy, though this can be hard to believe. It's like flipping a switch in your mind labeled "end-gaining" from ON to OFF.

As with everything we want, letting go begins as an idea in the mind. Letting go is a decision. Within that firm, whole-person, embodied decision to stop end-gaining lies the secret to truly letting go.

Imagine this . . .

What if, with the skill of healthy detachment, you could let go of the tension in ALL of you at once—not just in your body, but in your mind and emotions, as well?

And what if you could practice letting go in this way at any time of the day or night, not just when you feel tense or anxious, or when you have your instrument in your hands?

Imagine how much more valuable it could be for you to know how to use this simple self-mastery skill and apply it to your music—and everything else in your life!

In fact, learning how to let go like this is possible, and it isn't difficult. It's the skill Frederick Matthias Alexander finally discovered for himself in the late 1800s, when he started getting hoarse while speaking on stage, and was able to solve his problem after many years of self-observation, experimentation, and practice.

The surprising golden nugget that Alexander discovered by working to solve his performance problem can be distilled into one simple concept: *Alexander discovered how to consciously let go with his whole mind-body-self, in such a way that everything in his life was freed up to "go with the flow" with effortless ease, according to his natural human design.*

Going back to the origins in a new way

Most of us wander through our entire lives oblivious to the burden we carry of layers upon layers of habitual tension that just feels normal because we've adapted to it; after constant repetition over the years we've held fast to fixed ideas and limiting beliefs. "The hardest problems to get rid of are the ones that don't exist," said F. M. Alexander.

The good news is that we don't need a lifetime of therapy, endless massages and chiropractic adjustments, painkillers and muscle relaxants to finally let go of those layers of tension. Although there may be a place and a time for each of the above, what we *really* need is a much quicker, simpler way to let go—on our own—of the burdens we place on ourselves. And that solution is found "hidden in plain sight" within each of us.

The answer begins with paying attention to our Primary Concern, becoming a witness of the Self in this present moment, acceptance of a simple principle, the unity of the Self—drawing the logical conclusions from that and acting on those conclusions with an open mind, patience, and faith.

Mio Morales's Primal Alexander is a revolutionary new way of learning how to let go with maximum ease and awareness by going back to Alexander's original discoveries and, through systematic application of the process, *learning how to become your own best teacher*.

First, in stillness; then in activity. First, with simple movements; later with more complexity. First, without your instrument; later while making music. With practice, we uncover the freedom within structure, and we delight in developing, in any situation, more conscious, constructive control over ourselves.

The Art of Freedom Method brings it all together with an all-encompassing vision for life and music, by remembering the unity of the Self and focusing on the five Life-Pillars: Purpose, Mind, Body, Spirit, and Artistry.

I wrote this book to paint a picture of the endless ways end-gaining is getting in your way as a musician, and how you can easily and progressively learn to let go of that by practicing The Art of Freedom with Primal Alexander.

As I said in the Introduction, you don't have to *believe* that anything in this book works for it to work! But it does require that you have a curious, open mind, and a willingness to learn something new. That means being willing to examine some of your beliefs about yourself and things you've learned, and to experiment with letting go of some of what you're used to—discarding what doesn't work—in exchange for something that might enhance what you already know, helping you move forward with more ease, renewed energy, and joy.

Some of my readers will have very strong ideas about how to learn and play an instrument, and what it means to practice well, which might conflict with some of what's in this book. Hopefully, these readers will be able to suspend those ideas for a bit ("withhold definition"), just long enough to entertain some new ideas that could lead to real breakthroughs.

Others will have strong convictions that learning to do what Alexander did for himself to access the kind of ease and quality of Self-Use he possessed absolutely cannot be accomplished successfully without the skilled touch of a highly trained, certified Alexander teacher, administered over a long period of time; or that, without that hands-on experience, it would require a student at least as many hours and years of self-work as it took Alexander to make his discoveries himself.

Again, I'm not asking anybody to *believe* that the practical tools I'm sharing in this book work. Just like Alexander's original work, the ideas I present are based on flipping that end-gaining switch to "OFF," having an open mind that is willing to be wrong, self-observation, experimentation, and self-verification. Not belief or habit.

Let us remember that there are endless unrecognized potentials in this world, and Primal Alexander *just might be* a different path to the same end—a much quicker, easier route to self-learning that we now have available, thanks to more than a century of exposure to Alexander's work, and so much more.

If you can open up to the possibility of something utterly new—maybe even miraculous—happening within you that you can access in an even simpler way than what you're used to, and if you're curious to discover whether such a thing actually exists beyond the scope of your previous experience, then you'll need to be willing to take a bit of a risk.

Engaging with the ideas will require letting go of some of your well-earned and very useful ideas to step into the Unknown, trying on a new and unfamiliar approach, and perhaps going a little further after finishing this book to get some extra feedback and more personal support on your journey. That could be just the ticket to show you how to do all of these things in a way that's fun and exciting instead of confronting, difficult, or scary.

A word of encouragement

It is my sincere wish that reading this book has inspired you to experiment with applying what you've learned so you can start to feel better in your whole self and make better music very soon. I want you to know that nothing in this book is difficult or out of your reach! I've worked with hundreds of musicians of all kinds—all instruments—all skill levels—and *not a single one of them* has not found benefit in what I've taught them when they followed my simple instructions, especially when done in the generous and welcoming, all-inclusive spirit of LOVE.

I've included numerous client success stories throughout the book in the hopes that you may recognize yourself in some of them, so that you can get a feel for how this work could help you too.

Of course, you can only go so far in learning experientially from a book. This work is simple and infinitely wide in its application. To experience the full benefit of these words, I very warmly encourage you to go deeper—words can only scratch the surface, pointing you in the direction of that deeply personal, holistic experience of the unexpected "natural miracles" that are possible for YOU.

If you've found this book useful, feel free to reach out to me for more information. You can contact me directly through my website or use this form to inquire about my private coaching and group programs: www.ArtofFreedom.me/apply. I invite you to access the free materials I've created to supplement this book: the video training, the audiobook, and all the bonus materials. I look forward to supporting you on your journey towards greater freedom, joy, and musical mastery!

May you be blessed to discover afresh each day how to make great music with ease, and live a happier life through being, knowing, loving, and sharing your True Self with the world.

Acknowledgments

I am profoundly grateful for the warm support and positive presence of the many remarkable individuals in my life. Though it's impossible to acknowledge each person individually, I want you all to know that your contributions have played an invaluable role in bringing this project—one of the most challenging I've undertaken—to fruition.

First and foremost, endless gratitude goes to the timeless spiritual teachers I hold dear in my heart, and to my family, especially my parents, Philip and Marianne Wion, for your constant love and for filling my life with music; to my children, Gabriel and Rafael, who inspire me, teach me, and bring me so much joy; and to Miguel Roig-Francolí, for giving me a new perspective on life many years ago, for encouraging me never to give up the violin, and for your constant care of our family over many years.

A deeply heartfelt expression of thanks goes to my partner, Mio Morales. Your lifelong dedication to Alexander's discoveries, your brilliant teaching, and your creation of Primal Alexander are priceless gifts. Thank you for your loving presence, your constant encouragement, and your unwavering belief in me. You inspire and challenge me in the very best of ways!

I extend abundant thanks to the following violinists who have played significant roles in shaping my musical journey: Paul Landefeld, my first violin teacher, who, along with my mother, made learning the violin fun; Kypros Markou, my first non-Suzuki violin teacher, whose lessons taught me the essence of true musicianship; Dr. Shinichi Suzuki, who taught me daily for a month in Japan when I was ten, exemplifying his belief in nurturing students with love; David Cerone, who warmly nurtured my musical spirit while teaching me the value of structure, efficient organizational systems, and excellent practice skills; Nathan Milstein, my most influential and inspiring musical role model as a child and teenager; Josef Gingold, who lovingly trusted me to teach myself; and Stanley Ritchie, who introduced me to the early music scene at Indiana University, handed me a baroque violin, and instructed me to play at A=415 Hz before I'd even heard of original instruments, thus opening up a whole new world of lively musical creativity in which "everything is in ONE!"

I would like to express deep gratitude to the Alexander Technique teachers who have influenced my understanding and practice of the Technique in their unique ways. Erik Bendix, thank you for creating a safe space for me to be and express myself as described in this book. Helen Hobbs, your embodiment of inhibition and dedication to Principle have provided invaluable lessons for me. Tommy Thompson, your ability to withhold definition and provide profound healing on multiple levels is deeply appreciated. Missy Vineyard, thank you for elevating my thinking and practical understanding of the Alexander Technique. Yehuda Kuperman, your teaching encouraged me to keep exploring the intersection between Alexander Technique and spirituality. And Pedro de Alcantara, the enjoyable experience of having you work with me backstage before my performance at Carnegie Hall is something I will never forget!

Special thanks to Neil and Vivien Schapera, who directed the Alexander Technique teacher training that granted my first certification. I am also grateful to my Alexander friends and colleagues in Cincinnati, who supported me with warmth and compassion during my training and continue to explore the Technique with me to this day.

To all the students who have crossed my path, I extend my heartfelt appreciation. Thank you for bringing your best selves to the exploration of The Art of Freedom, for indirectly teaching me how to become a better teacher and a better human being. Your stories, shared in this book and elsewhere, have enriched my life. Above all, thank you for trusting me. It is a genuine privilege to witness your growth, celebrate your insights, and applaud your success!

Abundant gratitude goes to my exceptional editor, Margaret Harrell. Your excellent and insightful work, along with your meticulous attention to detail, has significantly enhanced this manuscript. I also want to thank my friends and social media connections who have encouraged me to see this book through to completion—your unwavering support means the world to me. Special appreciation to Amira Alvarez, Joy Bufalini, and Megan Barnhard for your stellar coaching, which has made it possible for me to successfully share my message with a wider audience.

Lastly, dear Reader, I express my heartfelt thanks to you. I am truly grateful that you have chosen to invest your time in reading this book, and I sincerely hope the ideas within it will inspire you for many years to come!

. . . And all praise belongs to Love!

About the Author

Jennifer Roig-Francolí (formerly Jennifer Claire Wion) is a prize-winning musician and double-certified Alexander Technique teacher (AmSAT, ATI). As the creator of The Art of Freedom® Method for conscious living and masterful artistry, Jennifer combines her extensive professional experience with a lifelong love of meditation and perennial wisdom. Her unique pedagogical approach, offered online since 2012 and exclusively touch-free since 2018, has empowered countless musicians with reliable tools to break through obstacles to personal and professional fulfillment and success.

Jennifer's career as a modern and baroque violinist has taken her to concert halls around the world, including solo performances at Carnegie Hall and collaborations with esteemed orchestras like the Pittsburgh Symphony Orchestra and Berlin Symphony Orchestra. She was honored as a "Rising Star" by *TIME* magazine and has held the positions of Concertmaster and Associate Concertmaster in various ensembles, including the Grammy Award-winning ensemble Apollo's Fire. She can be heard on recordings with Apollo's Fire and as a soloist on most digital streaming platforms.

A dedicated educator, Jennifer has taught the Alexander Technique on the faculties of the University of Cincinnati College-Conservatory of Music and Xavier University. In Ohio, she has established two professional associations for Alexander Technique teachers, providing a platform for growth and collaboration within the community. In 2010, her groundbreaking research study on the integration of Alexander Technique into laparoscopic surgery at Cincinnati Children's Hospital Medical Center resulted in a prize-winning paper presented at the American Academy of Pediatrics and publication in the *Journal of Urology*.

Jennifer studied violin with Nathan Milstein in Switzerland, Dr. Shinichi Suzuki in Japan, David Cerone at the Cleveland Institute of Music, and both Josef Gingold and Stanley Ritchie at Indiana University. A dual citizen of the USA and Switzerland, Jennifer lives in Cincinnati, Ohio, and enjoys traveling to far-off places such as Switzerland, Spain, and India. Some of her favorite things to do include playing Big Boggle with her grownup kids, swimming in the Mediterranean Sea, curling up by the living room fire, and taking walks in nature.

URGENT PLEA!

Thank You for Reading My Book!

I really appreciate all of your feedback and
I love hearing what you have to say.

I need your input to make the next version of this
book and any future books better.

Please take two minutes now to leave a helpful review on
Amazon, letting me know what you thought of the book:
https://www.artoffreedom.me/bookreview

Thanks so much!

~ Jennifer Roig-Francolí

NOW IT'S YOUR TURN

Claim Your Bonus Materials!

Now that you've completed this book, don't let the learning stop! Reading stories about transformation is one thing . . . but engaging with a process and experiencing the results for yourself is something else entirely!

There's a whole new world of marvelous ease and transformation waiting for you, once you start practicing what's in this book!

I've created three ways to help you pick up momentum and learn more for FREE:

1) Access the Video Training here: https://www.artoffreedom.me/book/training
2) Get more Bonus Materials here: https://www.artoffreedom.me/book/bonusmaterials
3) Listen to the Audiobook here: https://www.artoffreedom.me/audiobook

Of course, if you'd like more personalized guidance, tailored to your unique situation, just reach out to me. Share a little about yourself and tell me what you're most interested in learning. I look forward to hearing from you and I'll respond as soon as I can.

You can contact me personally through my website at https://www.artoffreedom.me/contact or use this form to inquire about my private coaching and group programs: at https://www.artofFreedom.me/apply. You can also reach me through Facebook at https://www.facebook.com/jroigfrancoli or through my YouTube channel at https://www.youtube.com/@JenniferRoigFrancoli. I look forward to connecting with you soon and helping you *Make Great Music with Ease!*

Made in the USA
Middletown, DE
19 February 2024